RUSSIAN THOUGHT
AFTER COMMUNISM
AFTER COMMUNISM

Also from *M.E. Sharpe*

VEKHI (Landmarks)
A Collection of Articles About
the Russian Intellegentsia
Nikolai Berdiaev et al.
Translated and edited by
Marshall S. Shatz and Judith E. Zimmerman
With a Foreword by Marc Raeff

REMAKING RUSSIA
Voices from Within
Edited by Heyward Isham
With an Introduction by Richard Pipes

RUSSIAN THOUGHT
AFTER COMMUNISM

THE RECOVERY OF A PHILOSOPHICAL HERITAGE

Edited by

JAMES P. SCANLAN

M.E. Sharpe
Armonk, New York
London England

Library of Congress Cataloging-in-Publication Data

Russian thought after communism: the recovery of a philosophical heritage /
James P. Scanlan, editor.
p.   cm.
Includes bibliographical references and index.
ISBN 1-56324-388-1 (hardcover).—ISBN 1-56324-389-X (pbk.)
1. Philosophy, Russian.
2.Philosophers—Russia (Federation).
3. Russian (Federation)—Intellectual life.
I. Scanlan, James P. (James Patrick), 1927–
B4201.R86   1994
197—dc20
94-27343
CIP

Printed in the United States of America

The paper used in this publication meets the minimum requirements of
American National Standard for Information Sciences—
Permanence of Paper for Printed Library Materials,
ANSI Z 39.48-1984.

BM (c)   10   9   8   7   6   5   4   3   2   1
BM (p)   10   9   8   7   6   5   4   3   2   1

The authors dedicate this volume to

GEORGE L. KLINE

in recognition of his unique and invaluable scholarly
contributions to the study of Russian philosophy and in grateful
acknowledgment of the generous help and encouragement he has
given to so many other scholars in the field.

Contents

About the Editor and the Contributors

STANISLAV BEMOVICH DZHIMBINOV teaches at the Gor'kii Institute of Literature in Moscow. His areas of scholarly interest are Russian and foreign literature and Russian philosophy. Among his many publications is the volume *Vechnoe solntse* (Eternal Sun) (Moscow, 1979), an anthology of Russian utopian writings.

CARYL EMERSON, professor of Slavic languages and literatures at Princeton University, is a specialist in the thought and work of Mikhail Bakhtin. Her publications include translations and editions of Bakhtin's writings as well as the 1990 book *Mikhail Bakhtin: Creation of a Prosaics*, coauthored with Gary Saul Morson.

PIAMA P. GAIDENKO, a specialist in continental European philosophy as well as the history of Russian philosophy, heads a department at the Institute of Philosophy of the Russian Academy of Sciences in Moscow. Her essay *"Landmarks*: An Unheard Warning" was published in English translation in *Russian Studies in Philosophy* (Summer, 1993).

PHILIP T. GRIER is professor of philosophy at Dickinson College (Carlisle, Pennsylvania), where he specializes in Russian philosophy. Among his publications is *Marxist Ethical Theory in the Soviet Union* (1978) and an article on the work of George L. Kline in the book *Philosophical Sovietology: The Pursuit of a Science* (1988).

ALEXANDER HAARDT, who teaches at the Westfälische Wilhelms-Universität in Münster, has done extensive research on the phenomenological movement in twentieth-century Russian philosophy, with emphasis on Gustav Shpet and Aleksei Losev. In 1993 he published *Husserl in Russland: Phänomenologie der Sprache und Kunst bei Gustav Špet und Aleksej Losev.*

BERNICE GLATZER ROSENTHAL, professor of history at Fordham University, specializes in twentieth-century Russian intellectual history. She is the author of *D.S. Merezhkovsky and the Silver Age: The Development of a Revolutionary Mentality* (1975) and editor of *Nietzsche in Russia* (1986) and *Nietzsche and Soviet Culture: Ally and Adversary* (1994).

JAMES P. SCANLAN, professor emeritus of philosophy at The Ohio State University, was a coeditor (with James M. Edie, Mary-Barbara Zeldin, and George L. Kline) of the three-volume anthology *Russian Philosophy* (1965). His book *Marxism in the USSR: A Critical Survey of Current Soviet Thought* was published in 1985. Scanlan is editor of the quarterly translation journal *Russian Studies in Philosophy*.

ANDRZEJ WALICKI is professor of history at the University of Notre Dame in South Bend, Indiana. His many books on Russian intellectual history include *The Slavophile Controversy: History of a Conservative Utopia in Nineteenth Century Russian Thought* (1975) and *Legal Philosophies of Russian Liberalism* (1987).

GEORGE M. YOUNG, JR., who received his Ph.D. from Yale University, is the author of the monograph *Nikolai F. Fedorov: An Introduction* (1979) and other works on the philosophy of Fedorov. Formerly on the faculty of Grinnell College and Dartmouth College, he is now president of the Young Fine Arts Gallery in North Berwick, Maine.

TARAS D. ZAKYDALSKY of the Canadian Institute of Ukrainian Studies at the University of Toronto wrote master's and doctor's theses at Bryn Mawr College under the direction of George L. Kline. He is the author of works on the philosophy of Grigorii Skovoroda, Nikolai Fedorov, and other Russian and Ukrainian thinkers.

Preface

A striking feature of the cultural upheaval accompanying the demise of communism in Russia has been an explosion of interest in the history of Russian philosophy and particularly in the ideas of those Russian thinkers who were consigned to oblivion by the communist authorities during the Soviet period. The names of Vladimir Solov'ev, Nikolai Berdiaev, Lev Shestov, and a host of other independently minded philosophers, earlier expunged from reference books and library catalogues in the USSR, are now encountered at every turn in Russian journals, conferences, university courses, and most of all in a storm of publications of their own works—in almost every case the first publications of their writings in Russia since the Bolshevik revolution of 1917. After three-quarters of a century, Russia's philosophical heritage is once again alive in the land of its origin.

The present volume is an examination of that heritage from the point of view of its actual and potential impact on Russian culture in the postcommunist world. The essays that comprise the volume approach the rediscovered Russian philosophical heritage in various ways, on a continuum ranging at its extremes from exclusive focus on features of the heritage itself to exclusive focus on the processes and character of its rediscovery. Most of the essays fall somewhere in between, and all are intended to illuminate the range and wealth of philosophical ideas that are once again available to the Russian intellectual community.

Section I takes a broad look at the return of Russian thought to its pre-Soviet traditions, with special attention to causes and consequences. The editor's introduction and the essay by Stanislav Dzhimbinov address the nature of Russia's philosophical past, the circumstances of its suppression, the history of its reemergence in recent years, and some aspects of its significance in Russian culture today.

Each of the four remaining sections of the book deals with a particular historical segment of the Russian philosophical heritage in which there is special interest today, with emphasis on major representatives of that segment whose ideas are once again prominent in Russia. Each section is introduced by a sketch of the attention these central figures are receiving, along with basic biographical and bibliographical information about them where needed.

Section II goes back to what many consider the beginnings of original Russian philosophy in the nineteenth century. In the essays by James P. Scanlan and George M. Young, Jr., the thinking of the early Slavophile philosophers (Ivan Kireevskii and Aleksei Khomiakov) and of Vladimir Solov'ev and Nikolai Fedorov—all seminal figures in the development of Russian philosophy—is examined with an eye to their present-day relevance.

Section III focuses on thinkers of Russia's "Silver Age"—the early twentieth-century period of the flowering of intellectual and artistic culture in Russia that was no less momentous for philosophy than it was for literature, music, and the visual arts. The essays by Andrzej Walicki, Piama Gaidenko, and Bernice Glatzer Rosenthal examine philosophical aspects of this remarkable era in Russian culture, with special attention to the thought of its major representatives, such as Nikolai Berdiaev (perhaps the single most quoted philosopher in Russia today) and Dmitrii Merezhkovskii.

After the triumph of bolshevism in Russia, a large number of non-Marxist Russian philosophers, especially the religious thinkers, either emigrated or were banished from the country. Many continued their philosophical work abroad, and in this way the Russian philosophical heritage was maintained outside the country if not within it. The work of these thinkers, too, figures prominently in Russia's current philosophical renaissance, and section IV is devoted to it. Essays by Philip T. Grier and Taras D. Zakydalsky focus on the current impact of two important émigré philosophers who are generating much interest in postcommunist Russia —Ivan Il'in and Lev Shestov.

Finally, section V is devoted to Russian philosophers who remained in Lenin's and Stalin's Russia but still managed, despite enormous obstacles, to maintain a modicum of independence and a link with the intellectual world of Russia's past. Largely unrecognized as significant philosophers throughout most of the Soviet period, these thinkers are now studied intently and their works are widely published. Essays on two of the most interesting of these figures, Aleksei Losev and Mikhail Bakhtin (by Alexander Haardt and Caryl Emerson), close out this examination of the Russian philosophical renaissance of the late twentieth century.

This volume was conceived as a tribute to an American scholar who did much to keep Russia's philosophical heritage alive in the West while it was being suppressed in Russia. As students, friends, and admirers of George L. Kline, the authors of this book—ten scholars from four countries, including Russia—rejoice with him at the return of this heritage to its homeland.

George L. Kline:
An Appreciation

Of few areas in modern Russian studies in the United States can it be said
that it is largely the creation of a single person, but that is true of the study
of Russian philosophy. George Kline is responsible for the development of
the field on at least three counts. First, his own pioneering analytical and
critical studies provided models of serious investigation of both the history
of Russian philosophy and contemporary Soviet Marxism. Second, Kline
produced, unassisted or with the aid of others, the basic reference works
and instructional materials that made possible the broad study of the field
and the training of younger specialists. Finally, Kline helped to nurture
those specialists (including many of those who have contributed to the
present volume), either by serving as their teacher in a formal setting or by
sustained informal counseling and encouragement.

Because a comprehensive description and assessment of George Kline's
work in Russian and Soviet philosophy (written by Philip T. Grier, one of
the authors of the present book) was included in the volume *Philosophical
Sovietology: The Pursuit of a Science* (1988), there is no need to recount
Kline's scholarly achievements here in detail.[1] The same volume also contains a bibliography of all of Kline's authored, edited, or translated works
in the field of Russian philosophy up to 1986; his relevant publications
since 1986 are listed in a note below.[2] We shall limit ourselves here to
brief comments on a few of the landmark publications produced by Kline
in the course of his career.

In his first book, *Spinoza in Soviet Philosophy* (1952), Kline provided
the English-speaking world with its initial exposure to some of the more
interesting writings of Soviet philosophers through translations of articles
on the philosophy of Spinoza by seven of the most talented representatives
of Soviet dialectical materialism. In a lengthy historical and analytical
introduction, Kline connected the work of these writers both with the pre-
Marxist history of Russian philosophy and with broader currents in contemporary Marxism, such as the debate, crucial for the future of Soviet

philosophy, between Deborinites and mechanists. Thus he used attitudes toward Spinoza to illuminate not only the facts of continuity and change in the history of Russian–Soviet philosophy but the major doctrinal rifts among contemporary dialectical materialists.

A great service to the profession was provided in 1953 by Kline's complete English translation of the two-volume *History of Russian Philosophy* published in Paris in 1948–50 by the Russian émigré idealist philosopher and religious thinker V.V. Zen´kovskii. This translation made available to English speakers an extremely valuable scholarly resource—a comprehensive, critical account of the entire panoply of Russian philosophical thought, beginning with the first emergence of independent philosophical reflection in the eighteenth century and ending with the mid-twentieth. Despite the subsequent appearance of other, more up-to-date histories, none is as rich in analysis and detail as Zen´kovskii's, and consequently Kline's translation retains its value today as the most authoritative treatment of the subject in English—in Grier's words, "the standard account of the subject for most philosophical purposes ... the single source most useful as a general survey and reference for the student of Russian philosophy."[3] This translation, it is interesting to note, may also have had an impact in Russia: when a Russian-language version of Zen´kovskii's work was published in Moscow in 1956, in a small, numbered edition for distribution to Soviet specialists, it appears that the work was back-translated from Kline's English version.[4]

The nature of George Kline's contribution to another basic publication —the path-breaking three-volume anthology *Russian Philosophy* (1965) —has been obscured somewhat by the formal designation of the work as being edited by James M. Edie, James P. Scanlan, and Mary-Barbara Zeldin "with the collaboration of George L. Kline." In fact Kline, in addition to translating several of the original texts included in the volumes, was in practice a full co-editor, involved in virtually every decision from the selection of philosophers and texts to their arrangement and editorial treatment. More than that, Kline was the project's guiding spirit and final authority, since by comparison with him the three named co-editors were neophytes at the time. The availability of this work, which has now been in print for some thirty years, has allowed generations of students to become acquainted with the broad sweep of Russian philosophy through the writings of some of its most important representatives, from Grigorii Skovoroda in the eighteenth century to the Marxists and non-Marxists of the twentieth.

Kline's 1968 book *Religious and Anti-Religious Thought in Russia* (a revised version of a series of lectures given in Cincinnati in 1964 under the auspices of the Frank L. Weil Institute for Studies in Religion and the Humanities) was the first extended treatment by an American philosopher of some important currents in late nineteenth- and early twentieth-century Russian thought. Dealing with the interplay of religious and atheistic ideas in the thinking of ten important Russian writers, the book served to generate interest not only in the philosophical thought of those particular writers (some of whom—most notably Gor'kii—had not typically been approached from a philosophical perspective before) but also in the broad themes of God-seeking and God-rejecting that marked Russian thought in the years leading up to the Russian revolution. Particularly influential was Kline's identification in this work of the category of "Nietzschean Marxists," which was to be followed by intensive study of the impact of Nietzsche on Russian thought by Bernice Glatzer Rosenthal (a contributor to the present volume) and others.[5]

One final way worthy of note in which Kline's writings laid the groundwork for the further study of Russian philosophy was through his authorship of articles on the subject in philosophical encyclopedias and other reference works. As early as 1956 he contributed an article entitled "Current Soviet Morality" to the *Encyclopedia of Morals* edited by Vergilius Ferm. This was followed in 1961 by the article "Philosophy" in Michael T. Florinsky's *Encyclopedia of Russia and the Soviet Union*, and more importantly in 1967 by the major article "Russian Philosophy" and separate articles on fourteen leading Russian philosophers in the authoritative eight-volume *Encyclopedia of Philosophy* edited by Paul Edwards. In addition to these early writings, but in the same category of basic reference materials, is Kline's lengthy chapter on "Russian Religious Thought" in the Cambridge University Press volume *Nineteenth Century Religious Thought in the West* (1985), as well as articles in several recent and forthcoming dictionaries, handbooks, and encyclopedias, including the new, multivolume *Routledge Encyclopedia of Philosophy*, the *Cambridge Dictionary of Philosophy*, and the *Encyclopedia of Time*.

George Kline's contributions to the field of Russian philosophy as a teacher also date from the early 1950s, when as a visiting professor at the University of Chicago from 1952 to 1953 he taught a course entitled "Russian Ethical and Social Theory"; subsequently he taught the same course at Columbia University during most years from 1954 to 1959. But it was at Bryn Mawr College, beginning in 1959 and extending for thirty-two years (until his formal retirement in 1991), that Kline had his greatest impact as a teacher. From 1962 on, his teaching at Bryn Mawr regularly included courses in the history of Russian philosophy and Russian and Soviet Marxism as well as various courses in Russian literature. During this period he

xvi GEORGE L. KLINE: AN APPRECIATION

also taught Russian philosophy as a visiting professor for a semester at the University of Pennsylvania and on another occasion at Douglas College of Rutgers University.

In many ways as important as Kline's formal teaching is the informal help he has provided to a multitude of students and colleagues in the field, not only in the United States but throughout the world. Anyone who has sought George Kline's advice or assistance on some matter relating to Russian philosophy is fully aware of his remarkable readiness to share information from his vast store of knowledge, go over a translation, review a paper, or comment on a research project—all with the most careful and patient attention, the highest scholarly standards, and the most humane sensitivity to the needs and interests of others. Still others have benefited from Kline's energy and generosity without knowing it, as indirect recipients of his tireless service to the many journals, professional organizations, and scholarly projects in the Slavic field with which he has been associated. Most recently this has included work on the editorial boards of such journals as *Russian Studies in Philosophy* (formerly *Soviet Studies in Philosophy*) and *Studies in East European Thought* (formerly *Studies in Soviet Thought*) as well as service in many capacities to the American Association for the Advancement of Slavic Studies.

George Kline's work in Russian philosophy has been so extensive and so constant over a period of more than forty years that some may be surprised to learn that his scholarly energies are not exhausted by that field, or even by the broader area of Russian literature and culture, to which he has also made significant contributions. In addition, Kline has written and edited a great many publications in other areas of philosophy, most particularly on Marx and Marxism (apart from its Russian incarnation), on the philosophy of Alfred North Whitehead, and on the philosophy of Hegel and modern Continental European philosophy generally. It is in recognition of these accomplishments that Kline has been selected as president of both the Hegel Society of America (1984–86) and the Metaphysical Society of America (1985–1986). Perhaps the best testimony to Kline's stature in philosophy outside the Russian field is the fact that another *festschrift*, quite separate from the present volume and compiled by a different set of former students, friends, and admirers, is being prepared under the editorship of Shaun Gallagher; tentatively titled *Hegel and Hermeneutics*, it honors Kline for his achievements in the other areas of philosophy. There already exists in print an analysis and appreciation of Kline's work on Marx and (non-Russian) Marxism by Tom Rockmore, accompanied by a bibliography of Kline's writings in that area.[6]

Even apart from his achievements in other fields, however, George

Kline's remarkable contributions to research and study in the field of Russian philosophy have earned him a place of honor in American and world scholarship. The following essays are offered in celebration of those contributions.

Notes

1. Philip T. Grier, "George L. Kline's Influence on the Study of Russian and Soviet Philosophy in the United States," in *Philosophical Sovietology: The Pursuit of a Science*, ed. Helmut Dahm, Thomas J. Blakeley, and George L. Kline (Dordrecht: D. Reidel, 1988), pp. 243–62.

2. "George L. Kline: Writings on Russian and Soviet Philosophy," in *Philosophical Sovietology*, pp. 204–13.

The following is a selected list of Kline's writings in the field of Russian philosophy published after the above bibliography was compiled (excluding reprints, translations, translated works already published in English, and book reviews):

Philosophical Sovietology: The Pursuit of a Science, ed. Helmut Dahm, Thomas J. Blakeley, and George L. Kline (Dordrecht: D. Reidel, 1988).

"Russische und westeuropäische Denker über Tradition, Gegenwart und Zukunft," trans. Edda Werfel, in *Europa und die Folgen: Castelgandolfo-Gespräche 1987*, ed. Krzysztof Michalski (Stuttgart: Klett-Cotta, 1988), pp. 146–64.

"Reuniting the Eastern and Western Churches: Vladimir Soloviev's Ecumenical Project (1881–1896) and Its Contemporary Critics," *Transactions of the Association of Russian-American Scholars in the U.S.A.*, vol. 21 (1988 [issued in 1990]), pp. 209–25.

"La Philosophie en Union Soviétique autour de 1930," trans. Marc Weinstein, in *Histoire de la littérature russe: Le XXe siècle, Gels e dégels*, ed. E. Etkind, et al. (Paris: Payard, 1990), pp. 256–66.

"Present, Past, and Future in the Writings of Alexander Herzen," *Synthesis Philosophica* (Zagreb), vol. 5 (1990), pp. 183–93.

"Soviet Ethical Theory," in *Encyclopedia of Ethics*, ed. Lawrence C. Becker (New York: Garland, 1992), pp. 1195–99.

"The Defence of Terrorism: Trotsky and His Major Critics," in *The Trotsky Reappraisal*, ed. Terry Brotherstone and Paul Dukes (Edinburgh: Edinburgh University Press, 1992), pp. 156–65.

"Changing Russian Assessments of Spinoza and Their German Sources (1796–1862)," in *Philosophical Imagination and Cultural Memory: Appropriating Historical Traditions*, ed. Patricia Cook (Durham, NC: Duke University Press, 1993), pp. 176–94.

"The Potential Contribution of Classical Russian Philosophy to the Building of a Humane Society in Russia," in *XIX World Congress of Philosophy (Moscow, 22–28 August 1993): Invited Lectures* (Moscow: XIX World Congress of Philosophy, 1993), pp. 34–50.

"The Hegelian Roots of S.L. Frank's Ethics and Social Philosophy," *The Owl of Minerva*, vol. 25, no. 2 (1994), pp. 195–208.

"Skovoroda's Metaphysics," in *Hryhorij Savvich Skovoroda: An Anthology of Critical Articles*, ed. Thomas E. Bird and Richard H. Marshall, Jr. (Toronto: University of Toronto Press, 1994), pp. 223–38.

3. *Philosophical Sovietology*, p. 246.

4. Stanisláv Dzhimbinov in his essay below implies that Zen'kovskii's original Russian text was used in this Soviet publication. But George Kline was informed by a

former editor at the press that issued the work (the "Inostrannaia literatura" [Foreign Literature] Publishing House) that it was back-translated from Kline's English version so as to facilitate editorial slanting. (Neither Kline nor the authors of the present volume have had access to a copy of the 1956 Soviet edition.)

5. See, for example, Bernice Glatzer Rosenthal, ed., *Nietzsche in Russia* (Princeton, NJ: Princeton University Press, 1986).

6. Tom Rockmore, "Kline on Marx and Marxism," in *Philosophical Sovietology*, pp. 218–42 (see pp. 214–17 for the bibliography mentioned).

RUSSIAN
THOUGHT
AFTER COMMUNISM

I

Overview

Although philosophy as a distinct intellectual enterprise was slow to emerge in Russia, by the end of the nineteenth century that country possessed a vital philosophical culture—a culture that was active, productive, and capable of sustained existence, despite the fact that it was overshadowed by Russia's stunning achievements in literature and music.

The earliest expressions of this Russian philosophical culture are found in the second quarter of the nineteenth century in the writings of Petr Chaadaev, the Slavophile thinkers Ivan Kireevskii and Aleksei Khomiakov, and Westernists such as Aleksandr Herzen and Vissarion Belinskii. Its development gained momentum with the modest liberalization of Russian society that followed the death of the "tsar-disciplinarian," Nicholas I, in 1855. The reopening or revitalization of philosophy departments in the major Russian universities contributed to the process, and by the end of the century Russian philosophy not only had become professionalized and institutionalized but could boast so brilliant a representative as Vladimir Solov'ev, whose original philosophical synthesis incorporated elements of both Slavophile and Westernist thinking. The Russian philosophical culture had come to maturity.

It was not a monolithic culture. Although Solov'ev's influence was far-reaching and profound, his synthesis as such was not widely shared. Most thinkers gravitated toward either the Slavophile (Christian, mystical, nationalist, conservative) pole or the Westernist (secular, scientific, internationalist, liberal) pole of the unique Russian philosophical spectrum. Tsarist censorship assured that the publicly available expressions of Russian philosophical thought were primarily religious and politically conservative, but there were also outstanding representatives of a secular orientation and of liberal and revolutionary political philosophies. Marxism had an early appeal in Russia; because of its stress on economic production and industrial development, it was to some degree even welcomed initially by the tsarist authorities (as Andrzej Walicki points out in his essay in this volume) as an alternative to the anti-industrial policies and terrorist tactics of the Populist movement. Furthermore, the Russian philosophical culture was thematically broad based, extending to all of the commonly recognized philosophical disciplines of the day. Its close ties with belles lettres (particularly in the persons of such writer-thinkers as Lev Tolstoi and Fedor Dostoevskii) were a reflection of Russian philosophy's strong focus on "man and his fate," and hence its special attention to ethics, the philosophy of religion, the philosophy of history, and social philosophy. But the more abstract philosophical disciplines were not neglected, although there was more interest in metaphysics than in epistemology or logic.

The flowering of Russian art, music, and literature in the first decades of the twentieth century—the period now commonly referred to as "the Silver Age"—by no means excluded philosophy; indeed, it marked the high point in the development of independent Russian philosophical thought up to the present day. Original thinkers such as Nikolai Berdiaev, Sergei Bulgakov, Dmitrii Merezhkovskii, and Vasilii Rozanov, all closely allied with the worlds of literature and art but at the same time in contact with philosophy's institutional, academic base, contributed powerfully to the intellectual ferment of the time. The publication of philosophical books expanded greatly, especially after the easing of censorship that followed the Revolution of 1905. Russia's first philosophy journal, *Voprosy filosofii i psikhologii* (Problems of philosophy and psychology), founded as early as 1890, provided a lively forum for original philosophical investigations and the exchange of opinions. In keeping with the spirit of the times, religious searchings were particularly prominent in the philosophy of the Silver Age; Russian philosophers, many of them by then fallen-away Marxists, sought to ground their thinking in Christian doctrine (often dramatically reinterpreted) or at least to achieve an accommodation with Christian doctrine—constrained to do so no longer by tsarist pressures but by their own profound belief in the apocalyptic salvation of Russia.

The apocalypse came in 1917, but salvation did not follow. The devastation inflicted on Russian culture by Communist rule was nowhere more complete than in the field of philosophy, as Dzhimbinov recounts in his essay below. As early as 1922, a large group of prominent, religiously minded Russian philosophers, including Berdiaev, Nikolai Losskii, and many others, were among the more than 100 non-Marxist intellectual and artistic figures forcibly expelled from the country on Lenin's order.[1] This action was followed by increasing censorship and restrictions on new publications, leading eventually to the total elimination of opportunities to express opposition to Marxist philosophy (particularly after the state was given a monopoly on printing in 1930), as well as to the banishment of all elements of Russia's philosophical past that could be deemed inimical to Marxism or an obstacle to the triumph of the proletarian revolution. "Dangerous" works of the past were no longer republished; the books of Russia's greatest philosophers were removed from academic curricula and from public library shelves (to be sequestered in restricted collections), and the philosophers' very names were expunged from library card catalogs and from reference books.

In this way the religiously oriented stream of Russian philosophy, the dominant stream at that time, was effectively cut off—rather, was diverted abroad, where it continued to develop, but now in isolation from the living culture of the Russian people in their homeland. For many years the Russian émigré philosophical community, centered in Paris, was an intellectually lively and creative one, which produced many original and profound philosophical works. But over time its aging ranks, despite some replenishment by later émigrés, eventually lost their vision and dynamism.

The portion of the Russian philosophical heritage that was closer to its secular pole fared somewhat better under communism, since many of its representatives could be co-opted by Marxism-Leninism and presented as true believers in, or at least forerunners of, Russian Marxism—unless, of course, they had contrived to run afoul of Marx (as Bakunin had), or of Lenin (as Plekhanov had), or of Stalin (as Trotskii had). In this way, thinkers such as Herzen, Belinskii, Pisarev, and Chernyshevskii (not to mention still earlier figures such as Lomonosov and Radishchev) were not only saved from oblivion, they were lionized and all but deified. Their works (with suitable omissions and heavily ideological commentary) were published repeatedly in massive editions and were studied in every high school. Still, in its own way this mandated, selective overexposure killed the secular side of the Russian philosophical heritage as effectively as banishment killed the religious side. The ideas of these "approved" philosophers were distorted in order to force them into the ideological mold, and they were deadened by the ritual repetition of this conceptual violence.

Thus by the mid-twentieth-century Russian philosophical culture, which had taken on independent life more than a century before, appeared to be essentially moribund, in both its religious and its secular dimensions, having been replaced in Russia by a dogmatic, ideologized philosophy with its own largely uncritical and uncreative culture. Indeed, the Marxist alternative seemed so entrenched that as late as 1985 many would have thought it foolhardy to predict that Russia's pre-Marxist past would soon be a major intellectual force in that country.

Actually, however, the appearance of philosophical desolation was de-ceiving. Even within the orthodox Marxist-Leninist mainstream there was some genuine intellectual vitality, nourished in part by surviving links with the pre-Soviet past.[2] And as Dzhimbinov points out, the return to the Russian philosophical patrimony was already under way before the onset of glasnost. Dzhimbinov describes the growing cracks that began to appear in the Marxist monolith soon after the death of Stalin in 1953, and that led in 1970 to the surprising liberalism displayed in the treatment of the history of Russian philosophy in the fifth and final volume of the Soviet *Philosophical Encyclopedia*. A conservative contraction followed; but, by fits and starts, the trend of liberalization subsequently resumed with the appearance of other adventuresome publications, so that even before perestroika began there was a significant body of literature having to do with the previously scorned Russian philosophers. Dzhimbinov closes his account with the epochal 1988 decision on the part of the Communist Party Politburo (persuaded, it is said, by the arguments of Aleksandr Iakovlev) to issue, as an appendix to the journal *Voprosy filosofii* (Problems of philosophy), a series of volumes containing works "from the history of Russian philosophical thought"—volumes to be printed by the "Pravda" Publishing House, no less.

Within a few short years the voices of the forgotten Russian thinkers were not simply being heard but had virtually drowned out the Marxists who had enjoyed a philosophical monopoly for more than half a century. What seemed moribund had in fact merely been dormant, or in a state of suspended animation, and given the opportunity Russians returned to their philosophical heritage with alacrity. The *Voprosy filosofii* appendix project became several annual series of volumes; although beset by publishing complications and delays, it has made a huge contribution to the dissemination of knowledge about the Russian philosophical past. The first series, dated 1989, included volumes of selected works by Mikhail Bakunin, Nikolai Berdiaev, Petr Chaadaev, Konstantin Kavelin, Dmitrii Pisarev, Aleksandr Potebnia, Gustav Shpet, and Vladimir Solov'ev (two volumes). In 1990, the authors were Pavel Florenskii (three volumes), Semen Frank, Pamfil Iurkevich, Petr Kropotkin, Aleksei Losev, Vasilii Rozanov (two volumes), and Petr Tkachev. The third series, bearing a 1991 imprint, included volumes of works by Vladimir Ern, Nikolai Losskii, and Pavel Novgorodtsev as well as a volume containing two famous and influential collections of essays by idealist philosophers—*Vekhi* (Landmarks) and *Iz glubiny* (From the depths). The fourth series of volumes, announced for 1993 but not all yet published in 1994, includes Sergei Bulgakov (two volumes), Ivan Il'in (two volumes), Viacheslav Ivanov, Aleksei Khomiakov (two volumes), Lev Shestov (two volumes), Evgenii Trubetskoi (two volumes), and Boris Vysheslavtsev.

Russian philosophical and literary periodicals, too, played a major role in bringing the ideas of these rehabilitated thinkers to a broad public. Beginning in 1988, almost every issue of *Voprosy filosofii* has contained one or more essays by or about them, in sections headed "Philosophical Heritage" or "From the History of Russian Philosophical Thought." Somewhat later the other principal philosophical journals followed suit; one of them—*Filosofskie nauki* (Philosophical sciences)—was compelled to cease publication for financial reasons in 1991, but each of the two principal Russian universities—Moscow State University and St. Petersburg State University—continues to issue a series of its *Vestnik* (Bulletin) that deals with philosophy and in which the history of Russian philosophy has a prominent place. And the literary periodicals, such as the weekly *Literaturnaia gazeta* (Literary gazette), have been if anything still more open to the history of Russian philosophy than the philosophical journals.[3] The subject is also treated regularly in a former official journal that has had a remarkable transformation: what was the theoretical organ of the Communist Party of the Soviet Union—*Kommunist*—is now published and widely read as an independent journal entitled *Svobodnaia mysl'* (Free thought). Finally, a large number of new philosophy journals began publication in the early 1990s, and many of them look to the history of Russian philosophy as a prime source of material; one in particular—*Nachala* (Beginnings)—deals exclusively with problems of Russian philosophy.[4]

What accounts for the great enthusiasm with which Russian philosophy was rediscovered in Russia? Among many contributing factors, some stand out. There is, of course, the lure of formerly forbidden fruit. In the contemporary philosophical renaissance the first and greatest attention was paid to writings—the works of Nikolai Berdiaev are a prime example—that were essentially unavailable or even unknown to Soviet readers, and many readers were initially fascinated by them in part simply because these works had been considered too dangerous for public consumption.

A second, more serious motive was the desire for historical fairness and completeness, intensified by a sense of the need for justice to those who were repressed, exterminated, or at least arbitrarily excluded from the historical record. Gorbachev encouraged this impulse with his pledge that there would be no "blank spots" in history, and the impulse is responsible for what has become a broad-scale program of recovering Russia's past through new publications and the expansion of access to archives, restricted collections of suppressed books, and other previously hidden records of the past. In philosophy, the ambitious *Voprosy filosofii* appendix project was one of the principal fruits of this drive for historical openness.

In addition to serving personal curiosity and historical fairness, however, the writings of the older philosophers have had great appeal because of their inherent quality. On the whole the level of their intellectual and literary merit is immeasurably higher than that of the Marxist-Leninist writings they have replaced. The ideas they express are far more imaginative and stimulating, and their language is not merely a breath but an entire atmosphere of fresh air in comparison with the impoverished vocabulary, the sloganeering, and the bureaucratic obfuscation of the typical Marxist-Leninist text. Stylistically almost any change from the language of "diamat" (dialectical materialism) would be welcome, but in fact many of the thinkers that have been rediscovered—Rozanov and Shestov come to mind immediately—are particularly noted for the vigor, richness, and inventiveness of their style.

Of course the substantive content of the thought of the earlier philosophers was also an important factor in their reemergence. For the most part they are thinkers of a religious, Russian Orthodox cast of mind, and as such they have found a sympathetic audience in a society that is not only newly freed of restraints on religion but positively drawn toward it. The freedom of scholars to explore the religious dimension of Russian philosophy coincides with a government policy that favors religion and a public attitude of heightened intellectual and devotional interest in the Christian faith, both Orthodox and non-Orthodox.

Added to the religious appeal of the earlier philosophers is another substantive appeal of their writings—one that derives from a historical parallel between their situation and the present day. The birth and evolution of Russia's modern philosophical culture was nearly contemporaneous with the origin and spread of Marxism, which became influential in Russia early in its history. Many of the suppressed Russian philosophers were severe critics of Marxism, including some who had been Marxists themselves but abandoned that faith early in the twentieth century. The present-day rejection of Marxism in Russia can thus be seen as a vindication of the earlier thinkers, with whom the disillusioned Marxists of the present day feel a kinship and in whose writings they find a rich and prophetic source of anti-Marxist reflections. Andrzej Walicki, in his essay in section III of this volume, examines the newly relevant case against Marxism as presented by several prominent Silver Age thinkers.

Of course other, non-Russian critics of Marxism are not ignored in today's open intellectual environment; a striking sign of how open that environment had become by 1990 was the publication in *Voprosy filosofii* of a complete translation of Friedrich von Hayek's classic antisocialist treatise, *The Road to Serfdom*.[5] But in addition to the attraction of their anti-Marxism, the earlier Russian thinkers are also the beneficiaries of the widespread belief that Marxism had drawn the country away from its own true culture and its native path of development, the nature and special virtues of which were understood by the Russian thinkers. Thus a return to the Slavophiles, Solov'ev, and Berdiaev is an attempt to find native material to fill the cultural vacuum left by the collapse of Marxism. Of course many would argue that Marxism generated merely a pseudoculture that never really replaced genuine Russian culture in people's hearts, however much it filled their textbooks and newspapers. In any event, whether it is a question of refilling cultural space or simply revivifying what is already there, the earlier Russian philosophers are seen as a storehouse of uniquely appropriate and valuable insights.

In the first flush of victory over Marxist ideology, the enthusiasm for the early thinkers was particularly great, and some Russian commentators now believe that it generated unrealistic expectations. People who opposed the "totalitarian ideology," Sergei Khoruzhii writes, "believed that the collapse of this ideology would produce a new world-view for a free country and that this world-view would be based on the teaching of our great Christian thinkers, the philosophical tradition founded by Vladimir Soloviev." Khoruzhii is disturbed by what he sees as an attitude of disillusionment that arose when the ideas of these great philosophers did not magically and immediately resolve Russia's urgent social and cultural problems, so that in fact the philosophers of the past did not fill "the vacant positions of spiritual teachers for the whole society."[6] And he is still more disturbed that public attention in Russia appears to be shifting more toward their extremist epigoni and popularizers, who, rather than seeking to understand "the Tradition," as he calls the religious philosophical heritage, merely use it for their own essentially political purposes:

> In the background of the Tradition, among its weaker and dubious elements, a hotchpotch of ideas and figures is being thrown together to produce a nationalist-Orthodox ideology for the new "Time of Troubles": the fabulous quasi-Orthodox quasi-mystics of Sergey Nilus, the authoritarian ideology of Ivan Il'in, the fantastic monarchism of Ivan Solonevich, the theories of Eurasianism. . . . But now the crisis has gone deeper. The defenders of the Tradition today are not Berdyaev, Bulgakov and Frank, but journalists who swear in the names of Berdyaev, Bulgakov and Frank, barely read and largely misunderstood by them.[7]

Although Khoruzhii's pessimistic assessment of the present intellectual atmosphere is not universally shared, the phenomenon to which he points—the abuse of Russian religious philosophy to support illiberal political programs—is a reality that will figure in a number of the essays below, particularly the essays on the Slavophiles and Il'in. On the whole, however, the book will concentrate on the major thinkers of the past who are once again prominent in Russia's intellectual life and on the significance of their ideas in Russia today. Each essay examines some aspect of the Russian philosophical heritage that is now being reappropriated by Russian thinkers, in the hope of mutually illuminating both the heritage and the present day.

Notes

1. For an account of their expulsion, see S.S. Khoruzhii, "Filosofskii korabl'," *Literaturnaia gazeta*, 9 May 1990 and 6 June 1990.

2. See James P. Scanlan, *Marxism in the USSR: A Critical Survey of Current Soviet Thought* (Ithaca, NY: Cornell University Press, 1985).

3. The Spring 1990 issue (vol. 28, no. 4) of the translation journal *Soviet Studies in Literature* (now *Russian Studies in Literature*) consists of articles from *Literaturnaia gazeta* on seven prominent Russian philosophers of the past.

4. Other new philosophy journals are entitled *Stupeni* (Stages), *Paralleli* (Parallels), *Chelovek* (Man), *Logos*, *Voprosy metodologii* (Problems of methodology), *Filosofskie issledovaniia* (Philosophical investigations), *Put'* (The way), and *Vybor* (Choice).

5. *Voprosy filosofii*, 1990, no. 10, pp. 113–51; no. 11, pp. 123–65; no. 12, pp. 103–49.

6. S.S. Horujy, "Russian Religious Philosophy: Present State and Future Prospects," unpublished paper presented at the Transnational Institute Conference on "The Renewal of Russian Spiritual Life," Dartmouth College, Hanover, NH, 8–11 July 1992, p. 2.

7. Ibid., p. 5 (ellipses in original).

STANISLAV BEMOVICH DZHIMBINOV

1 | The Return of Russian Philosophy

In order to understand what happened to Russian philosophy in our country, let us perform a thought experiment: let us imagine that the same thing
happened to Russian literature.[1] That is, that we were left with only "revolutionary democrats" and the writers in agreement with them—the materi-
alist atheists. To keep the experiment pure and simple, let us take only the
greatest names. Thus we will publish, esteem, and study only "progressive"
writers in the above sense. Only two writers would perhaps remain:
Mikhail Saltykov-Shchedrin and Nikolai Nekrasov, and even with these
two we would be stretching the point a bit—Shchedrin is after all the
author of *Provincial Sketches* (Gubernskie ocherki) and Nekrasov is the
author of *Vlas*, in which there is so much love for holy *Rus´* with its God's
fools (*iurodivye*) and its beggars. Now let us look at whom we would leave
out, whom we would not publish or study. First, of course, there are Tolstoi
and Dostoevskii; their religiosity leaves not the slightest doubt. (Not very
many people know that in 1928, on the hundredth anniversary of the birth
of Lev Tolstoi, in Moscow the state publishing house "Atheist" published a
book under the title *Lev Tolstoi as the Pillar and Bulwark of Priestly Rule*
[Lev Tolstoi kak stolp i utverzhdenie popovshchiny], with the touching
subtitle *A Collection of Useful Materials* [Sbornik poleznykh materialov],
intended, of course, for "agitators, propagandists, and leaders." The book
was published in a huge run for that time—10,000 copies—but, alas, it
soon landed in the special archives, not because of its title—believe me, the
title was quite in the spirit of the times—but because, in addition to leading
articles by Rosa Luxemburg and Liubov´ Aksel´rod, a leading article by
Lev Trotskii was also included. But that is just an aside.)

After Tolstoi and Dostoevskii, Gogol´ would also disappear: everyone
knows how he ended up. And, following Gogol´, after some vacilla-
tions, it would have been necessary to relinquish Pushkin and Lermontov,
since it is impossible to rank them among the representatives of a material-
ist world view. And after them a torrent of others would no longer be
published or studied: Derzhavin, Zhukovskii, Batiushkov, Krylov, Karamzin,

Baratynskii, Tiutchev, Kol'tsov, A.K. Tolstoi, Goncharov, A.N. Ostrovskii, Leskov, Pisemskii. But what's the point of enumerating them? In all of the great Russian literature there were perhaps only two classic atheists—Turgenev and Chekhov—but even they were not particularly sympathetic with the progressive (destructive) currents of their time, so that one can liken them to the revolutionary democrats only against their wills. In a word, we would be left with Saltykov-Shchedrin and Nekrasov. Fortunately, all this is only a terrible dream, and nothing of the sort happened. (Although, parenthetically, I should mention in addition to the collection on Tolstoi one more striking and likewise little-known fact: not one collection of Pushkin's work was published in our country in the 1920's; there were only selected one-volume editions, and the first collection of his works came out only in 1930 in six volumes, with a leading article by Comrade Lunacharskii about Pushkin's historical limitations, as an appendix to the journal *Red Field* [Krasnaia niva]. I present this fact as material for reflection: we have always loved to idealize the twenties, but they got along splendidly without Pushkin's collected works, preferring to publish multivolume collections of the works of Vladimir Lidin, Mikhail Kol'tsov, and other giants of the epoch, many of whom at the time were not yet even thirty years old. It was a glorious time.) But the situation changed abruptly in the thirties, and 1937 was remembered by people of the older generation as the year of Pushkin. Pushkin was thrust upon them in hundreds of editions in manifest excess, as if forgetting that they were celebrating the hundredth anniversary of the poet's murder.

As for Tolstoi and Dostoevskii, their complete collected works were begun in the twenties (Dostoevskii's in 1926 and Tolstoi's in 1928; the works of Tolstoi stretched on for thirty years, for they consisted of ninety volumes).

In a word, it proved impossible to take literature away from the Russian people. It is all the more surprising, then, that this was managed so totally and completely in the case of philosophy. First, the history of Russian thought was divided into two flagrantly unequal parts: a revolutionary-democratic, "progressive" part (i.e., all those who contributed to the death of historical Russia), and a "reactionary," religious part. To give a graphic idea, the qualitative and quantitative relation between these two parts may be expressed as 5 percent and 95 percent. Five percent were published and commented upon to exhaustion (also less than brilliantly, incidentally; it would be the pinnacle of naiveté to think that we were capable of outstanding works on Dobroliubov and Chernyshevskii; suffice it to say that the chief specialist on Dobroliubov before the war was the chief censor of all of *Rus'*, P.I. Lebedev-Polianskii, head of Glavlit [Chief Administration of Literature and the Press]). As for the 95 percent, that is, essentially the bulk of Russian philosophy, it was virtually declared to be nonexistent: not only could these philosophers not be published and commented upon, one could not even rail against them in any detail. (It is no accident that the first book totally devoted to such verbal abuse, *Russian Religious Philosophy* [Russkaia religioznaia filosofiia] by Valerii Kuvakin, did not appear until 1980, that is, almost "as the curtain fell," and the author earnestly prided himself on breaking the "conspiracy of silence." Although which is better, silence or crude invective, is another question.)

Let us recall the main dates in just the twentieth century. After October 1905, censorship was essentially abolished in Russia. A vigorous flowering, now difficult to imagine, of Russian philosophical thought began. Not a year passed but that one or even two great philosophical books appeared. A new and fourth gift (after icons, literature, and music) from Russia to the world was born: Russian thought. As if sensing that there was little time left—only ten to twelve years—philosophers hurried, laying the foundations of the future edifice with granite slabs. The war began, but even it did not stop the intellectual creativity. Let me mention the main books in support of my point:

- 1914: *The Pillar and Bulwark of the Truth* (Stolp i utverzhdenie istiny) by Pavel Florenskii;
- 1915: *The Object of Knowledge* (Predmet znaniia) by Semen Frank;
- 1916: *The Meaning of Creativity* (Smysl tvorchestva) by Nikolai Berdiaev;
- 1917: *The Unfading Light* (Svet nevechernii) by Sergei Bulgakov;
- 1918: *The Meaning of Life* (Smysl zhizni) by Evgenii Trubetskoi; *On the Social Ideal* (Ob obshchestvennom ideale) by Pavel Novgorodstev; *The Apocalypse of Our Times* (Apokalipsis nashego vremeni) by Vasilii Rozanov.

1918 . . . The light was already being extinguished; it was not possible to write in the dark, but philosophers made haste, and books continued to come out by some miracle (the Bolsheviks simply "did not have enough time" to do everything in the first years). It was said that if Russia had not been destroyed in 1917, within two decades (i.e., by 1937) it would have become the richest and the most flourishing country in the world. I do not know, but I fully allow for such a possibility. But what I do know with certainty is that if Russian philosophy had been given the chance to develop freely for another whole two decades in its homeland, treasures of worldwide significance, difficult now to imagine and comparable to Russian literature of the nineteenth century, would have been created.

Rozanov spoke better than anyone about the significance of Russian literature:

> Strictly speaking, the only brilliant thing, in a sense *monstrously* brilliant, in Russia was *literature*. Not our faith, not our church, not the state—nothing was as brilliant, as expressive, and as strong. Russian literature, despite the fact that *it existed for only one century*, rose to become a quite universal phenomenon unsurpassed in beauty and in its merits by any nation, not excluding the Greeks and their Homer, not excluding the Italians and their Dante, not excluding the English and their Shakespeare, and, finally, not yielding even to the Jews and their Holy Scriptures, their "hieratic parchments." Here it is a question of self-perception, of the soul, of the heart. The century Russia lived through *so passionately* in literature was a century in which it believed totally, it believed in every line written, that it was living through some sort of holy scripture, some sacred manuscripts. . . . And this was true to the very last minute, until almost all the newspapers were shut down, until the fateful 1918.[2]

Rozanov wrote this with a failing hand in Sergiev Posad in 1918, a year and a half before dying of hunger, in the article "From the Top of a Thousand-Year-Old Pyramid (Reflections on the Course of Russian Literature)" (S vershiny tysiacheletnei piramidy [Razmyshlenie o khode russkoi literatury]), which could no longer be printed anywhere, and the article patiently awaited publication for seventy-two years.

Is it a coincidence that the best statement about Russian literature came from a philosopher? Of course not. Philosophy is precisely what in science is called basic research, without which the entire empirical side would not be able to develop intelligently.

Not long before World War I, the first Russian philosophical publishing houses were established. It is pleasant to recall that the two best and most serious publishers, "Put'" and "G. Leman and S. Sakharov," were founded in Moscow and not in glittering St. Petersburg. "Put'" is the one that began the unprecedented series of monographs *Russian Thinkers* [Russkie mysliteli]. Altogether only three books managed to appear: *A.S. Khomiakov* by Berdiaev, *A.A. Kozlov* by Sergei Askol'dov (the author was Kozlov's illegitimate son), and *G.S. Skovoroda* by Vladimir Ern, the preface of which provides perhaps the best definition of the distinctive features of Russian philosophy. Pending publication were books by V. Borodaevskii on Konstantin Leont'ev, by Berdiaev on Nikolai Fedorov, by Viacheslav Ivanov on Fedor Tiutchev, by Florenskii on Father Serapion Mashkin, by Vasilii Zen'kovskii on Gogol', by Rozanov on A.M. Bukharev . . . "Put'" Publishers managed to exist for seven years (1910–17) and published a total of forty books, but what books they were! Gershenzon's complete editions of Ivan Kireevskii and

Petr Chaadaev (in two volumes each); Trubetskoi's book *Vladimir Solov'ev's World View* (Mirosozertsanie Vl. Solov'eva) (in two volumes), still unsurpassed; Bulgakov's two-volume *Two Cities* (Dva grada) and his *Philosophy of Economics* (Filosofiia khoziaistva); *The Struggle for Logos* (Bor'ba za Logos) by Ern; and the already-mentioned *Pillar* by Florenskii and *The Unfading Light* by Bulgakov.

Indeed, there is no comparison with the scribblings of "Politizdat" (Publishing House for Political Literature) that for seventy years replaced Russian thought for us.

But let us return to history. It is 1922. "People of ideas" are being exiled. The most striking thing is that all had to be exiled by force, under the threat of the death penalty (each signed a declaration that he would be shot if he tried to return). No one left the homeland of his own free will. Here is a list of exiled philosophers: Berdiaev, Bulgakov, Frank, Nikolai Losskii, Ivan Il'in, Lev Karsavin, Boris Vysheslavtsev, Fedor Stepun, Ivan Lapshin . . .

Lev Shestov was already living abroad before the revolution; Dmitrii Merezhkovskii left earlier, in 1920; Rozanov died in 1919 . . . Who was left? Of the great philosophers, only Father Pavel Florenskii and the quite young Aleksei Losev (he was 29 in 1922) remained. Arrest and the camp awaited both, of course. (Florenskii was shot, and Losev survived for a half century after the camp and was nearly turned into a Marxist. It is painful to write about this.)

For some reason Mikhail Gershenzon, who inspired the collection *Landmarks* (Vekhi), was not exiled, but he soon died (in 1925).

It appears that the last "idealist" Russian book was the fourth volume of Vladimir Solov'ev's *Letters* (Pis'ma), which appeared in 1923. Thereafter came the desert of the twenties through the forties, albeit with a few oases. In 1927–30, no less than eight books by Losev appeared, although in small runs (from 500 to 1,500 copies), and in 1935 another remarkable event occurred: five previously unknown "Philosophical Letters" (Filosofskie pis'ma) by Petr Chaadaev were printed all at one time in one of the regular volumes of the *Literary Heritage* (Literaturnoe nasledstvo) series (nos. 22–24) (it was found that the letter "On Architecture" [O zodchestve], published earlier as no. 4 in Gershenzon's editions, did not belong in the *Philosophical Letters*, so that essentially only three of the eight letters had been known). There was one other priceless publication in the same volume of the *Literary Heritage:* Konstantin Leont'ev's long autobiography, *My Literary Fate* (Moia literaturnaia sud'ba). And there you have perhaps everything that was done in the prewar years.

Our famous literary "thaw" in the late fifties and early sixties (1955–62) is perhaps comparable to the twenties, which got along without Pushkin.

Literally nothing was done in those years to publish or produce a commentary on Russian religious philosophy. By a strange coincidence, 1956 (the height of the "thaw") was the hundredth anniversary of the birth of V.V. Rozanov. But no one dared "to think, much less to speak" of noting this date in any way in print. This may seem puzzling at first glance—but only at first glance. Our entire "thaw," as well as those who were its vehicles—the "people of the sixties," who came to power during the time of perestroika—were totally unreligious people, and hence for them Russian philosophy simply did not exist. But never mind 1956! Thirty years later, in 1986, another Russian thinker, Georgii Fedotov, had the hundredth anniversary of his birth. But, as before, it was too early "to speak or think"; another two full years had to pass. But let us not get ahead of ourselves.

And yet something was stirring, even if it was at great depths. In 1954—that is, essentially even before the "thaw," almost the day after Stalin's death—a Russian translation of N.O. Losskii's book the *History of Russian Philosophy* (Istoriia russkoi filosofii) was published by the "Inostrannaia literatura" (Foreign literature) Publishing House in Moscow. The edition was limited, with volumes being numbered and stamped "distributed according to a special list"; its print run was probably somewhere between 500 and 1,000 copies. It was, of course, distributed only to comrades who were "tried and true," but at least it was published, and one could cite it in bibliographic references. True, the translation was quite incompetent; even the names of philosophers were not always spelled correctly by the translator—for example, for Shilkarskii he wrote 'Stsilkarskii,' and for Kobylinskii 'Kobilinskii'—but what is especially curious is that the names of books by philosophers and quotations from them were translated from an English translation and "magically" transformed. (Two republications of this book came out in the past year, by "Sovetskii pisatel' " and "Vysshaia shkola"; in the first edition not one word was changed; in the second, the grossest blunders were eliminated, but the quotations remained retranslations from the English. A Russian original of the *History of Russian Philosophy* probably does exist, but it is out of reach for our two biggest publishers.)

Two years later, in 1956, in the same "Inostrannaia literatura" Publishing House and also in a limited, numbered edition, Zen'kovskii's *History of Russian Philosophy*—still the best to this day—appeared in two volumes. Here at least it was not necessary to retranslate.[3] Both books, Losskii's and Zen'kovskii's, were in the special archives of large libraries, but they began to be available to the general reader in pale xerox copies sometime in the seventies. . . .

That same year, 1956, was the hundredth anniversary of the death of

Chaadaev, and the Academy of Sciences Publishing House announced a one-volume collection of his works. But the years passed, the book never came out, and it soon became known that the book had been "killed." It is striking that even Chaadaev was "unacceptable" in our "thaw"! In fact, Chaadaev's works were forbidden before 1905, and now we understood that they were forbidden (at least in a separate edition) after 1917 as well. It is not difficult to check and confirm that all the separate editions of Chaadaev's works were published in the brief interval between 1906 and 1917. One is hard put to recall even one other figure such as this—forbidden before 1905 and after 1917 . . . Were there any such in the history of Russia?

It is not so difficult to explain this puzzling phenomenon: a definite touch of Russophobia made Chaadaev unacceptable to both the old and the new state power. "Sovremennik" Publishers did not put out the first, very incomplete, Chaadaev collection until thirty years after 1956, at the beginning of perestroika, in 1987, and this same publisher followed that a year later with a quite complete collection (both under the editorship of and with a foreword by B. Tarasov).

But let us return to the now already distant sixties. Starting in 1960, a "thaw" year, "Sovetskaia entsiklopediia" Publishers put out a fully official *Philosophical Encyclopedia* (Filosofskaia entsiklopediia). It contained articles about Russian idealist philosophers, but written in the most orthodox, tooth-cracking manner. But suddenly in 1967, with the fourth volume, something miraculous happened to the editors. This volume contained ten articles written by the then still young, thirty-year-old Sergei Averintsev. I remember how the words of one Moscow priest were passed on by word of mouth: after reading the article by Averintsev entitled "Orthodoxy" (Pravoslavie), he said that any one of us could have put his name to such an article without changing a single word. And this article—a long article of two and a half pages—was printed in an official Soviet encyclopedia! This was unheard of. . . . True, there was a short addendum to the article, signed with another name, in which the official atheistic point of view was presented; but who read this addendum, who paid any attention to it? It was clearly separated from Averintsev's article.

But the most important event took place three years later, in 1970, when the fifth and last volume of the *Philosophical Encyclopedia* appeared. This was a real sensation. It is too bad that the volume comprised only a few letters of the alphabet—from the middle of the letter 'S' to the end, to 'Ia.' I remember how a comrade of mine showed me the article on Vladimir Solov'ev not only with astonishment but even with trepidation and suggested comparing it with the article about Engels in the same volume. The article on Solov'ev was longer! There were four signatures under it, beginning with Valentin Asmus and ending with my friend Sergei Khoruzhii. But what was most important was not the size of the article but its tone: serious, businesslike, and thoughtful, without any vile Marxist abuse. I began to study the volume and first made a complete list of the articles by Averintsev (with a pencil) on the flyleaf at the back of the volume, so that later I could read them one by one and enjoy them at my leisure. Indeed, it was almost a physiological delight. Not only the tone but the very texture of the articles was completely different—dense, satiated, and satisfying. This was a voice from another world. A modern secular theologian was living and working among us, a person who was almost our peer in age. Such was Bulgakov, too, before he was ordained in 1918.

Averintsev had assimilated the experience of both European and Russian culture with equal thoroughness and rare harmony. He resurrected the type of the Russian European, the Russian wanderer in Europe, about whom Dostoevskii so much loved to write (because he felt this person in himself), and who, it seemed, had already been totally exterminated in our country in the prewar years. . . . The struggle against the spirit is useless after all: it is indestructible and ineradicable.

There were altogether twenty-seven articles by Averintsev in the fifth volume, and even their topics seemed unlikely for a Soviet (or, better, a "quasi-Soviet") publication: Sophia, Salvation, Theodicy, Chiliasm, Eschatology . . . These things could be written about only in an encyclopedia; try to imagine an article on Sophia in the journal *Voprosy filosofii*. . . .

Averintsev showed that one can make a name for oneself writing articles in a reference publication, where it would seem that the very nature of the articles precludes individuality. Of course, during these same years he also had a series of articles in *Voprosy literatury* (but not in *Voprosy filosofii*), and there were articles in small, short-run scholarly collections, but the articles in the encyclopedia were for some reason especially valuable; nor were they eclipsed by later articles in another encyclopedia, *Myths of the Peoples of the World* (Mify narodov mira). They could even be collected in a book, as Vladimir Solov'ev's articles from the encyclopedic dictionary of Brockhaus and Ephron were collected in the tenth volume of his works.

Incidentally, this had already been accomplished for one author, if only partially. In the early seventies, when I became acquainted with A.F. Losev, he gave me a truly rare book: *A. Losev. Articles on the History of Ancient Philosophy for the Fourth and Fifth Volumes of the "Philosophical Encyclopedia"* (A. Losev. Stat'i po istorii antichnoi filosofii dlia IV–V tomov "Filosofskoi entsiklopedii") (Moscow, 1965). In the publication data one could read an imperturbable "Printed in 250 copies." The book was printed in the same format and type style as the encyclopedia, but as a manuscript for discussion. I began to compare the articles in the book with those in the encyclopedia. The article "Neoplatonism" in the encyclopedia was abridged fourfold (from ten pages to two and a half); the article about Proclus, threefold, and so forth. What good fortune that this voice has been preserved for us, if only in 250 copies. . . . Of course, certain proportions had to be observed in the encyclopedia, but an exception could have been made for Losev even so. . . . Perhaps similar work had been done on Averintsev's articles? No, his intonations are audible in it. . . .

The hymn to the last volumes of the encyclopedia has imperceptibly become a critique, but I recall how the fifth volume was received then, in 1970. I remember that at a seminar on philosophy at the Literary Institute where I was studying at the time, our teacher loudly announced that a special resolution on the fifth volume of the *Philosophical Encyclopedia* had been passed "at the top": this sortie of the enemy had received a fitting evaluation, and a decision had been made to publish a new, totally revised edition of the fifth volume, infused with a strictly scientific, Marxist, and atheistic spirit. I remember after the seminar I said to our teacher that I had little faith in his prediction: the title page of the encyclopedia contained the name of the editor-in-chief, Academician Fedor Konstantinov, and he would hardly want to liken himself to the noncommissioned officer's widow who whipped herself. And so indeed did it turn out: years passed, but no second, "revised" edition of the fifth volume appeared. The person who was behind all the wonders of the fourth and fifth volumes was by then named publicly. It was, of course, not Konstantinov himself but his deputy Aleksandr Spirkin, along with the academic editors Iu. Popov and R. Gal'tseva.

The fifth volume contained many articles on Russian philosophers— Trubetskoi, Fedorov, Florenskii, Khomiakov, Shestov—all of them written about with unfailing respect. It is interesting that the authors of many of these articles, R. Gal'tseva and I. Rodnianskaia, did not even hold Candidate of Sciences degrees, and there was no need to explain why: one need only imagine the introduction and the conclusion to any philosophy dissertation of that time, with its forest of quotations from the founders of Marxism and its bibliography that opened (always, regardless of the topic of the dissertation) with the works of the same founders, to understand that, for a person who did not want to utter "even a little word of falsehood" (Bella Akhmadulina), the dissertation was a humiliating journey to Canossa and a passage under the yoke. Better to get along without a salary supplement. Only women were capable of that, it seems. Even my friend D. Lialikov (the author of articles on Fedorov, Fedotov, and many others in that same fifth volume) was a Candidate of Sciences, albeit the geographical sciences. Not long ago this remarkable man and scholar was honored with a special, posthumous publication of his articles from the *Philosophical Encyclopedia* and the *Great Soviet Encyclopedia*, but the print run of the book was not much greater than that of the Losev rarity—600 copies![4]

The shock from the two last volumes of the *Philosophical Encyclopedia* was nonetheless quite a strong one because nothing in any way remarkable on Russian philosophy was published over the whole of the next ten years, up to 1979 (with the exception of the two-volume collection of Grigorii Skovoroda's works in 1973). And suddenly (always suddenly!), in the long-known and fully loyal series *The History of Esthetics in Texts and Documents* (Istoriia estetiki v pamiatnikakh i dokumentakh), a weighty volume of the works of the true founder of modern Russian philosophy, Ivan Vasil'evich Kireevskii (under the editorship of Iurii Mann), was published in 1979. But apparently it was such a deadened time that the book provoked no special response. And yet, if one wanted to one could find in it two great articles that laid the foundation for Russian philosophizing: "On the Character of European Enlightenment and Its Relation to Enlightenment in Russia" (O kharaktere prosveshcheniia Evropy i ego otnoshenii k prosveshcheniiu Rossii) and "On the Necessity and Possibility of New Principles for Philosophy" (O neobkhodimosti i vozmozhnosti novykh nachal dlia filosofii) . . . Jumping ahead a bit, I will say that five years later, albeit still in the years of "stagnation," a somewhat more complete volume of Kireevskii was published by "Sovremennik" Publishers in the series *For Lovers of Russian Literature* (Liubiteliam rossiiskoi slovesnosti). The editor, V. Kotel'nikov, dared to include an extremely important fragment from the unfinished second half of the article "On the Necessity and Possibility of New Principles" in the section "Excerpts" (Otryvki).

But three years before this, a volume of articles on literary criticism by the brothers Konstantin and Ivan Aksakov (edited by A. Kurilov) appeared in that same series, *For Lovers of Russian Literature*. What a pathetic volume it was! One glance at the famous biography of Tiutchev (which had never been published during the Soviet period), all chopped up and abridged to less than half its length, would be enough to lay the book aside. It caused a scandal even so: how could anyone dare to publish two reactionary Slavophiles in such a mass run! A collection of writings by Khomiakov, which was being prepared by the same publisher, was prohibited and was published only during the time of perestroika, in 1988 (A. Khomiakov, *On the Old and the New* [O starom i novom], ed. B. Egorov).

But even more tumultuous events then came about. Suddenly, a volume of the seemingly forgotten N.F. Fedorov appeared in "Mysl'" Publishers' prestigious series *Philosophical Heritage* (Filosofskoe nasledie), which had published Kant and Hegel. The "philosophical community," headed by M. Iovchuk "himself," became seriously alarmed. They demanded repressions. It was decided to withdraw the unsold copies of the book, but "alas," owing to the customary sluggishness of the officials (and the unsluggishness of the readers), almost all copies had already been sold. Iurii Andropov, the *gensek* (General Secretary) "himself," had a chat about this book with Georgii Mokeevich Markov, who was utterly blameless (in this case). The repressions fell on the deputy of the editor-in-chief of the *Philosophical Heritage* series, Gulyga, who was demoted to a rank-and-file member of the editorial board. The name of Arsenii Vladimirovich Gulyga should be mentioned together with A.G. Spirkin among those very, very few members of the official philosophical establishment for whom the unenlightened materialism of the "revdems" (revolutionary democrats) was never able to obscure all of Russian thought. As early as the seventies, Gulyga, together with A.F. Losev, began preparing a large three-volume edition of the works of Solov'ev. The "earthquake" over Fedorov torpedoed this publication.

I remember going to see Losev; he was terribly distraught and kept repeating: "Why did this Fedorov have to be published? He's no philosopher. And now because of him Solov'ev won't be published."

That is how it has always been with us: Khomiakov was not published because of the Aksakovs, Solov'ev was not published because of Fedorov, "Bolivar will not endure two of them." How sad it all is. . . .

But life went on. In 1983 a small book by Losev on Solov'ev was being prepared for publication in the series *Thinkers of the Past* (Mysliteli proshlogo) ("Mysl' " Publishers). Once again an "earthquake": sedition was seen in this harmless, mercilessly plucked book ("Hamlet without the Prince of Denmark," Solov'ev without his religious philosophy—almost the entire book was devoted to the philosopher's colorful personality and not to his philosophy). The State Committee on Publishing (Goskomizdat) made a decision worthy of Solomon—to forbid the sale of the book in both capitals and in large cities and to send them all "to rural areas, to the provinces, to Saratov." Someone brought Aleksei Fedorovich a whole package of his books from the island of Sakhalin. . . .

The following year, 1984, saw another unexpected event: a volume of literary criticism by N.N. Strakhov (edited by N. Skatov) was published in the series *For Lovers of Russian Literature*, already mentioned more than once, by "Sovremennik" Publishers. Of course, it was a carved up volume; there were cuts throughout: Strakhov needed only to get into an argument with the "furious Vissarion [Belinskii]" for three dots to appear in brackets. . . . But even so, a whole volume of Strakhov! A year before the beginning of perestroika!

All this is being related with the sole purpose of leading the reader to the stunning conclusion that the return of Russian philosophy was inevitable, even if there had not been a perestroika. . . . Something was irreversibly set into motion at the end of the seventies. . . . The Iovchuks would forbid one thing, but something else would appear. They would forbid this something else, and a third would appear. . . . Repression no longer functioned as effectively as before.

But perestroika also did not mean a prompt revision of the history of Russian philosophy. It was not until three years after its beginning, in the summer of 1988, that surprised readers of *Pravda* read that at one of the sessions of the Politburo of the CPSU Central Committee a resolution had been passed "On the Publication of a Series of Books 'From the History of Russian (*otechestvennaia*) Philosophical Thought' " in the form of an appendix to the journal *Voprosy filosofii*. Since when had the Politburo begun to concern itself with such trifles? But for us this was like Beethoven's fate knocking at the door. The era of the Iovchuks was over. "Pravda" Publishers, the Party publishing house, was charged with the publication of Berdiaev and Florenskii. An irony of history. . . . The long-awaited light at the end of the tunnel.

The old, much-troubled edition of Solov'ev became the first books of the new era. Three volumes had become two, albeit very large ones. Their content was both a joy and a disappointment. "The Meaning of Love" (Smysl liubvi) and "Three Conversations" (Tri razgovora) are there, but almost half of the "Critique of Abstract Principles" (Kritika otvlechennykh nachal) was cut, including the entire criticism of socialism. And such important writings as "Lectures on Godmanhood" (Chteniia o Bogochelovechestve) and "The Spiritual Foundations of Life" (Dukhovnye osnovy zhizni) are missing altogether. The print run was ludicrously small: 30,000. In a word, the publication bore all the birthmarks of socialism.

And yet we were happy. A new era had begun. Before three years would go by, no less than ten different publications of Solov'ev and Rozanov and more than ten of Berdiaev would appear.

Notes

1. English text originally published in *Russian Studies in Philosophy*, vol. 32, no. 2 (Fall 1993), pp. 7–20. Russian text © 1992 by "Zdes' i Teper'." "Vozvrashchenie russkoi filosofii," *Zdes' i Teper'*, 1992, no. 1, pp. 76–84.

2. V. Rozanov, *Sochineniia* (Moscow: Sovetskaia Rossiia, 1990), pp. 463–64.

3. See "George L. Kline: An Appreciation" (above), note 3.

4. See D.N. Lialikov, *Raboty po filosofii, psikhologii, kul'ture. Tom 1 (Entsiklopedicheskie stat'i)* (Moscow: INION, 1991).

II

The Nineteenth Century Revisited

Although there are no longer any ideological obstacles to the exploration of Russia's entire philosophical past, contemporary study is strongly focused on the tradition of Russian religious philosophy that began in the nineteenth century with the writings of the early Slavophiles, especially Ivan Kireevskii and Alexei Khomiakov, and that included such major figures as Nikolai Fedorov and Vladimir Solov'ev. The two essays by James P. Scanlan and George M. Young, Jr., that comprise this section of the volume deal with this nineteenth-century segment of the Russian philosophical heritage.

By contrast, the current Russian literature gives considerably less attention to pre-Slavophile philosophers and to representatives of the secular, or "Westernist," trend in nineteenth-century Russian thought. There is interest in some members of the latter group and also in some nineteenth-century representatives of Russian legal liberalism, such as Boris Chicherin, who have drawn attention because of their defense of the idea of a state based on the rule of law and of the institution of private property.[1] But on balance the weight of attention heavily favors the Slavophile tradition of Russian religious philosophy.

Two circumstances help to explain this emphasis. One is that the Westernist thinkers, who had been influenced by the French Enlightenment and by subsequent French and German philosophy, could be claimed by Marxist-Leninist authorities (however dubiously) as Russian forerunners of Marxist materialism and socialism. As a consequence, this Westernist group of nineteenth-century thinkers, which included pre-Slavophiles such as Aleksandr Radishchev as well as contemporaries and successors of the Slavophiles such as Aleksandr Herzen, Vissarion Belinskii, and Nikolai Chernyshevskii, did not suffer oblivion during the dark decades of Soviet dogmatism. On the contrary, they were lionized to the point of surfeit, elevated to near-saintly status as "Russian revolutionary democrats." And in their case, postcommunist interest in correcting the philosophical record by freeing them from Marxist-Leninist misreadings has not yet fully overcome the aversion generated by their ideologically inspired distortion and overexposure.

A second circumstance helps to explain the relative neglect today of other, formerly suppressed thinkers who were not secular but religious in orientation—Grigorii Skovoroda and Petr Chaadaev come to mind—but who have nonetheless not become powerful magnets of philosophical attention in the present day. In their case, the relative lack of interest may be explained by the fact that they are not perceived as representatives of a coherent *Russian* religious-philosophical heritage. They did not create a characteristically *Russian* philosophy, and their ideas were not integrated into Russian philosophical life by a school or even by identifiable individual followers. Theirs were solitary voices that did not become part of a distinctively Russian philosophical tradition.

Both of these circumstances favored the emergence of the Slavophiles and their major nineteenth-century successors as the earliest segment of the Russian philosophical heritage to receive widespread contemporary notice. As religious thinkers, they were almost totally suppressed during the Stalin era, and as late as the onset of glasnost they still had the aura of forbidden fruit; as Scanlan points out in his essay to follow, none of Khomiakov's theoretical writings were published until 1988. Moreover, it can be argued that the Slavophile philosophers were the first thinkers in Russia to philosophize specifically as *Russians* and to generate a self-conscious Russian intellectual tradition, marked by an interrelated complex of concepts and issues—specifically, what is now known as the tradition of Russian religious idealist philosophy.

Scanlan distinguishes two types of contemporary interest in Slavophilism: a scholarly, theoretical interest in understanding the concepts and principles advanced by Kireevskii and Khomiakov; and a practical, polemical interest in using Slavophile views to support particular social attitudes and programs.

Writers who favor the former approach are exploring theoretical readings of Kireevskii and Khomiakov that were not acceptable during the communist era, when Slavophile philosophy was treated (when it was acknowledged at all) exclusively from the standpoint of its socioeconomic role as an ideological expression of the class interests of the Russian gentry. Scanlan selects two such contemporary readings to examine in some detail.

One is an approach, represented by Zinaida Smirnova, in which Slavophilism is regarded as an integrated system of social, national, and religious-philosophical doctrines. On this reading, the key to Slavophile philosophy—the element that ties the philosophy organically to the other components of the theory—is found in its antirationalism (as developed,

THE NINETEENTH CENTURY REVISITED   25

particularly, in Kireevskii's epistemology of "integral knowledge"), which is seen to be closely linked with its anti-individualism in social thinking and its anti-Westernism in national thinking.

The second, quite different approach, advanced by Sergei Khoruzhii, sees Slavophilism as more a recognition of the positive conceptual content of the Russian Orthodox faith than a negative reaction against Western rationalism. Focusing chiefly on Khomiakov's concept of *sobornost* (communality), which signifies a spiritual unification that is both unforced ("free") and interpenetrating ("organic"), Khoruzhii argues forcefully that this central notion of Slavophilism was intended to describe neither social unity nor national unity but the mystical unity of the Orthodox church. For Khoruzhii, then, Slavophilism is a religious doctrine above all, and its theoretical pronouncements are really theological rather than philosophical.

Writers whose interest is primarily in using Slavophile doctrines to buttress practical social and national programs are the "neo-Slavophiles" of the present generation, and they are found primarily among supporters of the Russian "national-patriotic" movement in its diverse manifestations. Scanlan examines the views of two such neo-Slavophiles—Pavel Tulaev and Evgenii Troitskii—and finds that despite their differences they share a number of attitudes. They are, above all, intensely patriotic, and their patriotism is expressed in a nationalistic confidence in the virtues of Russia's traditional, distinctive culture and the vices of Western culture. Although they profess devotion to the Russian Orthodox church and faith, they also assume a much closer connection than Khoruzhii does between the unity of the Church on the one hand and the unity of the Russian nation and state on the other. Indeed, they are concerned mostly with the secular embodiments of sobornost— social, political, ethnic—rather than its strictly religious manifestation. At the same time, however, they invoke for these secular embodiments the same kind of mystical sanctity that Khoruzhii reserves for the Church. Applied to society and the nation, their "sobornost" has autocratic, xenophobic, and even racist overtones that are a cause of concern to many contemporary Russian critics. Some of these critics' reservations about present-day Russian neo-Slavophilism are sketched in the last section of Scanlan's essay.

George Young's essay deals with two thinkers who, without being identified as Slavophiles or even as being particularly sympathetic to Slavophilism, continued the development of Russian religious philosophy in the latter nineteenth century using concepts that bore a family resemblance to Slavophile ideas. They are Nikolai Fedorov and Vladimir Solov'ev—both of them thinkers in whom current Russian interest runs high.

Nikolai Fedorovich Fedorov (1828–1903), one of the great eccentrics in the history of Russian thought, is best known for his dedication to extravagant schemes that smack of science fiction—the physical restoration to life of all our ancestors, gaining control of the earth's climate and of the evolutionary process, exploring and colonizing other worlds through space travel. Yet what Fedorov called the "Philosophy of the Common Task" that is to unite all mankind in these cosmic endeavors was elaborated by him in a deeply religious, Christian idiom that some now see as an inspired marriage of Russian spirituality and cosmic universalism—a combination even more urgently needed at the end of the twentieth century than when Fedorov formulated it at the end of the nineteenth.[2]

The history of the rediscovery of Fedorov in Russia in recent years follows a paradigm common in the current Russian philosophical renaissance. Under Stalin, silence; Fedorov never existed. After Stalin's death, hesitant attempts to rationalize attention to a thinker's ideas by finding approaches to them that conform to Marxist-Leninist dogma. In the case of Fedorov, these approaches at first took the form of arguing that among Fedorov's radically inconsistent ideas, some had positive value; or that Fedorov was a predominantly secular thinker whose religious ideas were uncharacteristic and inconsequential; or that Fedorov was a thoroughly secular thinker, devoid of religious convictions, who simply used religious symbols and images to give metaphorical expression to his concepts. Still later it became possible to present a close analysis of Fedorov's religious beliefs, but only in the context of criticizing them. Finally, after the onset of glasnost, scholars could offer a sympathetic exposition of the religious core of Fedorov's philosophical conceptions.[3]

There is one respect, however, in which the post-Stalin reception of Fedorov departed from the general pattern: a volume of selections from his philosophical writings was published remarkably early—in 1982.[4] As Dzhimbinov pointed out in his essay above, the publication of this volume came as a stunning surprise to the Soviet intellectual and political communities, and it created a scandal that provoked the final conservative retrenchment in Russian philosophy before glasnost arrived later in the 1980s.

The controversial 1982 volume was prepared by Svetlana Semenova, and it is Semenova who has spearheaded the drive to bring Fedorov's ideas before the Russian public once again. Indeed it is through the efforts of Semenova and others that a whole series of Russian thinkers who share some of Fedorov's ideas are now being grouped together as exponents of what is called "Russian cosmism"—an outlook that focuses on the interrelationships between earthly life and the vast cosmos in which it is embedded. Membership in this group of thinkers expands or contracts (over a range reaching from Vladimir Solov'ev to Grigorii Rasputin) depending on the breadth with which the term 'cosmism' is conceived. Virtually every list, however, would include, in addition to Fedorov himself, the aeronautical inventor Konstantin E. Tsiolkovskii (1857–1935), considered the father of Russian rocketry and space travel, who in his youth was influenced by Fedorov and later propounded what he called a "cosmic philosophy"; Vladimir I. Vernadskii (1863–1945), the famed Russian naturalist and mineralogist who introduced the concept of the "noosphere"; and Aleksandr L. Chizhevskii (1897–1964), a scientist, poet, and painter who was interested in extraterrestrial influences on earthly biological and social processes.

'Extraterrestrial' here need not mean 'otherworldly' in the supernatural sense, and undoubtedly some of the present-day Russian devotees of cosmism are drawn to it for primarily scientific or technical reasons; this would include those with nonspiritualistic interests in astronautics, science fiction, the environment (Fedorov dreamed of controlling meteorological forces and preventing droughts and floods), and the prolongation of life (long a favorite topic of Russian physiologists as well as of Fedorov). Yet a spiritualistic, "otherworldly" motif is never far from the surface in the contemporary philosophical discussions of cosmism. Here is Vladimir Dudenkov's sympathetic description of Russian cosmism in a recent study:

> *Cosmism* is a movement in philosophy the central problem of which is human activity in its universality as testimony to the existence of another reality, a higher truth, a metahistorical perspective, transcendent panoramas. Cosmism proceeds from the idea of man as a being possessing a universality of inner content, an openness to people, to history, to being, to the universe, to God. Cosmism is a philosophy of the life, death, and immortality of man and the universe, of the earthly and unearthly in their inseparable unity. . . . To the philosophy of cosmism there corresponds a special—cosmic—consciousness, which includes a sense of the world order, an intellectual enlightenment, a genuine exaltation, and a confidence in the eternity of life.[5]

Given such a formulation of the outlook, which in some ways resembles Anglo-American "New Age" mentality, it is easy to understand how it can have a mystical or spiritualistic appeal to many Russians today. In this light, the attraction to cosmism is entirely consistent with the extraordinary popularity of astrology in present-day Russia (astrology being an exemplary case of supposed extraterrestrial influence on human life) and with the findings of a recent survey in which 35 percent of sixteen- and seventeen-year-olds in Russia reported that they "believe not in God but in some supernatural forces."[6]

The reference in the passage above to a special consciousness is a point of connection with another impulse behind cosmism—Russian national patriotism. Russian patriots are drawn to the outlook both out of pride in Russian space achievements and because of cosmism's supposed status as an original philosophical outgrowth of the Russian spirit; the "cosmic consciousness," in other words, is held to be part of a distinctively Russian mentality. Evgenii Troitskii, for example, calling Russian cosmism "one of the greatest discoveries of human culture," affirms that even in the remote past "the world presented itself to the Slav as a single, living cosmos, embracing heaven, the earth, the underwater and subterranean elements." The Russian nation is said to be inherently attuned to the cosmos; a feature of Russian cosmism is the "indissoluble connection of universal and atmospheric space with the ethnos, the nation." Patriotism blends neatly with several of the other impulses behind Russian cosmism when Troitskii reverently recounts the popular belief that no trace of Iurii Gagarin's body was found with his crashed aircraft because "he had been, as it were, raised aloft."[7]

The second philosopher treated in George Young's essay is by common consent the greatest and most influential of all of Russia's philosophical thinkers—Fedorov's nineteenth-century contemporary, the religious idealist Vladimir Sergeevich Solov'ev (1853–1900). Dzhimbinov described above the circumstances of the initial "rediscovery" of Solov'ev in the 1970s and 1980s, to which it need only be added that Solov'ev's comprehensive philosophical system, which is centered on the metaphysical concept of "total-unity" (vseedinstvo) but also encompasses epistemology, ethics, social philosophy, and the philosophy of history, continues to receive lively attention in the 1990s. Many of Solov'ev's works are now available in print, and a complete edition is in preparation at the Institute of Philosophy of the Russian Academy of Sciences.[8]

Not surprisingly, there is more than one assessment of Solov'ev's philosophical significance in the current Russian literature. Despite the nineteenth-century thinker's exalted reputation, Khoruzhii (as discussed in Scanlan's essay below) compares him rather unfavorably with the Slavophiles as far as his contribution to *Russian* philosophy is concerned. According to Khoruzhii, although Kireevskii and Khomiakov were primarily theologians rather than philosophers, they at least saw the need for a distinctively Russian philosophy and were intuitively in tune with the mystical doctrines of Russian Orthodoxy that must form the core of a genuinely Russian philosophy. In the hands of Solov'ev and his followers, however, Khoruzhii contends, true Orthodox sobornost was replaced by a rationalistic "total-unity"; the Orthodox nucleus was lost, and philosophy became a theory of "religion in general," based on abstract concepts borrowed from the West. Khoruzhii's Solov'ev thus differs from the Solov'ev who was described by one of his contemporaries (as quoted in Young's essay below) as "a mystic down to his toes" and a "visionary in rationalist clothing." For Khoruzhii the rationalism was not the clothing but the body of Solov'ev's thought, to the detriment of mystical insight and Orthodox truth.

Still another approach to Solov'ev is found in the monographs and articles of Russia's most distinguished modern interpreter of the nineteenth-century thinker's philosophy, the philosopher and classicist Aleksei Losev, himself one of the suppressed Russian thinkers "rediscovered" with the coming of glasnost (see section V of this volume). Between 1983 and his death in 1988, Losev completed two books and several lengthy articles on Solov'ev, whose philosophy had attracted him since his youth.[9] Losev's interpretation is in a sense a synthesis of the two mentioned in the preceding paragraph, for he regarded Solov'ev as *both* a consummate mystic *and* a consummate rationalist. In Losev's eyes it was Solov'ev's great virtue as a philosopher to be capable of elaborating and justifying rationally the same religious truths that mystical experience reveals to the visionary. On Losev's reading of Solov'ev, all philosophy—including mystical philosophy —requires the conceptual elaboration and logical formulation of concepts derived from experience, whether the "experience" itself be provided by the senses, by rational intuition, or by mystical intuition. No stranger to the latter, Solov'ev as Losev understands him was equally at home in the realm of rational intuition and understood the two as equally competent in discerning fundamental truths. And in either case the rationalistic form that the conceptual elaboration of the experience takes is not an abandonment of the original truth but a presentation of that truth in the logical form required of any philosophy.

George Young's essay brings together these two remarkable philosophical personalities—Fedorov and Solov'ev—on a subject on which for a time they appeared to be in agreement: the importance of resurrection from the dead as not merely an Orthodox Christian mystery (indeed, the central Orthodox mystery) but a universal Orthodox Christian project. By following their emerging disagreements on the issue, Young highlights the divergent perspectives of the two thinkers, Fedorov's being more technical and "scientific" and Solov'ev's more spiritual and mystical. In the strong current interest in the two thinkers, Young sees evidence that technological and spiritual forms of utopianism, both well known from Russia's past, are still alive in the country's postcommunist intellectual renewal.

Notes

1. As indicated earlier in this volume, Bakunin, Kropotkin, Pisarev, and Tkachev are included among the neglected Russian philosophers whose works have been published in the volumes issued as appendices to the journal *Voprosy filosofii* beginning in 1989. For a recent Russian discussion of Chicherin, see S.L. Chizhkov, "B.N.

Chicherin: The Idea of the Constitutional State and the Liberal Experiment in Russia," *Soviet Studies in Philosophy*, vol. 30, no. 3 (Winter 1991–92), pp. 7–24.

2. Two Western studies of Fedorov's ideas are George M. Young, Jr., *Nikolai F. Fedorov: An Introduction* (Belmont, MA: Nordland, 1979), and Michael Hagemeister, *Nikolaj Fedorov: Studien zu Leben, Werk und Wirkung* (Munich: Verlag Otto Sagner, 1989).

3. Some of the representative Soviet studies, in chronological order, are V.E. L'vov, "Zagadochnyi starik: Povest'-khronika," *Neva*, 1974, no. 5, pp. 65–122; S.G. Semenova, "Nikolai Fedorovich Fedorov (Zhizn' i uchenie)," *Prometei*, vol. 11 (Moscow: Molodaia gvardiia, 1977), pp. 86–105; V.P. Pazilova, *Kriticheskii analiz religiozno-filosofskogo ucheniia N.F. Fedorova* (Moscow: MGU, 1985); S.G. Semenova, *Nikolai Fedorov: Tvorchestvo zhizni* (Moscow: Sovetskii pisatel', 1990).

4. N.F. Fedorov, *Sochineniia*, ed. A.V. Gulyga, comp. and intro. S.G. Semenova (Moscow: Mysl', 1982).

5. B.N. Dudenkov, *Russkii kosmizm: Filosofiia nadezhdy i spaseniia* (Saint Petersburg: Sintez, 1992), pp. 57–58 (italics in original).

6. "Religion and Politics in Postcommunist Russia (A Roundtable Discussion)," *Russian Studies in Philosophy*, vol. 33, no. 1 (Summer 1994), p. 56.

7. Evgenii Troitskii, *Vozrozhdenie russkoi idei: Sotsial'no-filosofskie ocherki* (Moscow: Philosophical Society of the USSR, 1991), pp. 155–58.

8. Several editions of selected works by Solov'ev have been published since 1988. The two most comprehensive are Vladimir Solov'ev, *Sochineniia v dvukh tomakh*, ed. A.F. Losev and A.V. Gulyga, intro. A.F. Losev, 2 vols. (Moscow: Mysl', 1988); and Vladimir Solov'ev, *Sochineniia v dvukh tomakh*, ed. N.V. Kotrelev, intro. V.F. Asmus, 2 vols. (Moscow: Pravda, 1989).

9. Losev's principal writings on Solov'ev dating from this period are the following: *Vladimir Solov'ev* (Moscow: Mysl', 1983); the introduction to Vladimir Solov'ev, *Sochineniia v dvukh tomakh*, ed. A.F. Losev and A.V. Gulyga, 2 vols. (Moscow: Mysl', 1988), vol. 1, pp. 3–32; *Vladimir Solov'ev i ego vremia* (Moscow: Progress, 1990); and "Vl. Solov'ev: Zhizn' i tvorchestvo," in A.F. Losev, *Filosofiia, mifologiia, kul'tura* (Moscow: Politicheskaia literatura, 1991), pp. 474–92.

JAMES P. SCANLAN

2 | Interpretations and Uses of
Slavophilism in Recent
Russian Thought

Before Glasnost

Like the general emergence of Russian philosophy from Stalinist nonbeing
traced by Dzhimbinov in the first section of this volume, renewed Russian
attention to Slavophilism was noticeable well before the advent of glasnost.
Beginning in the 1960s, a number of Russian scholars, working within the
conceptual and institutional constraints of Marxism-Leninism, were able
nonetheless to publish articles and even books on Slavophilism and its
founding theorists, Ivan Kireevskii and Aleksei Khomiakov. By the time
glasnost was proclaimed in the second half of the 1980s, there existed in
Russia a substantial but relatively homogeneous body of literature on
Slavophilism as an intellectual and social movement—a literature marked
by a rough consensus as to where to place the movement within Marxism's
epic account of the world's march toward communism.

This attention contrasted sharply with the long silence on Slavophilism
that had characterized the Stalin era. As late as 1955 (two years after
Stalin's death), the standard Soviet one-volume philosophical dictionary
contained no entries for either Slavophilism, Kireevskii, or Khomiakov.
Such entries first appeared in that work in the 1963 edition, and even then
they were short and dismissive: Slavophilism was described as "a reactionary-
utopian program for the transition of the Russian gentry to the road of
bourgeois development with maximum preservation of its privileges."[1] A
somewhat longer article on Kireevskii, along roughly the same lines (it
quite unjustly suggested, for example, that Kireevskii resisted the abolition
of serfdom), had appeared in 1962 in the second volume of the five-volume

Philosophical Encyclopedia; this article did attribute to Kireevskii "some correct ideas"—namely, ideas in tune with Marxism-Leninism, such as the philosopher's thoughts on "the defects of metaphysical thinking" and "the negative sides of bourgeois society." The article also denied any original-ity to Slavophile philosophy, contending that "the evaluation of Kireevskii in prerevolutionary and contemporary bourgeois literature . . . as one of the founders of a 'unique' Russian philosophy distorts the course of devel-opment and the content of the history of philosophy in Russia."[2]

Substantial attention to Slavophile thought first appeared in 1969 with the publication of a volume of Khomiakov's poems and plays. Although the editor, B.F. Egorov, offered no sustained discussion of Slavophile philosophy, he did manage to describe Khomiakov as "a philosopher who created an original system" and to sketch the main lines of the Slavophile and Westernist philosophies of history without attributing venal motives to either side.[3] Ten years later, as Dzhimbinov mentions, Kireevskii's principal theoretical works were published, followed in 1982 by a volume of articles by the Slavophiles Ivan and Konstantin Aksakov, and in 1984 by a more complete edition of Kireevskii.[4] Hence by the mid-1980s, some major Slavophile texts were available for study, although they included none of the theoretical writings of Khomiakov; an edition of the latter did not appear until 1988, when glasnost was well under way.[5]

Over the same period the intellectual quality of the treatment of Slavophile thought by Russian writers showed distinct improvement, be-ginning most notably in 1970 with the landmark liberalization achieved in the final volume of the *Philosophical Encyclopedia*. By the luck of the Cyrillic alphabet, the entries "Khomiakov" and "The Slavophiles" both appeared in that volume, and each article was noteworthy for its length and philosophical substance. For the first time the ontological and episte-mological elements of the Slavophiles' thought were discussed along with their views of history and society, and in the article on Khomiakov his key religious-philosophical notion of "sobornost" received explicit attention. True, the emphasis was still on the sociocultural aspects of the doctrine, and the Slavophiles were still categorized as utopian advocates of "gentry liberalism," but for the first time they were given clear credit for opposing serfdom and were situated in a "creative current" of Russian thought. More than that, their thought as a whole was fairly assessed as providing the nucleus of Russian religious philosophy and as revealing "the distinc-tive face of Russian philosophy with its ontologism, the primacy it gives to the moral sphere, and its affirmation of the communitarian roots of personality."[6]

From the publication of those 1970 articles until the onset of glasnost, many articles and several books by Soviet scholars were devoted to the ideas of the Slavophiles—most notably the collection of essays entitled *Literary Views and Work of the Slavophiles, 1830s–1850s*, edited by K.N. Lomunov (1978); V.A. Koshelev's *Aesthetic and Literary Views of the Russian Slavophiles (1840s–1850s)* (1984); and N.I. Tsimbaev's *Slavophilism: From the History of Russian Sociopolitical Thought of the Nineteenth Century* (1986).[7] Despite differences in focus and in the degree of intellectual independence displayed by the authors of these works, they all reflect the Marxist-Leninist limitations that were imposed on publication in the controlled environment of pre-perestroika Russia.

Understandably, neither a religious nor a nationalistic reading of Slavophilism stands out in this literature. Tsimbaev, presenting a survey of Russian critical treatment of the Slavophiles as of 1986, recognizes the possibility of a religious reading, but he finds it only among prerevolutionary and "bourgeois" émigré thinkers, and he rejects it as an absurdity; neither Kireevskii nor the other Slavophiles, he argues, ever "reduced Slavophilism only to Orthodoxy, to interpreting the writings of the 'Church Fathers'." He does find evidence of a nationalistic interpretation even in Soviet thought (he cites Iu.Z. Iankovskii and V.P. Popov), but in the true spirit of Marxist-Leninist internationalism he condemns it as not only historically incorrect but "an insult to the memory" of the Slavophiles. The problem with it, of course, is that in Marxist terms "national sentiment" is something supposedly transcending class differences and specific social circumstances; in the Russian case it means, in Tsimbaev's words, going beyond "the bounds of the sociopolitical interests of the mid-nineteenth century" and "divesting the question of its social nature."[8] The clear implication is that only a *social*, as opposed to a religious or nationalistic, interpretation will do, and this view is reflected in the writings of the great majority of pre-perestroika Soviet students of Slavophilism.

Tsimbaev provides the social interpretation with a rationale that typifies not only the general approach but also the specific conclusions drawn from it by scholars in the late Soviet era. First there is the text from Lenin that is said to provide "the key to defining the chief content" of the phenomenon. In the case of Slavophilism, this is Lenin's pronouncement that in the Russia of the 1840s–1860s, "*all* social questions reduced to the struggle against serfdom and its remnants."[9] This "struggle" can be of only one sort—a *class* struggle—and consequently Slavophilism must be interpreted as an ideological expression of the class interests of its advocates. The class in question is the gentry, to which the leading Slavophile theoreticians did indeed belong, and its ideology is proclaimed to be a form of liberalism—"gentry liberalism," essentially a euphemism for what the

1962 dictionary more crudely but directly called a program of moving the gentry to bourgeois development "with maximum preservation of its privileges." (Why such an analysis should be considered any less "an insult to the memory" of the Slavophiles, Tsimbaev does not make clear.)

Tsimbaev credits S.S. Dmitriev with having first formulated this analysis, the acceptability of which to so many other scholars fully justifies Tsimbaev's generalization, made on the eve of glasnost, that in Soviet scholarship regarding Slavophilism "the main line in the evaluation of its class character has become the understanding of Slavophilism as one of the currents of early Russian liberalism." There were, of course, differences of shading and emphasis among the Soviet scholars who adopted this "standard interpretation" (as we shall call it) of Slavophilism during the late Soviet era, but the differences fell within acceptable limits of a class-based Marxist social analysis applicable to the Russian gentry. Among the writers of the time, only V.A. Koshelev appears to have deviated significantly from the standard view; Tsimbaev charges Koshelev with accepting an interpretation, which he traces to Plekhanov, according to which Slavophilism was not liberal but reactionary, "in the historical-philosophical sense."[10]

Glasnost and New Approaches to Slavophilism

The coming of glasnost affected the study of Russian philosophy no less than other fields, and the subject of Slavophilism was by no means immune to the general critique of previously unquestioned positions. At first, when the critics of Marxist-Leninist dogmatism merely blamed Stalin for distorting the thought of Lenin and Marx, Leninist approaches such as the standard interpretation of Slavophilism were not seriously shaken. But soon Lenin was being blamed for distorting Marx, and the way was open to abandon Leninist models. And when, in the ultimate move toward openness, Marx himself was blamed for distorting the truth, no obstacles remained to reexamining Slavophilism without preconceived Marxist categories. The possibility arose of genuinely new approaches to all the questions relating to the intellectual legacy of Kireevskii and Khomiakov in Russia—questions of the fundamental nature of Slavophilism as a philosophical system, of its "uniqueness" and place in the history of Russian philosophy, of the character and implications of the particular doctrines of its founders.

More than that, still another, quite different possibility arose—the possibility, unimaginable during the Stalinist era and for a long time after it, of openly espousing Slavophile views. It became possible again, in other words, to *be* a Slavophile, in the sense of advocating Slavophile views or using the classical Slavophiles as authority for a related position of one's own. Many Russians have in fact taken advantage of this second opportunity, so that a new generation of Slavophile-oriented thinkers has appeared on the intellectual scene. The term 'neo-Slavophiles', originally introduced to refer to later nineteenth-century followers of the "early Slavophiles," as they are now often called (above all Kireevskii and Khomiakov), may be extended to cover this most recent generation as well, provided we understand that we are talking about a postcommunist neo-Slavophilism, which may or may not differ in significant ways from the neo-Slavophilism of earlier generations.

By comparison with pre-glasnost Soviet attention to the phenomenon of Slavophilism, the more recent treatment of the subject is marked by several novel features. Perhaps the most striking is simply the heightened importance attached to Slavophilism as a set of ideas—an importance evident not only in the great increase in republications of the writings of the first Slavophile thinkers and their later followers but in the openly positive assessments of Slavophilism by scholars and other commentators. Largely, if not exclusively, these assessments result from attributing to Slavophile philosophy a number of positive features. Because these features are often only implicit and are sometimes confused with one another in the Russian discussions, it is worthwhile to distinguish them carefully at the outset.

First, many commentators assert that Kireevskii and Khomiakov were the true originators not simply of Slavophile philosophy but of Russian philosophy in general; let us call this the thesis of the philosophical *priority* of Slavophilism. Second, many believe that the thinking of the early Slavophiles was an original product of their own minds, not the result of borrowing from Western or any other philosophical sources; we may call this the thesis of the philosophical *originality* of Slavophilism. Third, since a philosophical theory may be an original creation without being unique to the culture in which it arises (since the same set of ideas may have arisen elsewhere, either independently or imitatively), it is a further qualification to say that Slavophilism distinguishes *Russian* thought from that of any other culture; this is the thesis of the philosophical *uniqueness* of Slavophilism. Fourth and finally, a philosophical theory might be unique without being an integral part of the culture in which it arises; thus when it is asserted that Slavophilism is especially fitting or appropriate to Russian culture, this is the further thesis of the philosophical *appropriateness* of Slavophilism. Although these four features are clearly distinguishable, in most current Russian treatments of Slavophilism they are assumed to entail one another or are simply lumped together without analysis. Most of the

Russian interpreters who now regard Slavophilism as a historically important body of thought subscribe to all four theses, without discriminating among them.

The priority thesis received much support in the writings of the Russian religious idealists of the early twentieth century who now enjoy such vogue in their homeland. Semen Frank, Nikolai Berdiaev, Aleksei Losev, and many other exiled or persecuted philosophers whose works are acclaimed in Russia today all regarded the ideas of Kireevskii and Khomiakov as seminal in Russian philosophy. Frank, for example, in laying out what he calls "the essence and leading themes" of Russian philosophy, essentially begins his account with the Slavophiles.[11] Berdiaev, the single most quoted philosopher in Russia today, wrote a book on Khomiakov in which he stressed the "Slavophile sources" of "our creative philosophical thought"; the "first intuitions" of this thought, he wrote, "were born in the soul of Kireevskii."[12] To many Russians the authority of these respected thinkers alone is sufficient to establish the priority of Slavophilism in the history of Russian philosophy. Prominent contemporary specialists such as Sergei Khoruzhii accept this judgment; Khoruzhii writes that "the pioneering mission of Slavophilism in relation to the Russian philosophical tradition is universally acknowledged in the history of philosophy."[13]

But what, then, of *pre*-Slavophile Russian thinkers such as Mikhail Lomonosov (1711–1765) and Aleksandr Radishchev (1749–1802)? To the extent that they are not simply ignored, as they often are in the present enthusiasm for the long-scorned religious thinkers, the answer seems to hinge on a subtle shift from the question of *priority* to the question of *originality*. That the early Slavophiles were *original* thinkers is a repeated theme in the writings of Frank, Berdiaev, and others; Gustav Shpet wrote in 1922 that "Slavophile problems are the only original problems of Russian philosophy."[14] By implication, the other philosophers borrowed their ideas from Western masters; and because their ideas were not arrived at independently, they were not genuinely *Russian*—that is, they had their intellectual source outside Russia. Thus the Slavophile thinkers were, in Khoruzhii's words, "the initiators of distinctive Russian philosophy," where the accent is on the word 'Russian'.[15] The philosophical priority of Slavophilism is saved by narrowing the context from "philosophical views held by Russians" to "*Russian* philosophy," where 'Russian' means having its sources in Russia.

Of course some contemporary commentators, as we shall see, object that the first Slavophiles were not in fact original. But on balance, present-day Russian treatments of the Slavophiles strongly favor regarding their outlook as an independent philosophical construct. The popularity of Berdiaev's analysis of the history of Russian philosophy has given currency to the view that the West exercised only a stimulative influence on Kireevskii and Khomiakov: dissatisfied with the legacy of European philosophical rationalism as epitomized in the philosophy of Hegel, the Slavophiles, it is said, set out to forge a new path in philosophy—for the first time, a *Russian* path.

The other general features commonly attributed to Slavophilism in current Russian discussions—its *uniqueness* and its *appropriateness* for Russia —are closely related to each other. The "uniqueness" (*svoeobrazie*) (or "distinctiveness" [*samobytnost'*]) of Slavophilism is invoked at every turn in the current literature, the apparent contention being that nothing resembling Slavophile philosophy is found in the intellectual life of any other culture.[16] On closer examination, however, it appears to be not uniqueness as such that is considered the critically important trait. A philosophy could, after all, be unique or distinctive by being an entirely fanciful or random intellectual construct that simply happens to have no match anywhere else in the world. What is valued in Slavophilism is not simply that it is different from every other philosophy but that it is different in an appropriately Russian way—that it is uniquely or distinctively *Russian* ("a distinctive *national* philosophy," in Blagova's phrase), in the sense of having a special appropriateness to Russian life or culture.[17] Thus the thesis of uniqueness gives way to the thesis of *appropriateness* in the current discussions of Slavophilism.

The Soviet "standard interpretation" of Slavophilism did not reject the thesis of appropriateness, but it interpreted the notion quite differently from the way in which it is understood in most of the postcommunist discussions. Tsimbaev, for example, although he acknowledged in his 1986 book that Kireevskii and Khomiakov drew heavily on their German idealist predecessors, nonetheless rejected the idea that the Slavophile movement had "Western roots." On the contrary, he insisted that it had *Russian* roots, in the sense of being appropriate to the Russian milieu in which it originated. But in Tsimbaev's Marxist framework, this kind of appropriateness is purely a matter of causal linkages among socioeconomic factors. Thus Tsimbaev writes, "Acknowledgement of the Russian roots of Slavophilism acquires concrete historical meaning only when it reveals the indissoluble connection of the doctrine with the problems of the Russian reality of the 1840s–1860s."[18] As we saw above, this "Russian reality" is interpreted in terms of the class struggle, with the result that Slavophilism becomes an ideological echo of the economic class interests of the Russian gentry. Generally speaking, postcommunist students of Slavophilism in Russia have abandoned not simply this particular causal scenario but the very idea of viewing Slavophilism as a causal response to socioeconomic conditions. They mean rather that it is a structure of concepts and principles that corresponds to a specifically Russian value system, a Russian mode of popular thought, a Russian way of life—a philosophical system that expresses the essence of those things and at the same time reinforces them and promotes their development. This would be a philosophy genuinely appropriate to Russian culture and life.

There is essentially no disagreement among current Russian commentators that the creation of such a philosophy was the early Slavophiles' objective. One of the most frequently quoted passages from the writings of Kireevskii is his statement that "*our* philosophy must be developed out of *our* life."[19] Contemporary commentators disagree, however, as to how successfully the early Slavophiles achieved their objective and what kind of conceptual system they actually created. By way of illustrating this disagreement, we shall examine expositions of the Slavophiles' thought by two Russian scholars who have gone far beyond the "standard interpretation"—Zinaida Smirnova and Sergei Khoruzhii.

Smirnova on Slavophilism as an Integrated System

Zinaida Vasil'evna Smirnova, an associate of the Institute of Philosophy of the former Soviet Academy of Sciences (now the Russian Academy of Sciences), published her article "The Debates about Slavophilism" in 1987. Although the article is thus a very early product of glasnost, it already shows an adventurous departure from the accepted position of Tsimbaev and others. This is immediately evident in Smirnova's refusal to describe Slavophilism as a form of gentry bourgeois liberalism. Without denying certain "bourgeois tendencies" in Slavophilism, such as its advocacy of free speech and of the use of free hired labor, she argues persuasively that on a number of fundamental issues the Slavophiles were anything but bourgeois. First, they were opposed to "absolute" private ownership of the bourgeois variety, the absence of which in Russia they considered one of the country's principal advantages over Western civilization. Second, they condemned the individualistic orientation associated with private ownership; they vehemently criticized the West for its lack of tradition-based social communities and its consequent alienation among individuals. Finally, they opposed the idea of the constitutional state (which *they* regarded as bourgeois—an expression of bourgeois individualism), arguing rather for social ties based on custom.[20]

Smirnova's characterization of the Slavophiles' social program is based on *a Gemeinschaft–Gesellschaft* distinction, though she does not use those terms of Ferdinand Tönnies. She sees the Slavophiles' program as "an attempt to counterpose a patriarchal type of social relations to relations of a capitalist type," where the main issue is whether social relations should be built on contract and law (*Gesellschaft*) or on custom and tradition (*Gemeinschaft*).[21] This opposition, she contends, is the central theme of the social thought of the early Slavophiles. In this light she summarizes her case against the interpretation of Slavophilism as "bourgeois," as well as her own competing analysis, as follows:

> The idealization of the patriarchal type of social relations, the negative attitude toward bourgeois property and the political and legal principles of bourgeois society, and the counterposing of "organic" life principles to "artificial" rational principles altogether support the view that sees Slavophilism as a conservative patriarchal utopia and a variant of the general European romantic protest against nascent bourgeois society and against enlightenment ideology. . . . In my view it was predominantly an idealization of the patriarchal traditions and turns of mind of the Russian peasantry.[22]

She also argues that there was no sympathy for democratic principles in the writings of the early Slavophiles.[23]

Smirnova does more than fault Tsimbaev and others for their particular version of the social content of Slavophile theory, however. More fundamentally, she objects to their exclusive focus on social content to the neglect of the integral system of Slavophile thought. Arguing that there are three clearly distinguishable components in Slavophile theory—a social component, a national or ethnic component, and a component of religious idealist philosophy—she contends that Russian commentators from Herzen to the present day have typically regarded one of these as a "core" component and neglected the others, thereby overlooking a cardinal feature of Slavophilism—the organic interdependence of its constituent elements.

One consequence of Smirnova's balanced approach to the components of Slavophilism is that it yields more attention to Slavophile philosophical (as opposed to social or nationalistic) doctrines than had been seen in Russian scholarship earlier in the Soviet era. Smirnova specifically criticizes Tsimbaev (and the point applies equally to other exponents of the Soviet Marxist "standard interpretation") for slighting the strictly philosophical dimension of Slavophilism.[24] Her own focus in dealing with Slavophile philosophy is on the antirationalism of Kireevskii and Khomiakov—their conviction that rationalistic thinking as developed in the Western philosophical tradition that produced Hegel is an impoverished, limited cognitive approach to the world. To the Slavophiles, Smirnova affirms, "logical cognition remains within the confines of reason and its

laws and is incapable of providing knowledge of objective, 'living' being."[25]
The positive alternative proposed by Kireevskii was "integral cognition," a
non-Western mode of knowing in which various human capacities—reason,
will, the senses, moral feelings, and aesthetic sense—come together to
achieve "living" knowledge. As understood by the Slavophiles, Smirnova
states, this integrated mode of knowing was inescapably fideistic and even
mystical; in her words, "the integrated character of cognition acquired a
religious, mystical interpretation in the conception of 'integral knowledge':
the integration of man's spiritual forces was understood as a unity which
necessarily had to be pervaded and imbued with religious faith."[26]

Smirnova establishes the interdependence of the philosophical and social components of Slavophile thought by pointing out that a fundamental
motif of early Slavophile theory was the existence of a close link between
rationalism and individualism. To the Slavophiles, rationalism was "a mode
of thought inherent in an atomized society based on the autonomy of the
individual, in which ties between people were only 'external,' and at the
same time as a mode of thought which justifies and grounds such a society, since it is guided by calculation and egoistic strivings."[27] In the absence
of traditional, customary social relations, bonds could be effected only by
"calculations and inventions of human reason." Conversely, rationalism
with its cognitive limitations was *not* endemic in a cohesive society based
on "natural" or "organic" (i.e., vital, whole) institutions rather than "artificial," legalistic institutions—a society, for example, such as the patriarchal
society of the Russian village commune (*obshchina*).[28] This integrated,
organic society permitted and abetted the flourishing of an appropriately
integrated mode of cognition.

Reference to the Russian commune suggests the place of the third
component—the national or ethnic component—in the system of Slavophile thought as Smirnova reconstructs it. The Slavophiles found the
two great modes of thought and types of social systems—rationalistic-
individualistic and integral-organic—to be characteristic of different peoples
—Western European and Slavic. It was the opinion of all the Slavophiles
that, in Smirnova's words, "in Russia the state developed along peaceful
lines, that there was no hostility among estates (in other words, class
struggle) in Russia (before Peter the Great), that Christianity in Russia
was genuine Christianity, not corrupted by rationalism, and that narrow
rationalism is a property of Western and not Russian thought."[29] Hence
arose the notion of Russia's national distinctiveness and "special character," which, as Smirnova points out, included the assumption of not simply the difference but the superiority of Russian culture in comparison
with Western.

Although Smirnova's essay by no means presented a full treatment of the philosophical component of Slavophilism, it did give that component equal status with others and incorporated philosophy into the intellectual complex of the outlook without making it dependent in unilinear fashion upon socioeconomic factors; in that way she avoided the class-based analysis of the standard interpretation. With regard specifically to the thesis of appropriateness, Smirnova accepts not only the appropriateness of Slavophile philosophy to what the Slavophiles *thought* was Russian reality but its appropriateness to that reality itself. The Slavophiles, she wrote,

> counterposed the Russian rural commune to the bourgeois society that had become entrenched in the West; at that time the Russian rural commune was still almost untouched by decay and represented an actually existing type of social relations of a nature distinct from that of capitalism. . . . The consciousness of the patriarchal peasantry, which was still relatively untainted by the power of money, stood in contrast to egoistic calculation, which was the driving force of the consciousness of the bourgeois in practice.[30]

Thus Smirnova contends that Slavophile theory was appropriate to at least a significant part of Russian culture at the time the theory was formulated. Writing as a student rather than an advocate of Slavophile doctrine, she makes no claims about its appropriateness in the present day.

Khoruzhii on Sobornost as an Ecclesiological Concept

An illustration of a different post-Marxist approach to the Slavophiles is provided by two essays by Sergei Sergeevich Khoruzhii, a scholar whose work at the Institute of Mathematics of the Soviet Academy of Sciences was supplemented by studies in the history of Russian philosophy that before glasnost were politically unacceptable for publication. His essay, "The Philosophical Process in Russia as the Intersection of Philosophy and Orthodoxy," written in 1974 or 1975, first appeared in print in 1991. The second essay, "Khomiakov and the Principle of Sobornost," was published in 1992.[31]

Khoruzhii is more openly sympathetic than Smirnova to the Slavophile complex of ideas, and he leaves no doubt that he regards the kind of thinking exhibited by the Slavophiles to be uniquely appropriate to Russian culture not only in their day but for all time, including the present. He also does not share Smirnova's objection to the identification of a core component in Slavophile theory. Far from regarding Slavophilism as an intellectual complex in which social conceptions, national or ethnic conceptions, and conceptions of idealist religious philosophy have essentially equal

weight, Khoruzhii views it as fundamentally a system of *religious* thought
in which the other so-called "components" are decidedly secondary. Consequently he delves much more deeply than Smirnova into the religious-
philosophical content and significance of the Slavophile system.

Khoruzhii's starting point is a general theory of cultural development
according to which a national culture evolves from a nucleus of some sort,
which it then elaborates: "The essence of the historical process includes
the discovery, unfolding, and actualizing of a certain initial content, the
original principles of the historical existence of the cultural subject." In
the case of Russian history, he contends, this nucleus or "initial content" is
provided by Russian Orthodoxy, considered "in the totality of its aspects:
as a faith and a Church, as a doctrine and an institution, as a vital and
spiritual formation." Philosophy, as a cultural phenomenon, is part and
parcel of the culture's development and plays a critical role in the "unfolding" of the initial content. Hence, in Russia, philosophy's fate is inextrica-
bly bound up with the cultural material furnished by Orthodoxy: "The
meaning content of the philosophical process in Russia of necessity includes the appropriation and elaboration of Orthodoxy by means of and in
forms of philosophical reason."[32] Although Khoruzhii acknowledges that
philosophy in Russia (as elsewhere) may have other tasks as well, they are
far less important: "We simply state, following Pushkin, that 'the Greek
confession gives us a special national character,' and we conclude that the
immediate duty of philosophy is to think about and disclose this 'special
character.' . . . The *authentic* Russian philosophical tradition cannot but
proceed from the experiential soil of Orthodoxy."[33]

At this point Khoruzhii has already made contact with Slavophilism, as
he interprets it. For he regards Slavophilism as precisely the intellectual
system that took up the challenge of building on the "soil of Orthodoxy."
Khomiakov's thinking, he affirms, was addressed to "perhaps the most
essential features of the life and organization of the Orthodox church."
And among the most central theses of Kireevskii, Khoruzhii argues, is the
idea that "the elaboration of 'distinctive Orthodox thinking,' the creation
of an original philosophy on the ground of Orthodox experience, constitutes the destiny and the duty of Russian thought."[34]

To what extent has this destiny been fulfilled? Khoruzhii clearly regards Slavophilism as the beginning of the process; in that regard he
subscribes to the priority thesis, as we saw above. But while he accepts as
accurate on the whole the view that Kireevskii and Khomiakov were the
originators of a distinctive Russian philosophy, he believes that this judgment requires qualification. What the Slavophiles created was not exactly
the philosophy itself but "the idea of it," following their recognition of the

need for a specifically Russian philosophy.[35] Their actual elaboration of Orthodoxy, he contends, was more theological than philosophical. Their ideas flowed from "living experience" of Orthodoxy; when Khomiakov spoke of the Orthodox church, Khoruzhii contends, he was "not so much constructing a theory as expressing the personal experience, plumbed to its depths, of his own life in the Church."[36] Furthermore, their ideas were not laid out philosophically—"not expressed in true philosophical form, in the categorial system of professional philosophy." Although the *content* of these ideas could be called philosophical, according to Khoruzhii, in the Slavophile doctrines this content "took the form of theology."[37]

Not surprisingly, the heart of Khomiakov's theory as Khoruzhii reconstructs it is what the latter calls "the theology of sobornost." Following Khomiakov's definition of the kind of union that sobornost represents—"a free and organic union, the vital principle of which is the Divine grace of mutual love"—Khoruzhii insists that the concept's proper sphere of application is in *religious* life and experience. Specifically, it must be understood as signifying the union that is the *Church*: "Sobornost is a theological concept, or more concretely an ecclesiological one. '*Sobornyi*' [the Russian adjectival form of 'sobornost'] is one of the four attributes of the Church indicated in the Nicene Creed; it is synonymous with the old term 'catholic' . . . signifying 'universal'."[38] For Khoruzhii the reference in the definition to Divine grace clearly indicates the supraempirical, mystical character of this union. In the doctrine of sobornost, he states, we are confronted with "not simply an ecclesiological doctrine but in the first instance a doctrine of the *Church mystical* and invisible, the Church as the mystical Body of the Lord." This mystical vision of the Church, according to Khoruzhii, "lying in the depths of the doctrine of sobornost," is expressed in many of the themes and features of the doctrine.[39]

In light of this approach it is understandable that Khoruzhii would relegate the purely social and national implications of sobornost to a distinctly secondary status. He admits that the concept has such implications and had them even for Khomiakov. But he regrets the secular emphasis often placed on them, and especially the frequent identification of the concept with socialism; he refers to the socialist interpretation of the concept as "this sad chapter in the history of sobornost." Khoruzhii has nothing but scorn for what he terms "all the communoid variations on the themes of collectivism, Sov-patriotism, or Nats-bolshevism." Referring specifically to the thought of contemporary Russian national patriots who claim the authority of the Slavophiles for their outlook—he calls it "the zoological philosophy of today's 'nativists' [*pochvenniki*]"—he denies them any Slavophile legitimacy: "There is no sobornost here, just as there is nothing in common with the spirit of the thought and faith of Khomiakov."[40]

Still, for all his virtues Khomiakov presented only the *theology* of sobornost, based on his profound personal experience, not its philosophy. The subsequent development of Russian philosophy as Khoruzhii views it was carried out by Solov'ev and others, who moved from immediate intuition to the conceptual elaboration of these religious notions, employing genuinely philosophical categories. But Khoruzhii believes that in the process these post-Slavophiles unfortunately lost the distinctive appropriateness of Russian thought to its true *Orthodox* culture. At the hands of Solov'ev and his followers, Russian religious philosophy became what Khoruzhii labels "general religious philosophy"—a philosophy dealing with religious themes "along traditional lines of Western speculative metaphysics, based on abstract conceptual constructs," without reference to the specific character of the Orthodox faith as it is revealed, for example, in the theological constructions of the Hesychast mystic Gregory Palamas in fourteenth-century Byzantium.[41] Only in some of the later efforts of Florenskii and other representatives of the "religious-philosophical renaissance" of the early twentieth century was there a genuine effort to "bring within the orbit of philosophical reason the phenomenon of Orthodoxy in its wholeness."[42] But these efforts were crushed by political developments in Russia.

Thus Slavophilism represents for Khoruzhii a philosophical promise not yet fulfilled. Its ideas were pioneering and are correct, fruitful, and uniquely appropriate to Russian culture, but Russian thought must go beyond them. This by no means entails political action or the whipping up of national sentiment in the guise of "implementing" Slavophile concepts. What it entails, rather, is what Khoruzhii describes as "thought thinking Orthodoxy"[43]—thought that goes beyond the profound but philosophically unarticulated insights of the Eastern church fathers and early Slavophiles to assimilate and develop philosophically the Orthodox legacy that is the foundation of Russian culture, leading to "the understanding of Orthodox positions on all anthropological and existential questions."[44]

Neo-Slavophilism and Russian National Patriotism

The attention to Slavophilism in current Russian thought is not limited to scholarly study of the sort we have been examining. Although a scholar like Khoruzhii is in a certain sense an "advocate" of Slavophile thought as well as a student of it, his focus is on philosophical understanding rather than advocacy. But for many other Russian writers in the present day,

Slavophilism is something closer to a blueprint for national salvation. These are the contemporary "neo-Slavophiles" mentioned above—the latest generation of Russian thinkers who directly champion Slavophile positions. Some, like Viktor Shapovalov, appear to use Slavophile conceptions simply to buttress a general conviction of the need to preserve Russia's "uniqueness" as one voice in "the symphony of human history."[45] The majority, however, are motivated more by a concern for Russia's stature as a great nation with not only unique but superior characteristics. Hence they employ Slavophile conceptions as part of an ideology of national patriotism—the "zoological philosophy" mentioned by Khoruzhii. We shall concentrate here on two writers—Pavel Vladimirovich Tulaev and Evgenii Sergeevich Troitskii—for whom Slavophile conceptions, and especially the conception of sobornost, play a prominent role in their patriotic reflections on the theme of Russia and the West.

There are many points of difference between the two, as there are among writers of the patriotic school generally. Tulaev, a young linguist and specialist in the history of Russian culture, is drawn more to the philosophical and theological aspects of Slavophilism, whereas Troitskii, a philosopher who founded the Association for the Complex Study of the Russian Nation, is interested more in social and national questions. Troitskii is more openly nationalistic (though he vigorously denies it) and is more concerned with Russia's physical might and with the outward trappings of patriotism such as flags and emblems; he also sets greater store by the supposedly "genetic" differences among national groups. Tulaev is more ready than Troitskii to find at least some virtues in Western culture that could benefit Russian Orthodox culture as well. Yet these are primarily differences in emphasis, and they are less important than the basic similarities in the two writers' approach to the East–West division and the relation of Slavophilism to it.

The first and most obvious similarity is simply the extreme dedication each displays toward "the Motherland" (*Rodina*) or "the Fatherland" (*Otechestvo*), as they variously call their country. "Our native land," Tulaev writes, "is for us not a territory over which we move but a bride, a wife, demanding love and attention."[46] Troitskii shares this sentiment about the country as a whole and lauds its inhabitants for their superlative traits; even "enlightened foreigners," he contends in *The Rebirth of the Russian Idea* (1991), value "Russianness, its humane, spiritual-cultural features, its tenderness and warmth."[47] In the case of both writers these expressions are symptomatic of an ill-concealed conviction of not simply the value and uniqueness but the superiority of "Holy Russia" over Western society and culture, echoing a similar conviction on the part of the early

Slavophiles. Less clear in the case of Tulaev, this conviction nonetheless comes out in such statements of his as that "in Russia, *on the high road of the evolution of thought*, a search is going on to unite the aspiration toward Freedom and the service of God," and in his reference to the "narrow-minded and mercantile civilization" that the spirit of Russia stands against.[48] In Troitskii's case such suggestions are more frequent and less subtle, manifesting themselves in a multitude of chauvinistic observations about the superior breadth and goodness of the Russian soul (for example, Russians are said to be kinder and more "universally human" than Germans) and in the view that the West has exhausted a greater share of its spiritual resources, whereas "the genius of Slavdom" is yet to be fully revealed.[49]

A second common feature in the writings of Tulaev and Troitskii is their reliance on Slavophile concepts, especially the concept of sobornost, for the conceptual framework of their patriotic programs. Troitskii explicitly places his book *The Rebirth of the Russian Idea* "in the context of the millennial discussions between Westernists and Slavophiles"—"millennial" because he argues that Slavophilism is as old as Russian history ("almost every century of Russian life has . . . had its Slavophiles"). In its origin, he writes, Slavophilism "was organically connected with the growth of the national-patriotic feelings of the Russian people."[50] Far from ignoring the classic Slavophile writers, however, Troitskii refers to them frequently and regards Khomiakov's conception of sobornost as an essential and supremely valuable constituent of "the Russian idea," both historically and in the present day.[51]

Tulaev concurs with this judgment. His long essay on sobornost is a paean of praise to one of the greatest achievements of Russian culture, and he takes as given "the striving of modern Russian consciousness for sobornost."[52] Writing lyrically of the contemporary rediscovery of sobornost and other concepts in Russian religious philosophy, Tulaev gives voice to a familiar theme among Slavophile-oriented writers: "Ultimately everything returns to its own place. And our life, like a river that had overflowed its banks, is again returning to its former bed. We are now assimilating long-hidden treasures, understanding forgotten truths, and regaining our sight and seeing what we were unable to see when we were blinded."[53] Russian thought, after its forced and tragic diversion under communism, is returning to what is natural, native, fitting, appropriate ("its own place").

In their interpretations of sobornost, both Tulaev and Troitskii acknowledge that the concept is at bottom a religious one—in Tulaev's words, "a theurgic and not a political principle." Yet in applying it to the present day, both find far greater social and political implications in the principle than someone like Khoruzhii would countenance. Tulaev believes that the principle has special social significance in the wake of the devastation wrought by Soviet rule on the family, rural communities, and the polluted cities, the inhabitants of which have been "cut off from their ancestral ties." Although basically a "spiritual principle," sobornost can function to transform "a heterogeneous populace into a unified people [narod]." More than that, sobornost has international promise as well, opening up new prospects "for the union of peoples"; characteristically, however, Tulaev gives Russia the central place in the anticipated union: he describes the peoples as "united *around Russia.*"[54]

A similarly social and Russocentric interpretation of sobornost is advanced by Troitskii, but with emphasis on the *ethnic* Russianness of the *sobornyi* union. Explicitly rejecting the view that "sobornost is only a religious category," Troitskii proceeds to apply the concept to Russian state unity—more precisely, to Russian *ethnic* unity under the protection of a Russian state. Thus he includes Russians living in other republics of the former Soviet Union as essential participants in true Russian sobornost; indeed, he affirms somewhat ominously that "the *sobornyi* consolidation of the ethnos is more and more becoming the categorical imperative of our time."[55] And although he speaks of the repatriation of Russians through compensated resettlement as a way of dealing with this problem, he also freely talks about Russia's "might." In what is surely the ultimate despiritualization of Khoruzhii's "ecclesiological concept," Troitskii includes Russian military power in his conception of sobornost. Escape from Russia's present crisis, he affirms in his book's final paragraph, requires "the *sobornyi* unification of all classes and strata of society, the patriotic organizations, and the armed forces." And lest the last words seem an inconsequential addition, Troitskii concludes with this statement: "In a word, without the application and strengthening of Russian power we are hardly likely to achieve the ideal of a better society."[56]

As to the contours of that better society, Tulaev and Troitskii share a clear preference for tight social unity over the unbridled liberty and individualism they attribute to the West. Although both pay lip service to the values of freedom and even democracy, the *sobornyi* freedom and democracy they have in mind (harking back to Khomiakov's requirement that a *sobornyi* unity be "organic") is one heavily qualified by the demands of community integrity. Troitskii states this corporatist inclination most baldly:

> The spiritual and political experience of the history of the Fatherland has shown that our chief, consummate concern about it must be unity, with

freedom secondary. Attempts to turn everything upside down have engendered a new time of troubles in which people, suffering from unemployment, inflation, the high cost of living, anarchy, and chaos ultimately lose freedom even as secondary, so that to a large extent it becomes practically meaningless, an empty category.[57]

Tulaev, too, argues that "the extreme development of human individuality" has had a socially pernicious effect for centuries, from the Renaissance to the present day, and he contends that the principal social benefit of sobornost lies in "the overcoming of individualism."[58]

How exactly the desired social unity is to be implemented is not entirely clear for either writer—in part because they believe that a concern with institutional structures is characteristic of the "cold, juridical arrangements of Western civilization."[59] Troitskii is particularly scornful of what he calls "parliamentarianism"; with typical bravado, he contrasts it unfavorably with the "Russian idea":

> The European countries that had a parliamentary system proved at a certain stage to be essentially powerless to oppose Hitler's fascism and collapsed like a house of cards under his blows and subversive activity. Only our people, inspired by this very Russian idea, smashed Hitler's military machine and saved not only their own country but the parliamentary system itself.[60]

If the lesson to be drawn from this statement is that the Stalinist one-man rule that purportedly defeated Hitler is superior to democratic rule, that would be consistent with many other passages in Troitskii's book that show substantial sympathy for both the tsarist and the communist varieties of autocracy. He urges his countrymen to study the history of the Russian autocracy, assuring them that in it, "as also in post-October [1917] development," they will find "as much good as there was bad." Count Uvarov's famous slogan, "Autocracy, Orthodoxy, Nationality," Troitskii contends, fulfilled "on the whole a positive function."[61] Tulaev, too, though without Troitskii's chauvinistic excesses, exhibits monarchist sympathies. But at the same time, again like Troitskii, he has more confidence in a special national, patriotic, and religious *spirit* than in specific socioeconomic or political institutions. He places his trust in the dedicated Russian who advances toward the flowering of Holy Russia "with God in [his] soul and the Tsar in [his] head."[62]

The mystical overtones discernible in many statements by our two representatives of contemporary patriotic neo-Slavophilism reflect a final point of agreement between them. Although sobornost as they present it is largely a social or national concept rather than a spiritual one, they seek to retain for it the mystical quality it had in Khomiakov's religious thinking. Thus when Troitskii speaks of Russian nationality (*narodnost'*) as "flowing from the deep essence of the Russian nation, from the priceless treasures of its biological, physical, spiritual-moral, and psychological characteristics," he appears to be subscribing to a kind of mysticized racial sobornost. This bio-mystical unity has little in common with the sobornost of the mystical Church as originally described by Khomiakov and developed in the present day by Khoruzhii.[63]

Both Troitskii and Tulaev freely invoke the mystical meaning of sobornost. According to Tulaev, "the economic, social, historical, and other aspects of community retreat into the background before its *mystical* content."[64] But both writers then proceed to treat the mystical element as not only the most prominent but as pervading all the others as well, so that to them a materialized, physically embodied unity such as a society or a people is as "mystically" united as is the supraempirical Church. Troitskii speaks of a *sobornyi* unity of individuals in society as a "perhaps somehow invisible joining together of people."[65] Thus, having taken a fundamentally spiritual, religious notion and given it material form, the patriotic neo-Slavophiles then call down the mystical aura of the original concept upon its earthly incarnation as well. In this way the "Church invisible" becomes the "Nation invisible," and the mystical body of Christ is replaced by the mystical gene pool. All of which suggests how far we have come from the "ecclesiology" described by Khoruzhii. In this light the latter's disdain for "Sov-patriotism" and "Nats-bolshevism" as claimants to the mantle of Slavophilism is readily understandable.

Contemporary Russian Criticisms of Slavophilism

Although currently enjoying a resurgence in popularity, the concepts and principles of Slavophile philosophy are far from immune to criticism in the newly opened intellectual marketplace of Russia. The critics appear to be fewer in number than the advocates, but they can be no less vigorous and categorical in their judgments. Here is the reaction of one of them, Evgenii Barabanov, to the wave of interest in Slavophilism and related doctrines:

> The *ideological* and *utopian* paradigms of Russian philosophical thought are acquiring a second life. Again the "Russian idea!" Again the "special way," again "originality," again doctrinal preaching instead of the pupil's desk.... Again an ideological orientation toward the expected, where the world of words is divorced from the world of things . . . all these things once again return us to magical consciousness.[66]

Each of the supposed virtues of Slavophilism identified by those who defend it—historical priority, originality, uniqueness, and appropriateness to Russian life and culture—is called into question by contemporary critics. On the subject of originality, for example, Barabanov calls the current fashion of stressing the independence of Russian philosophy "a pretentious characterization" and proceeds to detail the European influences that shaped Russian philosophy throughout its history, from Plato to Husserl.[67] Smirnova describes Slavophilism as a version of a broader romantic protest, common throughout Europe, against Enlightenment ideology and the development of bourgeois society.[68] And we must remember that even Sergei Khoruzhii, sympathetic as he is to the early Slavophiles, does not claim *philosophical* originality for their doctrines. His point, as we saw, is that although Kireevskii and Khomiakov recognized the need for an original Russian philosophy, they did not actually create one because their thought was essentially confessional and theological.

By far the greatest objections to Slavophilism, however, and the objections I shall highlight here, concern the question of *appropriateness*—the fittingness or adequacy of Slavophile doctrine to Russian culture, Russian nature, or Russian spiritual and social needs. In this connection contemporary attacks on Slavophilism take at least three different forms, which I shall characterize broadly as demographic, psychological, and sociopolitical.

Demographic Attacks on Slavophilism

The demographic attacks question the existence or the size of the supposed audience for Slavophile thinking in Russia. Most Russian commentators on Slavophilism agree that it was in some sense appropriate to the actual mentality of the Russian population at the time of its origin. Smirnova holds such a view, as we have seen, and even Barabanov admits that Russian philosophy arose with characteristic features that were rooted in active domains of Russian thought, such as Orthodoxy with its medieval Gnostic paradigms.[69] Yet there are also critics who question whether Slavophile philosophy adequately echoed Russian popular thinking even at the time of its formulation; T.I. Blagova writes that Khomiakov and Kireevskii "may be faulted for overestimating the degree of Christianization of the Russian people and of its dedication to the spirit of community and sobornost."[70]

But whatever the historical situation, many critics question the appropriateness of Slavophile philosophy to the Russian mentality of the present day. This demographic line of argument, often merely implicit in current debates about the value of earlier Russian thought, is directed not merely against the contemporary relevance of Slavophilism but against the applicability of Russian religious thinking in general to present-day conditions. It aims to establish that secularization has radically changed the face of Russian society over the last century and a half since the days of Kireevskii and Khomiakov, to the point that Russia is no longer a predominantly Orthodox or even Christian country. The implication is that no particular claim on the allegiance of the Russian people can be made by a philosophy grounded in Christian doctrine, let alone Orthodoxy.

Evidence for at least the first part of this claim—the purely demographic part—was presented in a roundtable sponsored by the journal *Voprosy filosofii* in 1992. In his lengthy presentation at the roundtable, D.E. Furman of the Russian Academy of Sciences' Analytical Center summarized survey results showing (among many other things) that as of 1991 only 29 percent of the inhabitants of Russia identified themselves as believers in God and only 19 percent considered themselves supporters of either the official Russian Orthodox church or the "free Orthodox church" abroad.[71] This was a significant decline even from the previous year, and it was accompanied by a precipitous drop in the proportion of Muscovites who believed that "religion is necessary for governing the state" (from 47 percent in 1990 to 21 percent in 1991).[72] In these and other survey findings, Furman sees a connection "between the retreat of Orthodoxy and the continuing movement of the mass consciousness toward the values of Western democracy." Surprisingly, he even ascribes part of the greater enthusiasm for Orthodoxy before 1991 to *Westernist* rather than Slavophile attitudes:

> Obviously, a large number of persons who declared themselves Orthodox in 1990 were people for whom Orthodoxy was a symbol and an expression not of "reactionary-romantic" [i.e., Slavophile] sentiments but of Western sentiments. These were people who knew that religion occupies an important place in the bourgeois-democratic societies of the West and who expected their religion, Orthodoxy, to play the same role of providing religious sanctification to democracy. . . . But . . . when democratically disposed people turned to Orthodoxy, they came upon a reality that had very little in common with their political attitudes.[73]

When they found in Russian Orthodoxy no great support for democracy, Furman argues, their enthusiasm quickly cooled.

Although some of the other participants in this roundtable were church representatives, including spokespersons for both Orthodox churches, on the whole the information and opinions presented were heavily weighted against the idea that Russian society is suffused with the kind of Orthodox religiosity associated with Slavophilism. In all likelihood it was opposition to this idea that motivated the journal's editors to arrange the roundtable.

Certainly the philosopher selected to moderate it, L.N. Mitrokhin, a veteran Marxist specialist on atheism and the history of religion, made clear in his concluding remarks that he distrusts the testimony of even the minority who call themselves "believers" and is convinced that current accounts of a "religious renaissance" in Russia are exaggerated. Mitrokhin criticized the Orthodox clergy who took part in the roundtable for "call[ing] on everyone except themselves to repent" and for holding that the Orthodox church is "the Russian people itself from the standpoint of its spiritual aspiration."[74] Mitrokhin and his colleagues appear intent on marginalizing Orthodox consciousness in Russia and hence minimalizing its significance as an anchor for Slavophile and other forms of religious philosophy.

If the demographic attack thus calls into question the conformability of Slavophile thinking to the actual mentality of the Russian population, the psychological and sociopolitical attacks find the two regrettably and even dangerously conformable.

Psychological Attacks on Slavophilism

Barabanov's article "Russian Philosophy and the Crisis of Identity," from which we have already quoted above, epitomizes the contemporary psychological critique of Slavophilism. For Barabanov, the current vogue of Slavophile concepts is a culturally conditioned neurotic response to contemporary circumstances. Actually, Barabanov's critique is an assault on the entire "distinctivist" mentality (which he traces to the early centuries of Russian life) that holds Russia to be unique among nations and endowed with a special historical role, and that consequently nourished the Slavophile opposition to Westernism. To Barabanov this mentality is pathological; he believes that mechanisms of repression have produced in Russia a widespread "neurosis of distinctiveness" that is manifested philosophically in the specific character of Slavophilism and related currents in Russian thought. The powerful manifestation of this neurosis in the present day, he contends, has been triggered by "an acute identity crisis."[75]

Clearly, Barabanov's psychological analysis is intended not simply as a diagnosis but as an argument against the notion that Slavophile thinking is an appropriate outlook for Russia today. For Barabanov, Slavophile and related religious thinking is itself a *cause* of a pathological Russian mental condition. "Utopian retrospectivism—the utopia of the renaissance of a purportedly paradisiacal past," he writes, "is again immersing consciousness in the dark myths of the collective unconscious." He explicitly associates this kind of philosophy with Orthodoxy: "Along with the spread of

Orthodox fundamentalism, this utopian myth-making is again—how many times already!—returning philosophy to the old *neurosis of distinctiveness.*" But it is not merely philosophy that suffers, for the human consequence of such thinking, he concludes, is pernicious attitudes such as xenophobia, delusions of persecution, and delusions of national grandeur.[76] In short, such philosophizing, although undeniably a feature of Russian reality, is not suitable for Russia because it is psychologically damaging.

Sociopolitical Attacks on Slavophilism

What I have called the sociopolitical critique of Slavophilism shares with the psychological critique the conviction that Slavophile thinking is both an outgrowth of Russian conditions and a negative feature of present-day Russian culture. Rather than viewing Slavophile thinking as a psychopathological phenomenon, however, the sociopolitical critique sees the danger of Slavophile thinking in its encouragement of mistaken social and political notions.

Without denying that the idea of sobornost expresses a sense of collectivism that is characteristic of Russian thought, A.T. Pavlov in his article "The Question of the Uniqueness of Russian Philosophy" (1994) argues that this outlook has had unfortunate consequences for Russia, including the promotion of socialism. Pavlov is particularly critical of the "antibourgeois" aspect of the Russian collectivist mentality that he finds not only among Slavophiles but among Westernists as well. This attitude, he believes, blinded Russian thinkers to the virtues of free enterprise and risk taking. In the case of the Orthodox thinkers such as the Slavophiles, it combined with an anti-Protestant bias to prevent an understanding of "the true social role of Protestantism in the genesis and consolidation of the spirit of entrepreneurship, personal initiative, and enthusiasm for work."[77] The special damage done by the Slavophile form of the antibourgeois spirit is summed up by Pavlov in this passage:

> The constant emphasis on the uniqueness of Russian historical development had the effect that the idea that Russia had to pave its own special way in history became fixed in the mass consciousness. The messianic idea of Russia's special predestination became embodied in the idea of building socialism in one country. This idea could so easily form the basis for the entire policy of the Soviet state because the idea of Russia's special role in this world, of Russia as a "third Rome," was alive in the mass consciousness and was actively stoked by philosophical reflections on the uniqueness of the Russian mentality.[78]

Pavlov also sketches a related sociopolitical argument against the Slavophiles and other representatives of Russian religious philosophy: their outlook, he believes, encouraged legal nihilism in Russia, or in other words the rejection or at least devaluation of laws, rights, and juridical structures. Pavlov traces Russian legal nihilism specifically to the thinking of Kireevskii and Khomiakov, and he identifies its origin as their elevation of "inner freedom" over the necessities imposed by external circumstances. The Slavophiles, he argues, saw the subordination of the individual person to external legal norms as a characteristic defect of Western civilization; they believed, on the contrary, that people should act as their conscience demands, guided by "a moral sense based on faith in God's supreme authority." During the revolutionary period, Pavlov contends, this Slavophile-inspired disregard of "external" legal controls on, and safeguards of, rights and liberties served to reinforce the Marxist scorn of law as a bourgeois device for maintaining class dominance. The result was "true legal anarchy" and the domination of "revolutionary expediency."[79] Pavlov finds it both ironic and tragic that Russian religious thought joined forces with Marxist doctrines in this way to destroy legality and respect for individual rights.

It must be noted that Pavlov is not denying the "appropriateness" of these social and political attitudes in the sense of their close linkage with widespread and characteristic Russian patterns of thought. On the contrary, he finds them anchored in the fabric of Russian life, "deeply embedded in the Russian consciousness."[80] His point, like Barabanov's as well, is that these attitudes are not appropriate to the Russia of today in the sense of being suitable or fitting for the growth and structuring of more important values—for the creation of a superior Russian culture. Both he and Barabanov are assuming, of course, that Russian culture is capable of change, and they are encouraging change in the direction away from Slavophile models. These two senses of 'appropriate' are pithily captured in Pavlov's concluding advice to students of Russian philosophy: they should realize that "not everything that is one's own is better than someone else's."[81]

The Interest in Russian Slavophilism Today: Some Conclusions

The foregoing examination of recent Russian attention to the ideas of Slavophilism, although far from exhaustive, provides grounds for a few general conclusions about the place of Slavophilism in postcommunist Russian thought.

The first is that the "new stage in the study of Slavophilism" (noted by

E. Dudzinskaia in 1983) that began in the 1960s and 1970s has continued into the postcommunist era with considerable vigor.[82] The publication of archival materials, reprints of original writings, and books and articles on the Slavophiles—not to mention, in more recent years, the increasing frequency with which Slavophile conceptions find expression in the popular press—all of this evidences a lively interest in the phenomenon of Slavophilism, its originators, and its relevance to the present. Two broad cultural processes in current Russian life have clearly abetted this rebirth of Slavophilism: one is the overall "religious renaissance," or growth of interest in religion and religious themes, and the other is the national-patriotic movement, which is distinguishable from the first process but sometimes coincides with it. To the extent that we can divide the interest in Slavophilism into scholarly and popular, its nationalistic appeal is largely restricted to its popular audience, while its religious appeal is more important to the scholarly community; indeed, surveys have shown that the religious renaissance is more vital and widespread among what *Voprosy filosofii* calls "cultural workers" than among the population at large.[83]

At the same time it should be noted, second, that Russian scholars have not yet produced major comprehensive studies of Slavophilism or its originators—nothing to rival Andrzej Walicki's *The Slavophile Controversy* or Peter K. Christoff's monographic studies of leading Slavophile thinkers.[84] K.N. Lomunov wrote in 1978 that "comprehensive study of the problem of Slavophilism is still a matter of the future,"[85] and in the Russian literature that future has not yet arrived. With regard specifically to philosophy, Smirnova noted in 1987 the complete absence of "special studies of the philosophy of Slavophilism" (for example, its relation to classical German philosophy), and aside from the few and relatively limited articles by Khoruzhii and others that have been cited above, that observation, too, remains in effect.[86] Thus there is much room in Russian scholarship for ambitious, philosophically oriented investigations into the nature and significance of Slavophile thought.

A third feature of the current Russian occupation with Slavophilism is the range of intellectual and programmatic interests it reflects and the broad spectrum of interpretations it produces. In today's intellectual environment in Russia, Slavophilism responds to a wide variety of concerns—philosophical, theological, religious, ecclesiastical, social, historical, national-ethnic—and accordingly is subject to many uses and interpretations, from Khoruzhii's spiritualistic, "ecclesiological" approach to the sabre-rattling jingoism of Troitskii. As we have seen, Russian writers today are providing readings of Slavophilism that differ considerably with regard to the priority of Slavophilism in the history of Russian philosophy, its originality and uniqueness, and its appropriateness to Russian culture, past and present.

Fourth, the debate between Slavophiles and Westernists in Russian thought is far from over, but continues today in a new form. Slavophile thought is not only studied but championed by a new generation of neo-Slavophiles, who once again find themselves opposed by thinkers who offer many of the same arguments against them as were articulated by previous generations of Westernists. The critical points by Pavlov examined above, for example, are not original to him but have been voiced by others in the past. The forceful repetition of these points today is vivid proof that the issues have not lost their relevance.

Still, the circumstances are different now, and they give the debate not only a new form but new urgency. The flavor of the debate is different today because it is renewed after the abject failure in Russia of Marxism —a Western ideology. Today's neo-Slavophiles can and do argue that the failed Communist experiment should be taken as the final refutation of the myth that Western notions can adequately cope with Russia's special, historically generated needs and problems. The tragedy of Russia's twentieth-century intellectual life, as Tulaev describes it, is that "the *messianic Russian idea* of Sobornost and the renewal of the Orthodox Empire" was replaced by "ideas of godless international communism and the bloody dictatorship of the proletariat." Communism, he asserts, "led our country into a reality that was contrary to its destiny."[87] When communism was shown to be an unmitigated disaster for Russia, what better argument could be given against the folly of ignoring or betraying one's own roots and traditions?

To all this the contemporary neo-Westernists can and do argue (as we saw in the case of Pavlov above) that the Marxist "experiment" is far from decisive because what was tried in Russia was an uncharacteristic Western ideology that furthermore was heavily shaped in Russia by Slavophile concepts and thought patterns. Specifically, the collectivistic import of sobornost both paved the way for the acceptance of Marxist socialism and guaranteed that Marxism's own inherent collectivism would be pushed to a destructive extreme. Similarly, without the moralistic tendencies toward legal nihilism present in Slavophile thought, Marxism's class-oriented, deterministic version of legal nihilism might not have taken hold or have triumphed so completely. On this view, true Westernism has not failed in Russia, because it has not really been tried. What was tried and failed was an eccentric Western ideology that unfortunately provided a convenient conceptual framework for the stimulation and implementation of the worst tendencies of Slavophilism.

But in addition to the fact that the present debate takes place in the shadow of Marxism, there is another circumstance that differentiates it from the historical opposition between the two intellectual currents. The original Slavophiles of the 1840s were developing their ideas in a young but at the same time relatively stable Russia, a Russia growing in strength and influence in the world and confidently asserting its national identity in a situation in which that identity was relatively unthreatened. The neo-Slavophiles of today, on the other hand, are writing at a time not of national promise but of national humiliation—a time of weakness and greatly diminished national stature. Their world has been shaken in virtually every imaginable respect, and their national identity is perceived as vulnerable to destruction at the hands of more powerful outside forces.

The depth of this sense of national vulnerability and insecurity in the world may be gauged by these recent remarks by the distinguished Russian academician and historian of culture, Dmitrii Sergeevich Likhachev:

> State power in Russia is at present extremely weak. Russia has constant relations with foreign countries, including the so-called neighboring foreign states. One need not be a prophet to say that, because of all this, our culture will lose its national origins and, all the more, its spiritual and mystical qualities. These our country had before the revolution and had managed to retain somehow, in a special way, under the Communist regime.[88]

Evidently the new foreign impact is feared by Likhachev as a force even more destructive than Western communism—as threatening finally to deprive Russia of its distinctive culture altogether.

Likhachev does not explicitly attribute this danger to evil intentions on the part of the West, but his statement has the ring of earlier Slavophile attitudes that were summed up by the poet Fedor Tiutchev when he wrote that virtually all the Slavophiles believed that "there is no single trend in the West which would not conspire against Russia, especially against its future, and would not try to harm us."[89] Walter Laqueur dubs this notion "the idea of Western Russophobia," defining it as "the suspicion that the West was plotting against Russia and holding it in contempt, openly or secretly." Laqueur is perhaps unfair to the early Slavophiles when he calls this idea "one of the chief motives of Slavophilism," but he is correct in finding it associated with Slavophile themes in Russian conservative thinking today.[90]

It would not be surprising if what Barabanov called the "neurosis of distinctiveness" in 1991, just before the collapse of the USSR, would be still more pronounced and dangerous today, after the final collapse of Communist power. In a geographically diminished, economically dysfunctional, and politically unsettled nation, some versions of Slavophilism provide ideologies that may promote not only "delusions of national grandeur" but a yearning for authoritarian control and a threatening posture toward the rest of the world. The authoritarian impulse is clearly present even in an eminent scholar such as Likhachev, who continues his mournful prediction as follows:

> The state as such will gradually be denationalized. It will no longer pretend to express the will of the people. For what is the will of the people, and how can it be known to the state? The deputies of the Russian parliament cannot invent a new state theory, not even a simple program of actions. *We need personal power for this.*[91]

Both the authoritarianism and the threat are clearly present in the thinking of someone like Troitskii, who tellingly quotes a neo-Slavophile of an earlier generation, the philosopher and critic Konstantin Leont'ev, in support of his case for the building of Russian might. In answer to the age-old Russian question, What is to be done?, Troitskii takes Leont'ev as his guide: "It is necessary to strengthen oneself, to think less about good and more about power. If there is power, some good will be possible as well."[92]

However benign these authoritarian and militaristic impulses may eventually prove to be, in today's wounded Russia they lend to the Slavophile-Westernist confrontation a gravity that was lacking in earlier times.

Notes

1. *Filosofskii slovar'*, ed. M.M. Rosental' and P.F. Iudin (Moscow: Izdatel'stvo politicheskoi literatury, 1963), p. 408.

2. *Filosofskaia entsiklopediia*, ed. F.V. Konstantinov, 5 vols. (Moscow: Sovetskaia entsiklopediia, 1960–70), vol. 2 (1962), p. 510.

3. A.S. Khomiakov, *Stikhotvoreniia i dramy*, ed. B.F. Egorov (Leningrad: Sovetskii pisatel', 1969), pp. 5, 27–29.

4. I.V. Kireevskii, *Kritika i estetika*, ed. Iu.V. Mann (Moscow: Iskusstvo, 1979); K.S. Aksakov and I.S. Aksakov, *Literaturnaia kritika* (Moscow: Sovremennik, 1981); I.V. Kireevskii, *Izbrannye stat'i* (Moscow, 1984).

5. A.S. Khomiakov, *O starom i novom*, ed. B.F. Egorov (Moscow, 1988).

6. *Filosofskaia entsiklopediia*, vol. 5 (1970), pp. 27–28, 443.

7. *Literaturnye vzgliady i tvorchestvo slavianofilov, 1830–1850 godov*, ed. K.N. Lomunov (Moscow: Nauka, 1978); V.A. Koshelov, *Esteticheskie i literaturnye vozzreniia russkikh slavianofilov (1840–1850-e gody)* (Leningrad: Nauka, 1984); N.I. Tsimbaev, *Slavianofil'stvo: Iz istorii russkoi obshchestvenno-politicheskoi mysli XIX veka* (Moscow: Izdatel'stvo Moskovskogo universiteta, 1986).

8. Tsimbaev, *Slavianofil'stvo*, pp. 99–100.

9. Ibid., p. 101 (italics in original).

10. Ibid., pp. 101–2.

11. S.L. Frank, "The Essence and Leading Themes of Russian Philosophy," *Soviet Studies in Philosophy*, vol. 30, no. 4 (Spring 1992), pp. 32–47, especially p. 38.

12. N. Berdiaev, *A.S. Khomiakov* (Moscow: Put', 1912), pp. 114–16.

13. S.S. Khoruzhii, "Filosofskii protsess v Rossii kak vstrecha filosofii i pravoslaviia," *Voprosy filosofii*, 1991, no. 5, p. 31.

14. Gustav Shpet, *Ocherk razvitiia russkoi filosofii. Pervaia chast'* (Petrograd: Kolos, 1922), p. 37.

15. S.S. Khoruzhii, "Khomiakov i printsip sobornosti," *Zdes' i teper'*, 1992, no. 2, p. 68.

16. In addition to the text by Khoruzhii just cited, see T.I. Blagova, "Filosofiia rannikh slavianofilov. I.V. Kireevskii o tsel'nosti dukha," *Vestnik Moskovskogo universiteta. Seriia 7. Filosofiia*, 1991, no. 4, p. 14; A.T. Pavlov, "The Question of the Uniqueness of Russian Philosophy," *Russian Studies in Philosophy*, vol. 33, no. 1 (Summer 1994), pp. 37–49; and James P. Scanlan, "Nuzhna li Rossii russkaia filosofiia?" *Voprosy filosofii*, 1994, no. 1, pp. 61–65.

17. Blagova, "Filosofiia rannikh slavianofilov," p. 14 (italics added).

18. Tsimbaev, *Slavianofil'stvo*, p. 101.

19. See, for example, Khoruzhii, "Khomiakov," p. 68. The quotation is from M.O. Gershenzon, ed., *Polnoe sobranie sochinenii I.V. Kireevskogo*, 2 vols. (Moscow: Tipografiia Imperatorskago Moskovskago Universiteta, 1911), vol. 2, p. 27.

20. Zinaida V. Smirnova, "The Debates about Slavophilism: Some Methodological Aspects of the Study of Early Slavophilism," *Soviet Studies in Philosophy*, vol. 27, no. 3 (Winter 1988–89), pp. 39–40.

21. Ibid., p. 40.

22. Ibid., p. 42.

23. Ibid., pp. 42–44.

24. Ibid., pp. 37–38.

25. Ibid., p. 54.

26. Ibid., p. 59.

27. Ibid., p. 56.

28. Ibid., pp. 41–42.

29. Ibid., p. 46.

30. Ibid., p. 56.

31. These are the essays cited in notes 13 and 15 above.

32. Khoruzhii, "Filosofskii protsess," p. 29. For a similar analysis of the nature of Russian culture, see Viktor Shapovalov, "The Categories of the Cultural-Historical Process in Russia," *Russian Studies in Philosophy*, vol. 33, no. 1 (Summer 1994), pp. 7–22.

33. Khoruzhii, "Filosofskii protsess," pp. 27, 29 (italics added).

34. Ibid., p. 32.

35. Khoruzhii, "Khomiakov," p. 68.

36. Ibid., p. 70.

37. Khoruzhii, "Filosofskii protsess," p. 32.

38. Khoruzhii, "Khomiakov," pp. 70–71.

39. Ibid., pp. 75–76 (italics in original).

40. Ibid., pp. 80–81. Khoruzhii's expression "zoological philosophy" is an allusion to Vladimir Solov'ev's scornful reference to "zoological patriotism."

41. Ibid., p. 78; Khoruzhii, "Filosofskii protsess," pp. 31, 34, 56.

42. Ibid., p. 31.

43. Ibid., p. 30.

44. Ibid., p. 56.

45. Shapovalov, "The Categories of the Cultural-Historical Process," p. 7.

46. Pavel Tulaev, "*Sobor* and *Sobornost'*," *Russian Studies in Philosophy*, vol. 31, no. 4 (Spring 1993), pp. 35–36.

47. Evgenii Troitskii, *Vozrozhdenie russkoi idei: Sotsial'no-filosofskie ocherki* (Moscow: Filosofskoe obshchestvo SSSR, 1991), p. 55.

48. Tulaev, "*Sobor*," p. 43 (italics added); Pavel Tulaev, "Rossiia i Evropa: Otkrytie prikrytogo," *Nash sovremennik*, 1991, no. 1, p. 162.

49. Troitskii, *Vozrozhdenie russkoi idei*, pp. 150, 185; see also pp. 131, 158.

50. Ibid., obverse of front cover, pp. 21, 59.

51. Ibid., p. 169.

52. Tulaev, "*Sobor*," p. 45.

53. Ibid., p. 25.

54. Ibid., pp. 46 (italics omitted), 34, 36 (italics added).

55. Troitskii, *Vozrozhdenie russkoi idei*, pp. 171, 177–78.

56. Ibid., p. 223.

57. Ibid., p. 171.

58. Tulaev, "*Sobor*," pp. 31, 34.

59. Troitskii, *Vozrozhdenie russkoi idei*, p. 171.

60. Ibid., p. 24.

61. Ibid., pp. 168, 186.

62. Tulaev, "Rossiia i Evropa," p. 162.

63. Troitskii, *Vozrozhdenie russkoi idei*, p. 154. Related to these views is Troitskii's notion that Orthodoxy is linked to the biological nature of Russians: "Genetically, Russia is the country of Orthodoxy" (p. 151).

64. Tulaev, "*Sobor*," p. 36 (italics in original).

65. Troitskii, *Vozrozhdenie russkoi idei*, p. 170.

66. E.V. Barabanov, "Russian Philosophy and the Crisis of Identity," *Russian Studies in Philosophy*, vol. 31, no. 2 (Fall 1992), p. 48.

67. Ibid., pp. 24–25.

68. Smirnova, "The Debates about Slavophilism," pp. 42, 55; see also Pavlov, "The Question of the Uniqueness," pp. 44–45.

69. Barabanov, "Russian Philosophy," pp. 28–29.

70. T.I. Blagova, "O filosofskom nasledii A.S. Khomiakova," *Filosofskie nauki*, 1991, no. 11, p. 133.

71. "Religion and Politics in Postcommunist Russia," *Russian Studies in Philosophy*, vol. 33. no. 1 (Summer 1994), p. 55.

72. Ibid., p. 61.

73. Ibid.

74. Ibid., pp. 92, 94.

75. Barabanov, "Russian Philosophy," p. 48.

76. Ibid, p. 48 (italics in original).

77. Pavlov, "The Question of the Uniqueness," p. 45.

78. Ibid., p. 46.

79. Ibid., p. 48; see also Smirnova, "The Debates about Slavophilism," p. 41.

80. Pavlov, "The Question of the Uniqueness," p. 47.

81. Ibid., p. 48.

82. E.A. Dudzinskaia, *Slavianofily v obshchestvenno i bor'be* (Moscow: Mysl', 1983), p. 21.

83. "Religion and Politics," p. 93.

84. Andrzej Walicki, *The Slavophile Controversy: History of a Conservative Utopia in Nineteenth-Century Russian Thought*, trans. H. Andrews-Rusiecka (Oxford: Clarendon Press, 1975). Peter K. Christoff's works include the following: *An Introduction to Nineteenth-Century Russian Slavophilism: A Study in Ideas. Volume I: A.S. Xomjakov* ('S-Gravenhage: Mouton, 1961); *K.S. Aksakov: A Study in Ideas* (Princeton, NJ: Princeton University Press, 1982); and *Iu.F. Samarin* (Boulder, CO: Westview Press, 1991).

85. *Literaturnye vzgliady i tvorchestvo slavianofilov, 1830–1850 godov*, p. 5.

86. Smirnova, "The Debates about Slavophilism," p. 52.

87. Tulaev, "Rossiia i Evropa," p. 159 (italics in original); Tulaev, "*Sobor*," p. 45.

88. D.S. Likhachev, "Two Streams of Russian Culture," *IHJ Bulletin* (Tokyo), vol. 14, no. 1 (Winter 1994), p. 3.

89. Quoted in Walter Laqueur, *Black Hundred: The Rise of the Extreme Right in Russia* (New York: Harper Collins, 1993), p. 8.

90. Ibid.

91. Likhachev, "Two Streams of Russian Culture," p. 3 (italics added).

92. Troitskii, *Vozrozhdenie russkoie idei*, p. 223.

GEORGE M. YOUNG, JR.

3 | Toward the New Millennium: Ideas of Resurrection in Fedorov and Solov′ev

Near the end of Gogol′'s "Overcoat," readers will recall, Akakii Akakievich returns from the dead to haunt the exalted official who has driven him to the grave. As he lays hand on the eminent personage's fine warm collar, the ghost says, in tones as close to "ghastly" as this particular ghost can manage: "Ah, at last, there—eh—you are! I've—er, um—collared you at last!"[1]

My question is: Come the resurrection, will Akakii Akakievich still dot his speech with stammering interjections? It is only fitting that as a ghost Akakii Akakievich should come back speaking the way he went out. This is part of Gogol′'s *realizm*. But, presumably, a resurrected entity is not the same as a ghost, and come the resurrection should he or should he not speak utterly without defect? If he has defects, can he be said to have been resurrected? If he has no defects, can he still be said to be Akakii Akakievich?

These are questions that have no doubt long troubled the sleep of every reader of this volume. Fortunately, if not these very questions, then others similar to them once occupied two of the most original minds in Russia—Nikolai Fedorovich Fedorov (1829–1903) and Vladimir Sergeevich Solov′ev (1853–1900). And the great attention being given to these thinkers in post-Soviet Russia suggests that such questions are coming to occupy the successors of Marxism in Russia as they did its predecessors.

For a period of a little more than ten years, from the early 1880s through the early 1890s, Fedorov and Solov′ev shared a conviction that the resurrection of the dead was not only an extremely urgent but also a highly practical matter. Fedorov was the first of the two, and perhaps the first thinker ever, to insist that the resurrection be viewed as an activity requiring universal human participation.[2] From at least as early as 1864, Fedorov held that the common task of all people now living is to resurrect all the dead. By this he meant not only a figurative or symbolic resurrection, not merely some kind of moral or spiritual renewal, but literal resuscitation of every one of our departed ancestors.

As Fedorov envisioned it, the task should be begun immediately, though its achievement would be long and gradual. Initially, resurrection would be little more than a common goal, a hope, an article of faith; then, at some future time, using future scientific technology all but unimaginable to nineteenth-century man, sons and daughters would first briefly, then for longer periods of time bring back to life a recently deceased parent. Then the activity would spread, technology would improve, until eventually people would travel to the moon and other planets searching throughout space for "particles" of disintegrated ancestral matter, single molecules or even atoms from which whole persons could be reconstructed. The task would unite all humankind: past, present, and future. Paradise, eternal life for all, would be literally established on earth and throughout the knowable universe. Although one of the least known, Fedorov's version of paradise on earth probably then was and now remains the most radical and comprehensive of any of the numerous utopian programs circulating in Russia at any given time.

Solov'ev first heard of Fedorov's idea through Dostoevskii in 1878 while delivering the *Lectures on Godmanhood*. At this time, according to Dostoevskii, Solov'ev had independently developed many ideas similar to Fedorov's and believed in a "real, literal, personal resurrection, and one that will come to pass on earth."[3] Scholarly opinion differs as to how much Solov'ev was influenced by the 1878 account of Fedorov's thought.[4] What is certain is that the account was at least sufficient to allow Solov'ev to sense a kindred mind. Four or five years later, Solov'ev received a much longer and more detailed presentation of Fedorov's thought, to which he responded, in part: "I accept your 'project' completely and without any discussion. Since the time of the appearance of Christianity, your 'project' is the first forward movement of the human spirit along the path of Christ. For my part I can only regard you as my teacher and spiritual father."[5]

But hope or try as he might, Solov'ev could not accept Fedorov's project "completely"—and certainly not after a face-to-face discussion. Shortly after one of their meetings, he wrote to Fedorov:

> The simple physical resurrection of the dead cannot, in its own self, be the goal. The resurrection of people in the same state in which they strive to

devour each other—to resurrect man in a stage of cannibalism would be both impossible and utterly undesirable. This means that the goal is not the simple resurrection of man in his personal organic structure but the resurrection of man in the form he ought to take. . . . Therefore, our task must have a religious and not scientific character, and it must rely on the believing masses, and not on disputatious intellectuals. So there you have a brief explanation of the feelings I was trying to express to you on my last visit to Moscow.[6]

Note that even after pointing out the major difference (spiritual as against scientific) that will eventually separate them, Solov'ev here still says "our" task. He believed that what he shared with Fedorov, at that time, was still more important than any minor points of disagreement. Their association culminated in 1891 when Solov'ev offered to present a joint summons to the common task at the October meeting of the Moscow Psychological Society. But the collaboration did not take place, and instead of a paper dictated by Fedorov, Solov'ev read "The Collapse of the Medieval World-Conception," a work heavy with Fedorovian matter but still not heavy enough to satisfy Fedorov. Though the paper made a considerable impact on its audience, Fedorov later wrote that Solov'ev had missed the entire point of the resurrection project and that "The Collapse of the Medieval World-Conception" presented almost nothing that he, Fedorov, recognized as true. This marked the end of their attempts to collaborate on a common task. Solov'ev continued for a while to place great emphasis on the idea of resurrection, writing for instance to Tolstoi in 1894, "Our [i.e., Solov'ev's and Tolstoi's] entire disagreement comes down to one concrete point—Christ's resurrection."[7] But Solov'ev's idea of resurrection from then on would have little in common with Fedorov's.

From the beginning, Solov'ev viewed the resurrection as a spiritual task. He agreed with Fedorov that the resurrection would be real, personal, and was to be accomplished by human effort over a long period of time. But he completely rejected the technological—that is, the most Fedorovian —side of the project. For Solov'ev, the "means" of resurrecting the dead are not space travel, cloning, genetic engineering, regulation of nature, and so forth, but fasting, alms giving, prayer, meditation. Spiritual exercises such as these, according to Solov'ev, have been given to man to enable him to develop the divinity within him and to unite his own share of divinity with the divine throughout the universe. In the letter to Tolstoi cited above, Solov'ev writes:

For man, immortality is the same as reason is for animals; the meaning [*smysl*] of the animal kingdom is the reasoning animal, i.e., man. The meaning of humanity is the immortal one, i.e., Christ. As the animal world tends toward reason, so the human world tends toward immortality. If the struggle with chaos and death is the essence of the world process, whereby the side of light and spirit ever so slowly and gradually takes control, then resurrection, i.e., actual and decisive victory of a living being over death, is a necessary element and indeed the culmination of that process. . . .

If by miracle we mean a phenomenon that contradicts the general course of things and is therefore impossible, then resurrection stands in direct opposition to miracle—it is a phenomenon that is absolutely necessary in the general course of things; if, however, by miracle we mean a phenomenon appearing for the first time, unprecedented, then the resurrection of the "firstborn from the dead" [*pervenets iz mertvykh*] is, of course, a miracle—accomplished in the same manner as the appearance of the first organic cell in the inorganic world, or the appearance of the animal in the midst of primordial vegetation, or the first human among orangutans. . . .

Victory over death is a necessary natural consequence of internal spiritual perfection; the person in whom the spiritual principle has decisively and conclusively taken power over all that is lower cannot be overcome by death; spiritual power, having attained its full degree of perfection, inevitably spills, as it were, over the edge of subjective mental life, fastens onto physical life, transforms it, and finally spiritualizes it completely, unites it constantly with itself. And it is precisely the image of complete spiritual perfection that I find in the Christ of the Gospels; I cannot consider this image an invented one for many reasons, which I don't need to list since you, too, do not consider the Christ of the Gospels to be a myth. If this spiritually perfect man did indeed exist, then he himself was the "firstborn from the dead" and there is no need to await another.[8]

For Fedorov, the long resurrection project is one in which children will resurrect their parents, who, in turn, will resurrect their parents, and so forth, back to Adam. The family is the basic unit of life, and in the project each family will grow backward through time, merging with other families, until all humankind is, literally, one family. Brotherhood becomes co-sonship, sisterhood co-daughterhood. Universal brotherhood will be as obvious a given as existence.

Solov'ev is much less specific about how the project will be conducted. Generally, instead of children resurrecting parents, he writes of a growing brotherhood based not on race, nationality, or family ties but on spiritual development. He seems to envision something like an Albigensian society of *perfects* mingling with the lay population, developing in the individual and in the population at large spiritual powers sufficient to overcome death.

Fedorov in more than one article attacks Solov'ev for valuing individual immortality over resurrection of the ancestors. To live forever without resurrecting one's parents is, for Fedorov, eternal adolescence, eternal orphanhood. But Solov'ev does not confuse immortality with resurrection, he merely states that the task of creating immortal spirits must precede any attempts to resurrect the dead, otherwise one would be bringing people back to life only to let them die again.

As Solov'ev stated in the letter to Fedorov cited above, "the simple physical resurrection of the dead cannot, in its own self, be the goal." For Fedorov, resurrection of the ancestors will coincide with the creation of heaven on earth, and this indeed should be the goal of all human action. For Solov'ev, resurrection is part of the greater task of "total-unity," a human and natural world wholly integrated and wholly infused with divine spirit. Resurrection is, for Solov'ev, the ultimate demonstration of divine-human spiritual power, the ultimate victory of order over chaos and of love over discord.

From the start, the two thinkers viewed nature very differently. Fedorov, an illegitimate son in a family of princes, consciously chose to view life from the perspective of the unlearned outsider and to view nature from the perspective of one who suffers from her hand. For Fedorov, nature is blind destructive force. Nature drives the world toward disintegration and death. Man's task is to regulate nature, to turn destructive force into life-restoring force. For Solov'ev, who does not pretend to view life from any other than an aristocratic perspective, nature is living matter infused with a soul. Man must not crudely set himself over or against nature but must live and work with nature.

In 1891, Russia suffered from a terrible drought and resulting famine. To Fedorov, the drought was a perfect example of nature's blind destructive force. The remedy was regulation of this force, in this instance either by melting part of the polar ice cap and channeling the runoff to irrigate the chronically dry areas of Russia, or, even quicker, by shooting cannons into the air to bring rain, as Fedorov read had recently been done in America. This redirecting of the cannon from horizontal to vertical aim represented for Fedorov the simple but radical change that would enable men to turn all instruments of destruction into instruments of salvation. Armies of soldiers could become armies of regulators; everything now directed toward war could be redirected toward controlling nature. The vertical over the horizontal is man over nature, the first monument over the first grave, the hope of resurrection over the everyday occurrence of death, history as a project over history as fact, the rocket over the railroad, the gun pointing at the cloud instead of at one's brother.

In his paper on "The Collapse of the Medieval World-Conception," Solov'ev also refers to the drought of 1891 but draws a very different conclusion:

> The unbelieving promoters of modern progress acted for the benefit of true Christianity, undermining the false medieval world–conception with its anti-Christian dogmatism, individualism, and spiritualism. They could not injure

Christ by their disbelief, but they have injured material nature, which many of them were championing. Against the pseudo-Christian spiritualism, which regards nature as an evil principle, they put forth another equally false view that nature is lifeless matter and a soulless machine. And earthly nature, as though offended by this double untruth, refuses to feed mankind. This is the common danger that ought to unite the believers and unbelievers. It is time that both recognized their solidarity with mother earth and saved it from deadness, in order to save themselves from death as well.[9]

The very idea that we should worry about "offending" nature or that we should seek oneness with mother earth was like a red flag to Fedorov. His refutation and "correction" of these few sentences runs to pages. But contrary to what Fedorov and his later disciples thought of him, Solov'ev was not merely misunderstanding and garbling Fedorov's idea. In fact, Solov'ev was incorporating into his own system as much of Fedorov as he could accept. He did not believe in regulating nature, but he did believe that man should do all possible to reestablish the total unity of God, man, and nature. The lecture on "The Collapse of the Medieval World-Conception" shows how far apart they were even when they were closest. To Solov'ev, Fedorov's projects for regulating nature, the entire technological side of the "common task," seemed grotesquely irrational, an attempt to incorporate a new pagan sorcery into Christianity. In his last work, "A Short Story of the Anti-Christ," Solov'ev parodies perhaps not Fedorov himself but a representative of the Fedorovian idea in Apollonius, "a man of genius, semi-Asiatic and semi-European," who

> marvelously combined a mastery of the most recent discoveries and technologies of Western science with a knowledge both practical and theoretical of all major tendencies in the traditional mysticism of the East. The results of this combination were amazing. Apollonius, for instance, had perfected the half-scientific and half-magical art of producing atmospheric electricity at will, so that it was said that he commanded fire down from heaven.[10]

This is actually not far from one of Fedorov's fantastic projects whereby enormous cones of some kind would be placed on earth in such a way that they would conduct electromagnetic force and allow men to steer earth like a spaceship through the cosmos in search of particles of departed ancestors.

But if Fedorov in Solov'ev's eyes tended toward half science and half magic, Solov'ev in Fedorov's eyes seems to have proceeded even farther down the same path, to advocate a resurrection that

> would be accomplished mystically, that is, by incomprehensible methods and unverifiable research; resurrection in this instance is to be accomplished not through scientific knowledge and the direction of blind force, not by way

of experiment or empirical knowledge, open knowledge, but by secret, occult methods, which might be presented in the guise of sorcery, as, for example, the materialization of spirits.[11]

According to Fedorov, Solov'ev issues not a general appeal for a common task involving all mankind but an invitation to intellectuals and adepts to indulge in occult exercises that separate them from the common man.

We have, then, in Solov'ev and Fedorov, two thinkers who for a time thought they believed in the same idea but who actually envisioned very different resurrections. Each thinker eventually rejected the most original parts of the other's idea. Both were enormously learned men, but each showed his learning in a different way: Fedorov pulled together obscure, disparate, apparently insignificant bits of overlooked information and made each little bit seem of great significance in the common task; Solov'ev drew attention away from erudition itself and toward only the conclusions of that erudition—one merely senses, without actually noticing, the mass of detailed information that lies behind a major idea. Fedorov's voice is that of the little man speaking up for those who cannot, the unlearned worker addressing a room full of learned men of leisure, the victim speaking to the ones in charge, the outsider who notices what the insider can no longer see. Solov'ev's voice is that of the prophet trying to be reasonable, the seer trying to speak in such a way that people will look up for themselves.

As Trubetskoi says, Solov'ev was a mystic down to his toes. His great gift was to write with logical precision about the most nebulous intuitions, to give credibility to the most unlikely revelations; he excelled as the visionary in rationalist clothing. Fedorov was just the opposite. His writings seem to be a series of fantastic aphorisms, striking italicized phrases strung together into interminable sentences, quotable here, unreadable there, turgid stretches of intermittent lucidity. But under the disconnected surface lies the click of inevitability, an argument that can start with any casual observation about tombstones or handwriting and not end until all humanity is resurrected, the step-by-step insistence that made Dostoevskii remark when he first encountered Fedorov's thought: "Rarely have I read anything more *logical.*"[12]

Solov'ev had a keen sense of humor, a levity directed first and most frequently at himself and at those ideas that he took most seriously. Fedorov could at times be ironical toward the ideas of others but by and large stood for sobriety and more sobriety.

Solov'ev devoted much of his life to the ecumenical cause, requiring compromise and sacrifice on the part of individual confessions for the greater unity and good of all. Fedorov's idea of the joining together of faiths was for the Orthodox to be truly Orthodox, that is, to practice the task of resurrection, and let all others abandon their persuasions and join the one true task. Neither compromise nor coercion is necessary in Fedorov—by working on the resurrection project everyone will eventually see the truth of Orthodox Christianity with his own eyes and will become an Orthodox Christian in fact rather than by lip service.

Both Fedorov and Solov'ev saw the sex drive as a problem in the world as it is. For Fedorov, the task of controlling the sex drive is part of the task of regulating nature. His emphasis throughout is on our duties as living children of departed parents. His solution is a literal unerotic brotherhood and sisterhood of everyone, without exception. With the resurrection of our ancestors, the need for childbirth, and all that precedes and follows, will end. Solov'ev's emphasis is on spiritualizing sex, integrating the masculine and feminine principles in ourselves and in the universe. His goal is not so much a universal brotherhood and sisterhood as a happy universal androgyny. Where Fedorov would shut down the erotic, Solov'ev would amplify, spiritualize, elevate, and transform erotic love into the force that will reunify all creation with the creator.

In personal life, both were bachelor ascetics who lived simply and gave away most of what they earned—saints perhaps, but with very different paths: Fedorov, the humble librarian who labored tirelessly to help others and sought only obscurity for himself; Solov'ev, the courageous martyr who repeatedly risked all in public controversy, repeatedly championed another noble lost cause, publicly stated the unwelcome truth regardless of whom it offended.

A hundred years after their agreements and disagreements on resurrection, Fedorov's technological projects may seem less fantastic than Solov'ev's spiritual tasks. We are probably further along in space travel, the creation of artificial organs, genetic engineering, and regulation of nature than we are in spiritual development, where we may even have lost ground in the last hundred years. As thinkers in today's post-Soviet Russia look back into the last century seeking intellectual guides for the future, one appealing feature of Fedorov's thought may be that the technological side of his vision no longer presents the barrier that it did to thinkers earlier in the century. We can appreciate the moral and spiritual side of his project today without having to dismiss the technological side as utopian eyewash. Our technological progress has made Fedorov's thought more plausible.

On the other hand, with Solov'ev, the *lack* of spiritual advancement over the last century may be one reason for the renewed interest in his thought that we find in today's Russia. Solov'ev offers practical steps for precisely the kind of spiritual development that has been missing in the age of Soviet Marxist thought.

That both Solov'ev and Fedorov are drawing lively attention in Russia now suggests that both technological and spiritual quests for perfection are still alive in Russian thinking and are finding nourishment in these earlier figures. The failure of the Marxian utopia has not meant the rejection of utopian thinking generally; the "new millennium" still beckons, in disparate forms of Christian utopianism. As Russian thinkers struggle today to rise again from the dead hand of Marxism, they have rediscovered the profundity of the idea of resurrection as it was formulated by two leading Russian thinkers a hundred years ago.

In an unnoticed debate of the 1930s, several members of the Eurasian movement argued about which thinker, Marx or Fedorov, should be the mentor for the movement's future intellectual development. The consensus was that, since socioeconomic questions were the dominant ones of the day, Marx would be the thinker for this century. But as technology would probably continue to advance and the questions of the relationship between technology and morality would become more urgent, the twenty-first century might well belong to Fedorov.[13]

If this is true, then perhaps we should be glad to see the twentieth century winding down and the twenty-first beginning to take shape. With Marxism largely consigned to the dustbin of history, today's Eurasians might argue that the real choice lies between Fedorov and Solov'ev. The questions near the top of many lists today are, indeed, Fedorovian questions: What happens if technology outpaces morality? Should we permit some people to enjoy extreme longevity, even approach immortality, while others die after a "natural" span of years? Can a democratic society undertake a task as grandiose as the resurrection of the dead, or must there be a benevolent autocrat to set and keep us on the long project? What is the point of space exploration when so many problems exist on earth? Who should decide questions involving genetic engineering, artificial organs, biological mutations? And on what grounds should such a decision be made? How much control should man attempt to exert over nature? How do we alter one part of an ecological system to our benefit without altering other parts to our detriment? If we insist on individual freedom, what are the alternatives to a pornocratic, parricidal culture?

If these are questions for a Fedorovian century, other questions, whose answers might depend on how the Fedorovian questions are answered, might best be reserved for a later, Solov'evian age. What kinds of entities will we be if someday we no longer need bodies? What is the least amount of "self" we will need to be "ourselves" and to be recognized as such by others?

Perhaps a hundred years from now it will be clear to all whether ancestral particles can and should be retrieved from outer space and whether Akakii Akakievich should or should not speak with stammering interjections in the resurrection. And if the answer is not clear near the end of the century of Fedorov, then perhaps it will become clear in the twenty-second century, which by all rights should see the beginning of the age of Solov'ev.

Notes

1. N.V. Gogol', *Sobranie khudozhestvennykh proizvedenii v piati tomakh*, 2nd ed., 5 vols. (Moscow: USSR Academy of Sciences, 1960–61), vol. 3, p. 217. Here, as elsewhere in this chapter, unless otherwise noted, translations are mine.

2. For a fuller discussion of Fedorov's life and thought, see George M. Young, Jr., *Nikolai Fedorov: An Introduction* (Belmont, MA: Nordland, 1979); Ludmila Koehler, *N.F. Fedorov: The Philosophy of Action* (Pittsburgh, PA: Institute for the Human Sciences, 1979); Irene Masing-Delic, *Abolishing Death: A Salvation Myth of Russian Twentieth-Century Literature* (Stanford, CA: Stanford University Press, 1992); Michael Hagemeister, *Nikolaj Fedorov: Studien zu Leben, Werk, und Wirkung* (Munich: Verlag Otto Sagner, 1989); Svetlana Semenova, *Nikolai Fedorov: Tvorchestvo zhizni* (Moscow: Sovetskii pisatel', 1990).

3. F.M. Dostoevskii, letter to N.P. Peterson, 24 March 1878, in *F.M. Dostoevskii. Pis'ma v chetyrekh tomakh*, ed. A.S. Dolinin, 4 vols. (Moscow: Gosudarstvennoe izdatel'stvo, 1928–59), vol. 4, p. 10.

4. See Young, *Nikolai Fedorov*, pp. 52–53; Semenova, *Nikolai Fedorov*, pp. 105–8.

5. *Pis'ma Vladimira Sergeevicha Solov'eva*, ed. E.L. Radlov (St. Petersburg: Obshchestvennaia pol'za, 1909), vol. 2, p. 345.

6. Ibid.

7. Ibid., vol. 3, p. 38.

8. Ibid., pp. 38–40.

9. Vladimir Sergeevich Solov'ev, *Sobranie sochinenii*, ed. S.M. Solov'ev and E.L. Radlov, reprint, 12 vols. (Brussels: Zhizn' s Bogom, 1966–70), vol. 6, pp. 381–93.

10. Ibid., vol. 10, p. 213.

11. *Filosofiia obshchago dela: stat'i, mysli, i pis'ma Nikolaia Fedorovicha Fedorova*, ed. V.A. Kozhevnikov and N.P. Peterson, photographic reprint, 2 vols. (Farnborough, England: Gregg International, 1970), vol. 1, p. 439.

12. Dostoevskii, letter to N.P. Peterson, p. 10.

13. Young, *Nikolai Fedorov*, pp. 188–89.

III

The Silver Age in Postcommunist Perspective

No part of Russia's philosophical patrimony is more important today than the thought of the country's vibrant "Silver Age"—the multifaceted outburst of cultural energies that stretched from the last years of the nineteenth century to the consolidation of Bolshevik rule after 1917. Unlike many of the literary and artistic luminaries of that period—Andrei Belyi, Aleksandr Blok, and others—whose work remained alive in Russian culture during the Soviet era through republication of their writings, the philosophers of the Silver Age (as Dzhimbinov pointed out in his essay in section I) suffered almost total suppression; most had not a single line published in the Soviet Union between the early 1920s and the coming of glasnost in the late 1980s. But now the long silence has ended with a vengeance, and the Russian public is inundated with writings by and about these philosophers. The essays in this section are devoted to their ideas, with special emphasis on the thought of Nikolai Berdiaev, Sergei Bulgakov, Pavel Novgorodtsev, and Dmitrii Merezhkovskii.

Nikolai Aleksandrovich Berdiaev (1874–1948) is unquestionably the best-known prerevolutionary Russian philosopher in the country today—"the central figure in today's 'philosophical renaissance,' " in the words of M.A. Kolerov and N.S. Plotnikov.[1] Piama Gaidenko in her essay below recounts the role played by the works of Berdiaev in her own philosophical education as early as the 1950s, when she was among the few Russian scholars able to gain access to writings by the religious philosopher that were preserved in the "special collections." Berdiaev's name surfaced in Soviet reference books in the 1960s, though always with negative characterizations ("bourgeois mystic," "reactionary"), and as early as 1976 a full-length critical monograph was published—Valerii Kuvakin's *Critique of Berdiaev's Existentialism,* a damning philosophical portrait, but a portrait nonetheless.[2] Not until 1988 did selections from Berdiaev's writings begin to appear in Russian journals, but at that point the floodgates opened. In 1989, Berdiaev's books *The Philosophy of Freedom* and *The Meaning of Creativity* were printed together as one volume in the first series of reprints published as appendices to the journal *Voprosy filosofii*.[3] Other full-length works quickly followed, so that by 1990 Kolerov and Plotnikov could report that "now every publishing house wishing to be *comme il faut* prints Berdiaev."[4]

Berdiaev's popularity, like that of many of the other Silver Age thinkers, is attributable in part to his prophetic and insightful criticism of the theory and practice of Soviet Marxism. Andrzej Walicki's essay below examines this aspect of Berdiaev's thought (along with that of Bulgakov and Novgorodtsev); Berdiaev's complex relation to Marxism also figures prominently in Gaidenko's essay on the value of his philosophy of freedom for the present day.

Walicki focuses on Berdiaev's recognition, elaborated as early as 1906 in the essay "Socialism and Religion," that Marxist socialism in the hands of the Russian Bolsheviks had become a substitute for religion, and that it was advanced as a fanatical, millenarian ideology (in keeping with Marx's own inclinations, Walicki argues). Berdiaev understood that this ideology incorporated an inhumane theory of progress—one that demanded sacrificing the present for the sake of a future ideal—and hence that it functioned as a cruel historical theodicy, justifying the treatment of existing human beings as mere means to an end. And even if we grant that Marx himself defined the *end* humanely as freedom and human development, the fanatical championing of what Walicki calls "ideocratic socialism" was destined, in Berdiaev's view, to result in the most oppressive and depersonalizing totalitarian slavery. To have foreseen this long before the Bolsheviks actually came to power is a distinction that understandably recommends Berdiaev to some, at least, of the first generation of Russians who are able to inquire openly into the circumstances of their former bondage.

Berdiaev's criticisms of Bolshevik Marxism are far from exhausting the attention now given to the Russian philosopher, however. As Gaidenko points out in her essay, Berdiaev never made a complete break with the Marxism of his youth, and in the 1920s and 1930s he returned to the very socialism and "utopian revolutionism" (as she calls it) that he had scorned in his 1906 essay and in his contribution to *Vekhi* (Landmarks), the famous 1909 attack on the radical left-wing intelligentsia. As a result, Berdiaev's legacy is somewhat clouded, not to say contradictory, and it can be mined for support by representatives of opposite points of view in the present-day ideological controversies over Russia's future. In the words of Kolerov and Plotnikov, "Berdiaev's ambiguous anticommunist–procommunist image makes his works a tool in the internal intellectual struggle."[5]

On the one hand, a writer such as Elena Stepanova, in an essay entitled "Exhausted Marxism" (1991), relies on Berdiaev's critique of "ideocratic" socialism to support her rejection of Soviet Marxism-Leninism. In keeping with Walicki's observations, she stresses Berdiaev's attack on the sacralization of the inhumane Marxist theory of progress. She writes:

> This religion of progress, as Berdiaev saw it, had no scientific, philosophical, or moral justification since it is a religion of death and not of life; it is absolutely hostile to the fate of every individual person, which remains completely outside its purview. Moreover, the coming happy future takes on an ominous meaning, for "in respect to every other moment in time, it is a devouring vampire because the future is a devourer of the past, a murderer of this past."[6]

As a result of the faults noted by Berdiaev, Stepanova concludes, "Marxism at the end of the twentieth century is a theory that has been exhausted above all by its own titanism, by the inhuman burden of its own universal historical mission, . . . by its constant search for enemies, and finally, by the loss of the very purpose for which it was created."[7]

On the other hand, V.N. Adiushkin in "The Social Philosophy of N. Berdiaev in Light of *Perestroika*" (1991) uses Berdiaev to support his opposition to radical change in the Soviet order. Quoting Berdiaev to the effect that there is more justice in communist society than in capitalist, Adiushkin fastens on the Russian philosopher's critique of private property and of bourgeois values in general. On the political side, Adiushkin invokes Berdiaev's name in arguing against "absolutizing" the idea of democracy; Berdiaev understood, he contends, that political power "cannot belong to everyone; it cannot be mechanically uniform. It must belong to the best, to the selected individuals who are entrusted with great responsibility and who take upon themselves great commitments."[8] Adiushkin's Berdiaev, in other words, could have been embraced by a Communist Party leader for whom perestroika by no means signified any fundamental abandonment of either the economic or the political principles of the Soviet order.

Gaidenko in her essay below is fully cognizant of the competing strains in Berdiaev's thinking, and she seeks to warn her compatriots against being lulled by the positive elements of his outlook into accepting the negative elements as well. Admittedly, she writes, Berdiaev defended the freedom and integrity of the individual personality and was an eloquent critic of totalitarian oppression. But he was also (except for a brief period in his middle years) a mystical anarchist whose philosophical principles led him to adopt a destructive, revolutionary posture not only toward capitalism but toward all social order, and indeed toward being itself. Gaidenko is appalled that Berdiaev refused to give up his utopian revolutionism and continued to praise aspects of communism even after he saw millions of innocents perish in the Russian revolution and civil war; and she is disturbed by the extremism that kept him from recognizing the relative merits of liberal democracy in comparison with other political structures. In another essay entitled *"Landmarks*: An Unheard Warning," published in 1991, Gaidenko sums up her warning against Berdiaev's utopian maximalism in the following words:

> The great danger for the contemporary Russian intelligentsia is to believe Berdiaev. The harsh lessons of the twentieth century will then come to nothing, and we will remain in the old rut of revolutions and civil wars, concentration camps, and mutual extermination. Bloody practice will again seem to confirm the validity of Berdiaev's prognosis—whereas in fact it is nihilistic revolutionism (and its "prognosis") that gives rise to bloody practice: in the beginning was the word.[9]

Although none of the other thinkers who figure in the essays in this section loom as large as Berdiaev in recent Russian philosophical discourse, the phenomenon of conflicting uses of a philosopher's writings is certainly not restricted to Berdiaev. Sergei Nikolaevich Bulgakov (1871–1944), for example—the second thinker whose case against Marxism is laid out by Walicki—is also subjected to divergent readings in current Russian debates. To Elena Stepanova, Bulgakov is on a par with Berdiaev in the depth and foresight of his critique of the Marxist "religion of socialism"; like Berdiaev, he believes that the Marxian theory of progress means that "the past and present of mankind, the infinite series of generations of people who had once existed or are existing at present is no more than the material out of which in some indefinite future a new generation will be born that will have the good fortune to resolve the riddle of history and will make the leap into the kingdom of freedom."[10] To Vladimir Akulinin, by contrast, Bulgakov is not an enemy but a defender of socialism, and moreover of *religious* socialism, albeit of an improved, Christian variety. This view is expressed in Akulinin's introduction to the first Soviet publication in 1991 of a book by Bulgakov, his *Christian Socialism*, which Akulinin saw as an important contribution to discussions about how to impart "a human face" to socialism.[11] Although these two approaches to Berdiaev are not formally contradictory, since Bulgakov could (and did) quite consistently reject Marxian socialism but accept Christian socialism, they nonetheless reflect two opposing perspectives among those who make use of Bulgakov's philosophy in Russia today—an antisocialist perspective and a socialist reformist perspective.

It should be noted that in the recent enthusiasm for relating the pronouncements of these two great religious thinkers to contemporary interests, neither of them has yet been given a full and penetrating philosophical examination by a Russian interpreter. A few articles have been published that deal specifically with their philosophical doctrines, and the recent book *Nikolai Berdiaev: Life and Work* (1993), by N.K. Dmitrieva and A.P. Moiseeva, contains summaries of several of Berdiaev's principal works. But no broad critical philosophical study has yet been made of either thinker.[12] Ironically, the most straightforward and comprehensive (though concise) expositions of the philosophies of Berdiaev and Bulgakov yet published by a present-day Russian have been written by the same writer— Valerii Kuvakin—whose typical Marxist-Leninist monograph condemned Berdiaev in 1976; chapters on both Bulgakov and Berdiaev are included in Kuvakin's two-volume work *A History of Russian Philosophy* (1994), published not in Russian but in English, by an American publisher.[13]

Pavel Ivanovich Novgorodtsev (1866–1924), the third of Walicki's critics of Marxism, is missing from the new *History of Russian Philosophy*, but that does not mean he is neglected in current discussions. As the respected head of the "Moscow school of jurisprudence," a founder of the Constitutional Democratic (Kadet) party, and a leading theoretician of early twentieth-century Russian liberalism, Novgorodtsev draws attention in intellectual circles that are more secular than religious and that consequently are somewhat less prominent in current Russian philosophical discussions. Novgorodtsev's major treatise, *On the Social Ideal*, was reprinted, along with several of his more important essays, in one of the *Voprosy filosofii* appendix volumes in 1991. A.V. Sobolev's remarks in his preface to that volume confirm the fact that one of Novgorodtsev's principal attractions in the present day is his prophetic critique of the failure of Marxism in its real-life application. "Novgorodtsev shows the incompatibility of the idea of Marxist socialism with the real functioning of society," Sobolev writes; "no intellectual arguments are effective against the Marxists, but if Marxist socialism is put into practice, it will perish once and for all, rejected by a recovering society."[14]

Many present-day Russians, finding themselves in that "recovering society," are turning to the writings of Novgorodtsev and other representatives of the Russian liberal tradition, such as Boris Chicherin and Bogdan Kistiakovskii, for arguments in support of constitutionalism, the idea of a state based on the rule of law, civil rights, and other liberal themes.[15] A center for the study of Russian liberalism was established in the Institute of Philosophy of the Russian Academy of Sciences in the early 1990s, and a Russian translation of Andrzej Walicki's seminal study, *Legal Philosophies of Russian Liberalism* (1987), is being prepared for publication. Symptomatic of the dominance of the religious interest in the current Russian philosophical renaissance, however, is the fact that the first published volumes of selections from Vladimir Solov'ev's writings in 1988 did not adequately reflect the considerable degree to which he shared the social views and attitudes of the more secular-oriented Russian liberals.

Dmitrii Sergeevich Merezhkovskii (1865–1941), the subject of the essay by Bernice Glatzer Rosenthal that concludes this section of the volume, was a pioneer among the Silver Age philosophers in Russia. With his wife, Zinaida Gippius, he founded in 1901 the Religious-Philosophical Society of St. Petersburg, which brought together leading thinkers of the day for philosophical discussions, and he first formulated the so-called "New Religious Consciousness" that Berdiaev also championed for a time. In light of Merezhkovskii's early prominence, it is surprising that there is not more discussion of his thought in the present day. A volume of Merezhkovskii's philosophical essays has been reprinted with a brief introduction, but Merezhkovskii thus far has not been included in the *Voprosy filosofii* appendix series of reprinted works, and even the periodical literature on Merezhkovskii is less extensive than that on the other major Silver Age thinkers.[16] Merezhkovskii's reputation as a fascist sympathizer during his years in emigration after 1920 may work to discourage greater current interest in him.

Rosenthal believes that as more of Merezhkovskii's writings become available to the Russian reading public the relevance of his ideas to present-day conditions will become evident. Her essay details the themes Merezhkovskii treats that are as much a part of the present-day conception of "the Russian idea" as they were in the Silver Age—the relation of Christianity to secular life, Christian views of sex and art, the relations of church and state. Rosenthal also finds "chillingly relevant" to postcommunist Russian society Merezhkovskii's observations on the appeal of autocracy in Russia and his praise of Napoleon. Gaidenko, too, in her *"Landmarks"* essay, finds Merezhkovskii as guilty of "revolutionary mysticism" as Berdiaev was;[17] on the other hand, in her essay below she credits Merezhkovskii with seeing the potentiality for "diabolical chaos" in Berdiaev's conception of freedom. Altogether Merezhkovskii's ideas are an intellectual resource not yet fully explored but eminently open to contemporary use and abuse.

Notes

1. M.A. Kolerov and N.S. Plotnikov, "New Publications of the Works of N.A. Berdiaev," *Soviet Studies in Philosophy*, vol. 30, no. 2 (Fall 1991), p. 76.

2. V.A. Kuvakin, *Kritika ekzistentsializma Berdiaeva* (Moscow: Izdatel'stvo Moskovskogo universiteta, 1976).

3. N.A. Berdiaev, *Filosofiia svobody. Smysl tvorchestva* (Moscow: Pravda, 1989).

4. Kolerov and Plotnikov, "New Publications," p. 76.

5. Ibid.

6. E.A. Stepanova, "Exhausted Marxism: An Examination of Marxist Doctrine in the Traditions of Russian Religious Philosophy," *Soviet Studies in Philosophy*, vol. 29, no. 4 (Spring 1991), p. 24.

7. Ibid., p. 31.

8. V.N. Adiushkin, "The Social Philosophy of N. Berdiaev in Light of *Perestroika*," *Soviet Studies in Philosophy*, vol. 30, no. 4 (Spring 1992), p. 59.

9. P.P. Gaidenko, "*Landmarks*: An Unheard Warning," *Russian Studies in Philosophy*, vol. 32, no. 1 (Summer 1993), p. 39.

10. Stepanova, "Exhausted Marxism," pp. 23–24.

11. S.N. Bulgakov, *Khristianskii sotsializm* (Novosibirsk: Nauka, 1991), p. 24.

12. N.K. Dmitrieva and A.P. Moiseeva, *Filosof svobodnogo dukha: Nikolai Berdiaev, zhizn' i tvorchestvo* (Moscow: Vysshaia shkola, 1993). Two interesting articles on Berdiaev's philosophy are Andrei Smirnov, "The Path to Truth: Ibn-'Arabī and Nikolai Berdiaev (Two Types of Mystical Philosophizing)," *Russian Studies in Philosophy*, vol. 31, no. 3 (Winter 1992–93); and R.A. Gal'tseva, "Sub specie finis (Utopiia tvorchestva N.A. Berdiaeva)," in Gal'tseva, *Ocherki russkoi utopicheskoi mysli XX veka* (Moscow: Nauka, 1992), pp. 10–76.

13. Valery A. Kuvakin, ed., *A History of Russian Philosophy*, 2 vols. (Buffalo, NY: Prometheus Books, 1994), vol. 2, pp. 570–93, 621–38. This book contains chapters by various Russian authors; Kuvakin is the author of the Berdiaev and Bulgakov chapters, in addition to others.

14. P.I. Novgorodtsev, *Ob obshchestvennom ideale* (Moscow: Pressa, 1991), p. 8.

15. See, for example, S.L. Chizhkov, "B.N. Chicherin: The Idea of the Lawful State and the Liberal Experiment in Russia," *Soviet Studies in Philosophy*, vol. 30, no. 3 (Winter 1991–92), pp. 7–24.

16. The volume *Suffering Russia* (Bol'naia Rossiia [Leningrad: Izdatel'stvo Leningradskogo universiteta, 1991]) contains essays from two collections of Merezhkovskii's essays originally titled *Griadushchii kham* (published in English translation as *The Menace of the Mob*) and *Bol'naia Rossiia*.

17. Gaidenko, "*Landmarks*," p. 30.

ANDRZEJ WALICKI

4 | Russian Philosophers of the Silver Age as Critics of Marxism

Introductory Remarks

It is no exaggeration to say that in nineteenth-century Russian thought the idea of progress was even more central and pronounced than in West European or American thought of the Victorian Age. Russian discussions about progress were especially passionate for a number of reasons, all of them connected with the specific nature and historical tasks of the Russian intelligentsia. To put it most briefly, we can distinguish three main causes of the peculiar intensity and richness of these discussions.

The first one is, obviously, Russian backwardness and the well-perceived, deeply felt need of modernization. In the absence of a modernizing bourgeoisie, after a series of disillusionments in the modernizing mission of the absolute monarchy,[1] the Russian intelligentsia—itself a product of modernization—came to see itself as the main vehicle of further progress. Its members, alienated from the ruling class and painfully aware of their inalienable responsibility for the fate of the "people" as well as for the position of their country in the family of civilized nations, enjoyed the cognitive "privilege of backwardness,"[2] consisting in the possibility of learning from the accumulated experience of more-developed nations. This made them conscious not only of the humiliating backwardness of their country but also of the price and contradictions of European progress. Hence the characteristic tension between their enthusiastic devotion to the idea of progress and their bitter criticism of the really existing, "bourgeois" forms of modernization. A good illustration of this is provided by the Russian populists: all their ideas revolved around a "formula of progress" while containing, at the same time, a strong admixture of a backward-looking utopianism.

Another cause is the close interconnection between conceptions of progress and the question of national identity. Despite all the processes of westernization, nineteenth-century Russia was very different from the West

European countries, and it was by no means obvious that these differences boiled down to the simple fact of backwardness: they could be interpreted as qualitative, culturally valuable, pertaining to a different *type* of national development. Hence the perennial dispute between Russian Westernizers, adhering, as a rule, to a universalist and unilinear conception of progress, and many different advocates of a principled antiwesternism, stressing Russia's cultural distinctiveness, usually bound up with a spiritual superiority and a "special way" of her national development.

Finally, Russian discussions about progress expressed an intensive search for the meaning of history, which emerged as a result of the disintegration of Russia's ecclesiastical culture and served as a substitute for a religious world view.[3] Different Russian utopias of earthly salvation and the corresponding conceptions of progress represented, therefore, a secularization and historicization of the idea of the Kingdom of God. The peculiar eagerness with which the Russian intelligentsia committed themselves to the search for a "horizontal" (historical) collective salvation was, in a sense, the other side of their intolerance of the traditional Christian ideas of a transcendent Absolute and a "vertical," individual salvation in the afterlife. A paradigmatic case of this intolerance was provided by the two "fathers" of the classical (i.e., leftist) Russian intelligentsia: Vissarion Belinskii and Aleksandr Herzen. The latter defined the "thinking Russians" as completely divorced from the past and, therefore, more independent, more radical than their Western counterparts, still paralyzed by the burden of inherited traditions. He was totally unable to understand the Polish revolutionaries who combined progressive ideas with religious faith, and he saw them for that reason as belonging, unwillingly, to the "old world." [4]

It is useful to point out that the idea of progress had two functions in this secularized millenarianism. On the one hand, it showed the direction, thus giving an answer to the "cursed question" of *what was to be done*; on the other hand, it explained the necessity of a development through stages, thus justifying the evils of the past and present by reference to the meaningful pattern of historical evolution as a whole, paving the way to the earthly triumph of truth and justice. It contained the promise that the sufferings of the present would be fully compensated in the more or less remote epoch of the ultimate fulfillment of human destinies; hence the idea of progress performed the role of a justification of evil, that is, of a secular theodicy, or, rather, historiodicy. Even more than that, it contained also an argument for the view that the present *had* to be sacrificed for the future, that the presently living individuals, and entire generations, *had* to see themselves as mere instruments of universal progress.[5] The painful contradictions of Russia's historical development made this view both attractive and repellent: attractive as historical consolation, repellent as reconciliation with moral evils.

As can be seen from the above, the centrality of the idea of progress in nineteenth-century Russian thought did not involve its universal, uncritical acceptance. The conception of progress as economic and social modernization found in Russia both enthusiastic advocates and powerful critics; very often these two attitudes toward modernization were combined somehow in the same thinker. The same is true about the idea of a universal, unilinear progress, allegedly common to all nations and identified, in practice, with the pattern of historical development of the West. And, most importantly for our topic, the same holds true of the idea of progress as a secular religion. The nineteenth-century Russian intelligentsia represented, no doubt, a peculiarly instructive exemplification of this phenomenon; at the same time, however, many of its members offered a passionate criticism of the "idolatry of progress." Suffice it to refer in this connection to Belinskii's and Herzen's revolt against the Hegelian conception of historical necessity, which justified the suffering of individuals in the name of universal progress.[6] A similar rejection of historiosophical theodicy can be found in Russian religious thinkers, particularly in Dostoevskii, who, as we shall see, powerfully influenced Russian philosophers of the Silver Age.

But let us turn now to the Russian reception of Marxism. At the end of the nineteenth century, Marxism became the dominant ideology of the Russian intelligentsia. Its widespread influence, as well as its initial tolerance by the authorities, was, in Lenin's words, "an altogether curious phenomenon": "Marxist books were published one after another, Marxist journals and newspapers were founded, nearly everyone became a Marxist, Marxists were flattered, Marxists were courted, and the book publishers rejoiced at the extraordinary, ready sale of Marxist literature."[7]

There were many reasons for this interesting episode in Russian intellectual history. The authorities saw Marxism as a welcome antidote to populist terrorism and also as welcome intellectual support for government-sponsored industrialization. The intellectual elite saw it as the last word in European thought, offering a convenient way of combining conditional support for Russia's capitalist development (in the present) with continuous loyalty to socialism (as the final ideal). The Marxist theory of progress was hailed as a critical form of westernism, endorsing, in principle, the Western model of development but giving at the same time an unsurpassed critical analysis of the multiple contradictions of capitalist society. It was valuable for the elite as a respectable form of breaking with the legacy of populist socialism, such as the programmatic methodological "subjectivism" that undermined the authority of rigorous, "objective" scholarship, and the radical egalitarianism that was hostile to all forms of intellectual aristocracy. It helped the Russian intelligentsia to overcome the deeply rooted populist prejudices against political freedom (as "bourgeois" in its class content and detrimental to "the common people"), thus legitimizing the struggle for it as a necessary phase of development. The Marxist endorsement of a capitalist economy and "bourgeois liberty" was, of course, qualified and relative; nevertheless, it was perceived as an important step toward the rehabilitation of political liberalism. This was not so in the case of Lenin, but in the 1890s Lenin's revolutionary and fundamentalist Marxism was still marginal and hardly visible. For the mainstream Russian intelligentsia, Russian Marxism was a current of thought having two intellectual leaders: Plekhanov in the emigration (publishing in Russia under the pseudonym "Beltov") and Petr Struve, head of the "legal Marxists," in St. Petersburg. Despite obvious differences (Plekhanov's dogmatism and Struve's revisionism), both of them (in contrast to Lenin) proclaimed the need for "objectivism" in social science and for an alliance with the liberals in the struggle for political freedom.[8]

Philosophically, the common denominator of Plekhanov's and Struve's Marxism was a scientistic interpretation of history, stressing the deterministic, law-governed character of social processes and opposed to all forms of deontological, normative thinking. This fully agreed with the spirit of positivistic scientism and naturalistic evolutionism that became dominant in European thought in the second half of the nineteenth century.[9] The Russian intelligentsia took seriously the scientistic pretensions of Marxism and, consequently, saw historical materialism as the most consistent application of positivistic science to historical evolution. However, this intellectual situation changed with the appearance of the revolt against positivism in Europe. In Russia it began with *transcendental* (neo-Kantian) idealism, which established the autonomy of ethics without relapsing into relativistic "subjectivism," and soon developed into *transcendent* (metaphysical) idealism, which provided metaphysical grounding for the human personality and its inalienable rights. This, in turn, paved the way for openly religious philosophical thinking and the religio-philosophical renaissance in Russia. The former "legal Marxists" came to be the leading spirits in this intellectual revolution. As might have been expected, an important aspect of their philosophical development consisted in settling accounts with Marxism.

The present article deals with the criticism of Marxism by three representative thinkers of the Russian religio-philosophic renaissance: two former Marxists, Nikolai Berdiaev and Sergei Bulgakov, and Pavel Novgorodtsev, a leading figure in the revolt against positivism and the main theorist of the new, rights-based Russian liberalism.[10] However, I will not try to present and analyze Bulgakov's criticism of the Marxist economy or the successive stages in Berdiaev's and Novgorodtsev's struggle against positivism. I will concentrate instead on what I see as their most important contribution to a critical understanding of Marxism: namely, on their criticism of Marxism as a substitute for religion, that is, as utopia, not positive science. This focus appeared in their thinking when the antipositivist breakthrough in Russian intellectual culture was already an accomplished fact and when Marxism ceased to be merely an instrument of thought, becoming instead an all-embracing ideology of an organized revolutionary movement, characterized, especially in its Bolshevik version, by the single-minded fanaticism and crude fundamentalism of a millenarian crusade.

Nikolai Berdiaev

Lack of space does not allow for a comprehensive outline of Berdiaev's intellectual evolution here. Happily, such an outline is not absolutely necessary in the present context. Berdiaev's most important insights about revolutionary Marxism have been fully and forcefully expressed in a single article, "Socialism and Religion" (1906), written in the aftermath of the revolutionary events of 1905 in Russia.[11]

In his other writings Berdiaev defined socialism as the inevitable and acceptable result of the "entire bourgeois development," a justified extension of the Declaration of the Rights of Man and of the Citizen.[12] This applied, however, only to one type of socialism: the religiously "neutral" socialism, solving the problem of daily bread without pretending to replace religion.[13] Such socialism, represented by Proudhon, the British Fabians, and the liberal socialism of Bernstein, was opposed by the Russian thinker to another type of socialism—socialism as religion, represented by orthodox, revolutionary Marxism. This "religious socialism" was, in his view, "a complete dogma, a solution to the question of the meaning of life, the purpose of history."[14] It aimed at strict ideological control of all spheres of human activity, thus crushing freedom of conscience and allowing no room for spontaneously shaped personal identities. In other words, it was an *ideocratic* socialism,[15] striving for an earthly salvation and, therefore, adamantly hostile to the idea of heavenly salvation. Following Dostoevskii, Berdiaev defined this aspiration as a passion for the deification of man, a thirst "to organize this world not only apart from God but in opposition to him."[16]

In developing these views Berdiaev dwelled on three aspects of the

Marxist religion: first, the element of crude theodicy, the justification of historical evils, including evil means for the realization of the final goal; second, the cold cruelty of its theory of progress, demanding a wholesale sacrifice of the present for the sake of an ideal future, treating presently living individuals as merely means for the future flourishing of the species; finally, "the poverty and wretchedness of its positive perspectives,"[17] boiling down to the achievement of universal affluence and thereby subordinating all aspects of life to daily bread. Let us briefly discuss these three points.

The first two aspects, closely interrelated with each other, were indeed important features of Marxism. There can be no doubt that the author of *Capital* conceived progress as a long and cruel historical process in which not only individuals but also entire generations and classes had to be ruthlessly sacrificed for the sake of the unfettered development of the human species in the communist society of the future. He himself emphatically endorsed the "historical law" according to which

> the development of the capacities of the human species takes place at the cost of the majority of human individuals. . . . The higher development of individuality is thus only achieved by a historical process during which individuals are sacrificed, for the interests of the species in the human Kingdom, as in the animal and plant kingdom, always assert themselves at the cost of the interests of individuals.[18]

It is obvious that this conception of progress provided a convenient way of justifying past evils as necessary, unavoidable steps in historical development; suffice it to recall Marx's utter contempt for "sentimentalism," his apologia for the progressive role of slavery (including nineteenth-century American slavery),[19] or his emphatic assertion of the necessary and ultimately progressive function of the atrocities of primitive accumulation. He did not hesitate to state that historical progress in the past had nothing in common with the increase of humanitarianism: it resembled rather "that hideous pagan idol who would not drink the nectar but from the skulls of the slain."[20] And it is evident that he attributed to evil passions the role of prime movers of progress not only in the past but also in the immediate future—after all, he made the victory of socialism dependent on the intensification and mobilization of class hatred, not on its gradual disappearance from human relations. Using the terminology of Nietzsche, we can say that "the love of the remote" (*Fernstenliebe*)—that is, the love of the imagined communist humanity—made Marx conspicuously indifferent to the fate of the imperfect human individuals of the capitalist present.[21] Berdiaev was therefore right in accusing Marxism of justifying cruelty and treating everything as merely a means for the future.[22]

Berdiaev's sensitivity to this aspect of Marxism was increased by his awareness of the distinctively Russian tradition of criticizing the idolatry of progress: He was influenced by N.K. Mikhailovskii, a thinker who passionately rejected the Marxist notion of historical inevitability and referred in this connection to Belinskii's rejection of the "rational necessity" in Hegelianism.[23] He quoted Ivan Karamazov's rebellion against historiosophical theodicy—his refusal to accept the future harmony, if purchased by the sufferings of the innocents. His (Berdiaev's) reference to the "bad infinity of progress," as leading to slavery in time to the cycle of birth and death,[24] reminds one of the views of Nikolai Fedorov, who treated progress as an immoral idea, involving the dismissal of past generations as mere stepping-stones to the happiness of future ones. But the most important factor influencing Berdiaev's attitude toward Marxism was his careful observation of the Bolsheviks. Their militancy, ideological fundamentalism, and unswerving devotion to the final goal sharply contrasted with the advances of revisionism and the rapid de-eschatologization of Marxism in German social democracy. Hence, Russian bolshevism offered a much better perspective for the understanding of Marxism as a horribly brutal (Berdiaev's expression) "religion of progress."[25] It was Berdiaev's merit to realize this and to predict that the victory of revolutionary Marxism in Russia would lead to totalitarian slavery.[26]

I fully realize that this conclusion is not convincing for all those who believe that German social democracy was more faithful to the original spirit of Marxism than Russian bolshevism. Such a view, however, is very superficial and misleading. Berdiaev's interpretation presupposes a clear distinction between Marxism as science and Marxism as the secular religion of communism;[27] if we accept this valid distinction, we have to concede that the development of German social democracy after Engels's death consisted in a gradual but steady abandonment of Marxist communism,[28] while Russian bolshevism remained fanatically faithful to it. Abandoning Marxist communism should not be seen as developing it, as being its legitimate heir. Hence, it is justified to say that Marxist communism— that is, Marxism as a "religion"—was being betrayed by German social democrats; this made the party of Lenin more representative of the original Marxism than the party of Kautsky.

Berdiaev's third point is somewhat less well taken. There is a certain contradiction in his view of Marxism's final goal. On the one hand, he saw in Marxism the potential for a new religion of superhumanity, that is, "the striving toward a new earthly God who will emerge at the end of progress and in whose name all humanity itself is transformed into a means."[29] On the other hand, he saw Marxist religion as superficial, as nonradical in its content, subordinating everything to the petty-bourgeois ideal of universal material security—an ideal whose realization would transform people into "millions of happy infants."[30] The first diagnosis was inspired by Nietzsche's vision of the superman, as well as by Dostoevskii's analyses of the hubris of theomachist atheism; the second took up the vision contained in Dostoevskii's "Legend of the Grand Inquisitor." In Berdiaev's view these two diagnoses were interconnected because the Promethean ideal of the deification of man was ultimately self-defeating, bound to usher in the utter degradation of humanity. Nevertheless, quite irrespectively of our view of the value and logical coherence of this interpretation, he should have been more clear about the basic *intention* behind the Marxist religion. Was it a striving for a regenerated, godlike humanity, or merely a desire to subordinate everything to the prosaic question of daily bread?

The discovery and publication of the works of the young Marx, especially his *Economic and Philosophic Manuscripts of 1844*, made it evident that Marx's ultimate concerns cannot be reduced to the question of daily bread. Unlike the system of Dostoevskii's Grand Inquisitor, Marx's communism was about freedom rather than bread: freedom conceived as conscious mastery over collective fate, putting an end to alienation and thus bringing about a tremendous increase of human species powers, a truly unheard of, unimaginable feast of universal liberation. Communism so conceived was to be nothing less than "the solution of the riddle of history," the true solution of "the struggle between existence and essence, between objectification and self-affirmation, between freedom and necessity, between individual and species."[31] It was to create a new race of people, superior to the present generation not only spiritually but physically as well. Young Marx boldly proclaimed the idea of a "complete emancipation of all human senses and qualities": the eyes and ears of the de-alienated people of the future will be completely different from the crude, inhuman eyes and ears of the dehumanized people of the present.[32]

We can see, therefore, that Marx's early writings supported Berdiaev's first diagnosis (the "religion of superhumanity"). Marx's "people of the future" were to be supermen, not "happy infants." This was clearly realized by sophisticated representatives of the militant wing of Russian Marxism. A telling testimony of this is Trotskii's vision of the communist man—totally transformed, capable of changing and controlling not only the social but also the biological life of the species. Under communism, he wrote, "man will become immeasurably stronger, wiser and subtler; his body will become more harmonized, his movements more rhythmic, his voice more musical. . . . The average human type will rise to the heights of an Aristotle, a Goethe, or a Marx."[33]

It is easy to see, however, that this final ideal could serve as a justification of the most brutal totalitarian tyranny. Trotskii exemplified this in his *Terrorism and Communism*, written in 1920, providing arguments for slave labor and the total militarization of life in the transitional period. He said explicitly that the dictatorship of the proletariat represented "the most ruthless form of state, which embraces the life of citizens authoritatively in every direction."[34] This was a perfect confirmation of Berdiaev's view that Marxist communism would call into being the most unrestricted state despotism and thus establish "the definitive and final slavery."[35]

On the whole, Berdiaev's analysis of Marxism deserves the close attention of Marxologists. It has not become antiquated; on the contrary, it can serve as an indispensable reminder of those features of Marxism that are, as a rule, conveniently forgotten. After the "discovery" of the young Marx, hundreds of authors, not necessarily Marxists, triumphantly argued that Marx, as was evident from his early writings, had always been a great humanist and libertarian, seeing the highest end in the unfettered, nonalienated development of individual human beings. What was forgotten, or deliberately ignored, was the simple fact that, according to Marx, the principle of treating human beings as ends in themselves was valid *only* under communism, that is, only at the final stage of progress; before the attainment of this stage the human individual was to be treated as "never a goal and always a means."[36] Remembering this effectively destroys all attempts to present Marxist communism as a form of radicalism that had nothing in common with totalitarianism and was compatible with the principles of modern democracy.

Sergei Bulgakov

Another ex-Marxist, the future Orthodox theologian Sergei Bulgakov, developed similar ideas but with a different emphasis. Like Berdiaev, he perceived Marxism as the last word in nineteenth-century theories of progress and, at the same time, as a surrogate of religion—the religion of positivism, combining scientistic pretensions with the ability to impart meaning to history and thus to satisfy an ineradicable human need.[37] Unlike Berdiaev—or, at least, unlike Berdiaev as the author of "Socialism as Religion"—he stressed the attractiveness of this "religion of millions"[38] and did not try to set against it the religiously "neutral" type of socialism. On the contrary: at the first stage of his evolution toward idealism he continued to value Marxism precisely as a doctrine with a utopian and eschatological dimension, powerfully attractive for "religiously minded atheists."[39] The religiously "neutral" evolutionary socialism of Bernstein represented, in his view, a degraded form of Marxist thought—"Marxism without wings."[40] He was alarmed by the successes of Bernsteinian revisionism and saw them as a symptom of the inevitable de-utopianization and de-eschatologization of Marxism. As a religiously minded man he did not welcome this development: Marxism without the faith in "the leap to the kingdom of freedom" was for him unworthy of allegiance. He reacted by concluding that the Marxist combination of positivistic science with religious mentality proved no longer workable, that science ceased to support the belief in the meaning of history, and, therefore, that to save this belief it was necessary radically to separate religion from science.[41] This diagnosis motivated his turn toward metaphysical idealism and theistic religiosity.

Thus, Bulgakov's religious philosophy emerged, partially at least, as a reaction to Bernsteinian revisionism, that is, as a reaction to the seeming disappearance of the Marxist religion, not (as in Berdiaev's case) to its inherent falsity. This does not mean that Bulgakov was insensitive to the inner contradictions and morally unacceptable aspects of the Marxist "religion of progress." There is no reason to doubt that he was increasingly aware of them. Like Berdiaev, he was well acquainted with the Russian tradition of criticizing the idolatry of progress; he devoted to it two important articles: one on Herzen, another on Dostoevskii's Ivan Karamazov.[42] But the fact remains that he wrote these articles in the first two years of the new century, that is, at the time when his Marxist faith had already been destroyed by Bernstein.

Bulgakov's article on Dostoevskii is philosophically more important than his article on Herzen and deserves a short summary in the present context. Its relevance for our topic derives from Bulgakov's practical identification of the theory of progress with socialism, and socialism with Marxism. Socialism, he wrote, was historically the most important, as well as the most widely accepted, theory of progress;[43] Marxism was, of course, the most important socialist theory; hence Ivan Karamazov, as a passionate critic of the theory of progress, was simultaneously a critic of socialism and in particular a critic of Marxism. He was, as Bulgakov put it, a "skeptical son of the epoch of socialism."[44]

The expression "epoch of socialism" may seem strange in its application to the nineteenth century. Bulgakov meant by this the centrality of the socialist idea in nineteenth-century intellectual life and popular expectations. In this sense socialism provided the frame of reference for all theo-

ries of progress and all future-oriented historiosophies of this century. Even
Nietzsche, with all his hostility toward socialism, was "a product of the
socialist world view, its illegitimate spiritual son."[45]

Ivan Karamazov dared to challenge the main dogmas of the nineteenth-
century religion of progress. He did so by questioning the principle of
"living for the future," by rejecting the price of progress as too high, as
morally unacceptable, and, finally, by putting in doubt the value of universal happiness as the final goal of history.[46] Bulgakov endorsed these
doubts, presented them as his own, and concluded that the problems of
historiosophical theodicy could be solved only through a metaphysical and
religious synthesis.[47] Nevertheless, he refrained from rejecting socialism as
such, limiting himself to saying that materialism and positivism were unable to mobilize ethical enthusiasm, necessary for the realization of socialist ideals. Did this mean that a Christian socialism, which became his own
ideological option,[48] would be more justified in demanding human sacri-
fices than the atheistic socialism? Unfortunately, Bulgakov's article did not
provide an answer to this question; it remained somewhat unclear whether
the principle of sacrificing the present for the future should be rejected or
merely softened by promising celestial rewards for the sufferers.

Bulgakov's most important text about Marxism was his pamphlet *Karl
Marx as a Religious Type*, published for the first time as a newspaper
article in 1906.[49] It was no longer a study of Marxism as the best exemplification of something broader, more general—socialism as such, or the
theory of progress—but a study of ideas and attitudes characteristic of a
single individual named Karl Marx. And it was intended as Bulgakov's
final attempt to settle accounts with the thinker who had so deeply influenced him in the past.[50]

Karl Marx, Bulgakov argued, was by no means an attractive individual.
Love of one's neighbor or spontaneous sympathy and compassion for other
humans were almost unknown to him. He was a "dictatorial type," motivated mostly by negative feelings, such as hatred, anger, envy, and contempt for all those who dared to disagree with him.[51] Consequently, his
polemical style was utterly aggressive, vituperative, trying to crush the
adversary and to intimidate his followers. He thought in abstract, sociological terms and showed no interest in the concrete and the individual, no
understanding of the absolute value of the irreducible human personality,
and no concern for its fate. Hence he would have been unable to understand Ivan Karamazov's protest against the cruel aspects of the theory of
progress.[52]

In his analysis of Marx's ideas, Bulgakov relied on his interpretation of
Marxism as an atheistic religion, deeply hostile to theistic religion, espe-

cially Christianity. The new elements in his interpretation consisted in concentrating on the philosophical sources of Marx's thought, on the importance of his early works, and on the differences between the Marxism of Marx and the official Marxism of German social democracy. This new emphasis was made possible by Mehring's publication of some works of the young Marx in 1902.[53]

Careful reading of Marx's two articles of 1843–44—"On the Jewish Question" and "Toward a Critique of Hegel's *Philosophy of Right* "—led the Russian thinker to conclude that these early writings contained Marx's "philosophical maximum" and provided the best key to the understanding of his world view.[54] At the same time, however, Bulgakov saw in them a decisive argument against the popular view of Marx's indebtedness to Hegel. Marx, he asserted, had never been a philosophical idealist; hence, he could not have been a disciple of Hegel. His true philosophical teacher was Ludwig Feuerbach. Marx's historical materialism was in fact little more than a translation of Feuerbachianism into the language of political economy.[55] Hence it was justified to say that Feuerbach was the untold secret of Marx, as well as the solution of this secret.[56]

This conclusion corroborated Dostoevskii's thesis that socialism, as the modern variant of humanistic atheism, aimed above all at the replacement of the religion of Godmanhood by that of Mangodhood—that is, by the deification of humanity. Bulgakov cautiously added that Marx took up the critical side of Feuerbach's philosophy without following him in the explicit commitment to the ideal of deification of the human species. Nevertheless, he found in Marx's early writings an unmistakenly Feuerbachian conception of man's ultimate liberation: a conception of liberating people from their "egoism" through transforming them into "species beings," or "communal beings," free from the alienating pluralism of the conflicting interests of civil society and capable of merging together in unanimous community. He discovered these views—the notion of "species being" (*Gattungswesen*) and the total rejection of pluralistic civil society—in Marx's article "On the Jewish Question." His comment on this article deserves to be quoted:

> It is easy to find here Feuerbach's idea about *Gattungswesen*, about the human species as the highest instance for man. In Marx this "love of the remote," for the not-yet-existing humanity of the future, takes the form of an outright contempt toward "one's neighbor," that is, really existing human beings. . . .
>
> Thus, only when people lose their individuality and society transforms itself into a Sparta, an ant-hill, or a beehive—only then will the task of human emancipation be completed.[57]

In other words, Bulgakov interpreted Marx's essay as a manifesto of collectivism, demanding the complete socialization of man. He saw this as the gist of Marx's utopia, the heart of Marxism as an integral, all-embracing world view.

In the remainder of his study Bulgakov reflected on the relationship between this world view and the Marxist teachings of the theorists of German social democracy. He stressed that the German workers' party was created by Lassalle, that its commitment to Marxism (whether its theorists were aware of this or not) was never total, and that its development in recent years consisted in gradual liberation from Marxist dogmas.

Showing the vital connection between Feuerbach and Marx was a strong side of Bulgakov's interpretation. It is true that Marx's critique of capitalism started "from the account of human nature set forth in Feuerbach" and that his philosophical communism was based on Feuerbach's conception of man as *Gattungswesen*.[58] In 1906 this aspect of Marxism was almost completely ignored and stressing it was an important contribution.[59] However, it was a great exaggeration to conclude from this that Marx owed nothing to Hegel. In fact, he borrowed from Hegel the central idea of the dialectical conception of the self-actualization of human "species being" in history—the idea of self-enriching alienation.[60] True, Marx's *Economic and Philosophical Manuscripts* were published only in 1932, and without this text it was impossible fully to reconstruct Marx's theory of alienation. Nevertheless, Bulgakov too hastily dismissed the significance of Hegel for Marx's thinking. After all, Hegelian dialectics underlay Marx's account of the development of man's "species being" and was, therefore, inseparable from his "Feuerbachianism." Bulgakov's utterly negative view of Marx's dialectics stemmed probably from its unconscious identification with the naturalistic distortion of dialectics in the works of Engels.

Focusing on Marx's final goal (and not merely his theory of progress) was another merit of Bulgakov's interpretation, sharply distinguishing it from the dominant "scientific" accounts of Marxism. Bulgakov was right in emphasizing that the Marxist "science" contained a soteriological myth, a quasi-millenarian religion of earthly salvation. However, strangely enough for a professional economist, he did not define the economic content of Marx's final ideal; he failed to see that Marx's conception of human emancipation involved a wholesale abolition of the market economy, as generating the divisive pluralism of conflicting interests and thus preventing the actualization of man's communal essence. In addition, his criticism of Marxist secular millenarianism stopped short of rejecting millenarianism as such. On the contrary: at the end of his study he quoted from the Lord's Prayer, interpreting the words "Thy Kingdom come" as tantamount to stating that the Kingdom of God on earth was the final end of human history.[61] He even expressed a hope that Marxist socialism, as opposed to Marxism as a religion, might prove to be working for the realization of this Kingdom.[62]

Such inconsistency characterized Berdiaev as well. In 1906, reacting to revolutionary violence, he pointed out the heretical nature of millenarian dreams, declaring that the eschatological dimension of Christianity should not be understood as salvation in history.[63] In the next year, however, resisting the statist spirit of "Stolypin's reaction," he embraced the idea of "anarchist theocracy" and proclaimed genuine socialism—that is, social-ism free from both theomachist revolutionism and Bernsteinian "bour-geois philistinism"—to be a right step in this direction: its task was to permeate the economic sphere with the divine spirit and thus to provide an economic foundation for the Kingdom of God.[64]

Pavel Novgorodtsev

Novgorodtsev, head of the Moscow school of legal theory, was the first thinker of the Russian religio-philosophical renaissance who elaborated a consistent philosophical critique of all variants of teleologically conceived progress. He saw them as secularized versions of millenarianism but did not concentrate exclusively on their analogy with religious thinking. His frame of reference in analyzing them was the problem of the social ideal and of the utopian belief in a paradise on earth.[65] In approaching this problem, he combined Kant's criticism (ideals as regulative guides, not goals to be fully realized in history)[66] with a religious perspective, critical of the immanentization of the Absolute as involving the mortal sin of idolatry. He followed also Trubetskoi's analysis of Solov′ev's theocratic utopia, endorsing the view that the error of utopianism consisted in the absolutization of the relative, that is, in attributing absolute significance to certain relative values and thus paving the way for the tyranny of false Absolutes.[67] In opposing all conceptions of an immanent meaning of his-tory in the name of a nontemporalized, transcendent Absolute, he antici-pated, to a great extent, Voegelin's warnings against "immanentization of the eschaton." [68]

Almost half of Novgorodtsev's book *On the Social Ideal* (1917) is devoted to Marx and the historical fate of Marxism. It was not just another polemical writing but a scholarly contribution to Marxology. Its original-ity consisted in concentrating not on Marxist science but on the Marxist utopia. This was, of course, very different from the established views on "scientific socialism" and especially from the self-image of the German

Marxists of the Second International. In the context of the Russian religio-philosophical renaissance, Novgorodtsev's originality was less striking because he was partially dependent on Bulgakov, whom he often quoted in his book. Like Bulgakov, he interpreted Marxism as the most perfect specimen of a religion of earthly salvation, deriving from the Feuerbachian conception of the immanent divinity of humankind; a religion without transcendence, seeking salvation in absolute collectivism, in reuniting individuals with the species through raising them to the level of species beings.[69]

Following Bulgakov, Novgorodtsev paid special attention to the works of the young Marx, especially his essay "On the Jewish Question." He focused on Marx's criticism of the rights of man as rights of egoistic individuals, asserting themselves against the community and thereby denying man's "communal essence." He rightly derived from this Marx's hostility to the law-governed state (*pravovoe gosudarstvo*), as sanctioning the divisive egoism of the civil society, and Marx's utopian vision of the "withering away of law and the state" in the communist society of the future.[70] But he did not question Marx's view of the relationship between the law-governed state and modern individualism. His disagreement with Marx concerned value judgments rather than facts. He used Marx's diagnosis as an indirect corroboration of the liberal view of the positive role of the modern, law-based state in the emancipation of the individual. He fully agreed that the total socialization of man would involve the disappearance of law and the state, but he refused to see this as the desired end of human history. The abolition, or withering away, of law and the state would leave no room for personal autonomy; people would be transformed from individualized beings into species beings. Marx, Novgorodtsev commented, "saw this as the absolute human emancipation. As a matter of fact, this would be the absolute subordination of individual to society. In the Marxist philosophy there is no place for a genuine idea of personality; hence, there is no room for personality in the Marxist ideal."[71]

Among the writings of the "mature Marx," the most revealing for an understanding of the Marxist utopia was, of course, "The Critique of the Gotha Program." In analyzing it, Novgorodtsev agreed with Marx that "right by its very nature can consist only in the application of an equal standard" and, therefore, that every right is inevitably "a right of inequality."[72] He saw these words as an expression of the realistic side of Marx's world view and, at the same time, as a good explanation of the radical incompatibility between the juridical point of view and Marx's utopianism. On the one hand, Marx had acknowledged that individuals were unequal, that they "would not be different individuals if they were not unequal,"[73] and, therefore, that they were bound to think in terms of "rights"; on the

other hand, Marx's ideal of the higher stage of communist society pre-
supposed the overcoming of "the narrow horizon of bourgeois right" and
of the standpoint of "right" as such.[74] If so, Novgorodtsev argued, the
realization of Marx's ideal meant, in practice, that people would cease to
feel themselves as different individuals, becoming instead species beings,
renouncing any appeals to right and justice, surrendering their freedom to
the supraindividual life of the species.[75]

Another feature of Marx's utopianism was its striving for the wholesale
rationalization of social life.[76] In this respect Marx's and Engels's attitude
toward law and the state was diametrically opposed to Stirner's anarchis-
tic irrationalism.[77] In contrast to Stirner, the founders of Marxism criticized law and the state as institutions sanctioning egoistic individualism
and therefore creating obstacles to the complete rationalization of social
life. Their ideal of freedom was utterly collectivist and rationalist, con-
ceiving freedom as conscious rational control over the conditions of life
and development of the species—that is, as conscious planning and a
perfect rational order. Their vision of "the leap from the kingdom of
necessity to the kingdom of freedom"[78] identified freedom with conscious, planned regulation and necessity with irrational spontaneity.
Novgorodtsev had no doubts that a realization of such a vision would lead
in practice to the maximum centralization of power and to the subordination of all spheres of individual life to the arbitrary will of those in
power.[79]

Awareness of the authoritarian dangers inherent in the communist ideal
turned Novgorodtsev's attention to the problem of Marx's attitude toward
democracy. He agreed with Bernstein that Marxism was compatible with
both democracy and dictatorship, owing to the lack of sharp contrast
between these two notions in Marxist theory.[80] The dictatorship of the
proletariat was, in Marx's view, a form of dictatorship and a form of
democracy at the same time. Novgorodtsev was one of the first thinkers
who subjected Marx's teaching about the dictatorship of the proletariat to
a close analysis, pointing out the possibility of its different interpretations.
He even claimed the priority in this respect, since he dealt with Marx's
conception of politics in the transitional period already in the first edition
of his book (1917), that is, before the appearance of the most important
works on this subject.[81]

At the top of the short list of these works Novgorodtsev put Lenin's
book *The State and Revolution* (1917); the second place he gave to Hans
Kelsen's *Sozialismus und Staat* (Leipzig, 1920).[82] Lenin's book, in his
view, deserved attention as a "detailed enumeration of almost all passages
from the works of Marx and Engels that deal with the state;" its main

shortcoming was leaving out of account Marx's essays of 1844 ("Zur Kritik der Hegelschen Philosophie" and "Zur Judenfrage") and Engels's "revisionist" introduction to Marx's *Class Struggles in France* of 1895.[83] This shows that he valued this book mostly as a useful collection of quotations. In the footnotes to the new edition of *Ob obshchestvennom ideale*, he took issue with some of Lenin's interpretations of the meaning of the quoted passages. But, amazingly, he failed to discuss Lenin's work as a whole, as a manifesto of militant communism, consciously and adamantly opposed to the social-democratic Marxism of the Second International. In his detailed, analytical account of the history of the workers' movement, he concentrated on Germany and France, completely ignoring Russian Marxism, bolshevism, and the Russian revolution.

The limitation of the scope of analysis allowed Novgorodtsev to arrive at very optimistic conclusions. German Marxism had split into reformist and revolutionary currents; the former had already abandoned its utopian faith in ultimate salvation on earth, embracing instead the idea of a law-based, democratic national state; the latter was bound to do the same under the threat of becoming discredited and rejected. This meant that Marxism as a total world view was dead and beyond resurrection.[84] But, Novgorodtsev added, it was dead only in its revolutionary and utopian strivings, not as an effort to improve the lot of the working people.[85] Its "vital truth" was the idea of man's right to a dignified existence, and this ideal became assimilated by the modern, socialized liberalism and the modern law-governed state. True, this idea was not specifically Marxist, and not even specifically socialist: it was formulated in the process of the organic development of liberal thought. Nevertheless, it was Marxism that necessitated its practical implementation. "We must recognize," Novgorodtsev argued, "that Marxism marks a point after which moral consciousness cannot return to the past, after which the modern law-governed state had radically to change its views on the tasks of politics, on the nature of law, and on the principles of equality and freedom."[86] Therefore, the death of Marxism as a utopia of earthly paradise could not entail the death of its "indisputable truth," its "vital kernel," which constituted the heart of all socialist teachings of the past and which Marx had felt, understood, and expressed with unusual force.[87]

It is somewhat strange that Novgorodtsev's book ended on this note. It was not consistent with his analysis of Marxism, which showed that the heart of Marxism was precisely its utopian dimension, permeating all aspects of Marx's thought,[88] that "scientific socialism" was in fact not a scientific overcoming of all utopianism but the most widespread and intense utopian faith of modern times. It contradicted his brilliant interpretation of Marx's and Engels's vision of the revolutionary "leap to the kingdom of freedom," which uncovered the logical hiatus between the conception of necessary, objective laws of history and the ideal of liberating people from their yoke through establishing an effective, conscious direction of historical processes.[89] In particular, it contradicted his revealing analysis of the problem of law and the state in Marxism—an analysis that established beyond doubt that Marxism had nothing in common with thinking in terms of "rights" and with the intention to contribute to the development of the law-governed state.

Novgorodtsev's conclusions were based upon his close study of the fate of Marxism in Germany. His presentation of the history of German social democracy was excellent, but it is not quite clear why he chose to treat this history as a sufficient basis for broad generalizations about the death of Marxism. After all, his own analysis has shown that the intellectual heritage of the German Social Democratic Party was not homogeneously Marxist and that the evolution of its ideology consisted in fact in the gradual renunciation of Marxist tenets, in the gradual abandonment of Marxism both as a "science" and (even more) as a communist utopia.[90] If so, the increasing commitment of German social democrats to democracy and the rule of law should not be treated as providing an insight into the essential truth of Marxism. And the death of Marxist communism in Germany should not be seen as tantamount to the death of Marxist communism in general. If Marxist communism was dead in Germany, it did not follow that it was dead in Russia.

The third edition of Novgorodtsev's book was published after the Bolshevik revolution; after Lenin's rejection of the compromised name "social democracy" and his proud proclamation that now his own party, calling itself "Communist," was the only legitimate successor of the entire legacy of genuine Marxism; after the Bolshevik experiment with war communism, an exercise in revolutionary utopianism directly inspired by the Marxist idea of a "leap to the kingdom of freedom." Novgorodtsev, however, did not take these events into account. He was uniquely equipped to interpret the Bolshevik revival of Marxist utopianism, but he failed to undertake this important task.

The same is true of Bulgakov, who at that time ceased to be interested in Marxism. His interpretation of Marxism was less rich than Novgorodtsev's but was on the whole similar. Both thinkers had the merit of drawing attention to the texts of the young Marx; both—in sharp contrast to the later phenomenon of the Western reception of the "early Marx" —interpreted these texts as the expression of an adamantly antiliberal "absolute collectivism"; both concentrated on the quasi-religious function of the Marxist "science" and on the presence of a powerful utopian drive in Marxist thought. At the same time, both were rather insensitive to the economic aspect of Marxist utopianism: both insisted on the positive side of socialist reforms and remained silent about the dangers of the communist idea of a total suppression of the market economy. Finally, both had grossly underestimated bolshevism as the possible successor of Marxist revolutionary communism.

Many features of Bulgakov's and Novgorodtsev's view of Marxism were present also in Berdiaev's conception of "socialism as religion." Berdiaev can be credited with a greater awareness of the vitality of the revolutionary, militant trend in Marxism and with a prophetic insight into the nature of its "ideocratic" aspirations. Nevertheless, he also failed to produce an interpretation of bolshevism as the most consistent version of militant Marxism. His well-known explanations of the Russian Revolution revolved around the problem of its distinctively Russian roots, thus turning attention away from the continuity between Lenin and the founders of Marxism.

On the whole, however, the three thinkers offered a valuable, original critique of Marxism—a critique reflecting the specific historical experience of the Russian intelligentsia, including its persistent presentiment of the revolution. The results of their thinking about Marxism deserve to be known and assimilated by intellectual historians and by all those who want to have a better understanding of the greatest and most dangerous utopia of our century.

Notes

1. The first disillusionment of Russia's intellectual elite with the modernizing autocracy is symbolized by the name of "the first Russian *intelligent*," Aleksandr Radishchev. The next long step on this way was, of course, the Decembrist Uprising of 1825.

2. See A. Gerschenkron, "Economic Development in Russian Intellectual History," in *Economic Backwardness in Historical Perspective* (New York: Praeger, 1965), pp. 167–70. Also A. Walicki, *The Controversy Over Capitalism: Studies in the Social Philosophy of the Russian Populists*, 2nd ed. (Notre Dame, IN: University of Notre Dame Press, 1989), pp. 107–31.

3. See V.V. Zenkovsky, *A History of Russian Philosophy*, trans. George L. Kline, 2 vols. (London: Routledge and Kegan Paul, 1953), vol. 1, pp. 70, 77.

4. For a detailed analysis of this aspect of Herzen's "Russian socialism," see my *Russia, Poland and Universal Regeneration* (Notre Dame, IN: University of Notre Dame Press, 1989), pp. 39–69.

5. George L. Kline subjected this view to thorough philosophical criticism. See his articles: " 'Present', 'Past', and 'Future' as Categoreal Terms, and the 'Fallacy of the Actual Future,' " *Review of Metaphysics*, vol. 40, no. 2 (December 1986), pp. 215–35;

and "The Use and Abuse of Hegel by Nietzsche and Marx," in *Hegel and His Critics: Philosophy in the Aftermath of Hegel*, ed. William Desmond (Albany, NY: State University of New York Press, 1989), pp. 1–34.

6. See Belinskii's letter to V.P. Botkin of 1 March 1844 (in *Russian Philosophy*, ed. J.M. Edie, J.P. Scanlan, and M.B. Zeldin with the collaboration of G.L. Kline, 3 vols. [Knoxville: The University of Tennessee Press, 1965], vol. 1, pp. 304–6) and Herzen's *From the Other Shore*, especially his famous words: "If progress is the end, for whom are we working? Who is this Moloch who, as the toilers approach him, instead of rewarding them, only recedes, and as a consolation to the exhausted, doomed multitudes crying 'morituri te salutant,' can give back only the mocking answer that after their death all will be beautiful on earth[?]" (A. Herzen, *From the Other Shore and the Russian People and Socialism* [London: Weidenfeld and Nicolson, 1956], p. 36).

7. V.I. Lenin, *Collected Works*, 45 vols. (Moscow: Progress Publishers, 1960–70), vol. 5, p. 361.

8. Struve's article "Die Marxische Theorie der sozialen Entwicklung" (in *Archiv für soziale Gesetzgebung und Statistik*, vol. 14 [Berlin, 1899] echoed Bernstein in its radical critique of the "utopian side" of Marxism. Lenin's early work "The Economic Content of Populism and Its Criticism in Mr. Struve's Book" (referring to Struve's *Critical Remarks on the Economic Development of Russia*, 1894) rejected Struve's "objectivism" in the name of a class standpoint in scholarship. It contained also an elaborate argument for the alliance with the peasantry and *against* the alliance with "bourgeois liberals."

9. Plekhanov, like Engels, tried to combine scientism and Darwinian naturalism with Hegelian dialectics. This led, of course, to a deep distortion of genuine dialectics. Nevertheless, this quasi-Hegelian component in Plekhanov's Marxism justified the search for a rational pattern and meaning in history, which was not quite consistent with naturalistic positivism. According to Ivanov-Razumnik, this peculiar feature of the Marxism of Engels and Plekhanov helped Russian thinkers to pass from historical materialism to philosophical idealism (see Ivanov-Razumnik, *Istoriia russkoi obshchestvennoi mysli*, 2nd ed., 2 vols. [St. Petersburg: M.M. Stasiulevich, 1908], vol. 2, p. 450).

10. For a detailed presentation of Novgorodtsev's ideas, see chapter 5 of my *Legal Philosophies of Russian Liberalism* (Oxford: Clarendon Press, 1987; paperback edition published by the University of Notre Dame Press, 1992).

11. It was published in *Voprosy filosofii i psikhologii*, vol. 17, no. 85 (1906), pp. 508–45.

12. See his article "Pravda sotsializma," in *Novoe religioznoe soznanie i obshchestvennost'* (St. Petersburg: M.V. Pirozhkov, 1907), pp. 102–3.

13. See N. Berdiaev, "Socialism as Religion," in *A Revolution of the Spirit: Crisis of Value in Russia, 1890–1924*, ed. B. Glatzer Rosenthal and M. Bohachevsky-Chomiak (New York: Fordham University Press, 1990), p. 108.

14. Ibid., p. 109.

15. The term 'ideocracy' is not yet used in this article. Berdiaev introduced it in his later works, especially in *The Origins of Russian Communism*, where he defined 'ideocracy' as "pseudomorphosis of theocracy" (see N. Berdiaev, *Istoki i smysl russkogo kommunizma* [Paris: YMCA Press, 1955], p. 137).

16. Berdiaev, "Socialism as Religion," p. 109.

17. Ibid., p. 119.

18. K. Marx, *Theories of Surplus Value*, 2 vols. (Moscow: Progress Publishers, 1969), vol. 2, p. 118.

19. In his letter to P.A. Annenkov of 28 December 1846, Marx wrote: "Without slavery North America, the most progressive country, would be transformed into a patriarchal land. You have only to wipe North America off the map of the nations and you get anarchy, the total decay of trade and of modern civilization. But to let slavery disappear is to wipe North America off the map of nations" (K. Marx and F. Engels, *Selected Works*, 3 vols. [Moscow: Progress Publishers, 1977], vol. 1, p. 524).

20. K. Marx, *Selected Writings*, ed. D. McLellan (Oxford: Oxford University Press, 1985), p. 336 (the quotation is from "The Future Results of British Rule in India," an article Marx wrote for *The New York Daily Tribune* in 1853).

21. This similarity explains the phenomenon of so-called "Nietzschean Marxism." See G.L. Kline, "Nietzschean Marxism in Russia," *Boston College Studies in Philosophy*, vol. 2 (1969).

22. Berdiaev, "Socialism as Religion," p. 112.

23. Berdiaev was well acquainted with Mikhailovskii's ideas because his first book, *Sub"ektivizm i individualizm v obshchestvennoi filosofii* (published in St. Petersburg in 1900), was devoted to Mikhailovskii's social philosophy. Belinskii, especially as a critic of Hegelian historiodicy, was one of Berdiaev's favorite thinkers.

24. Ibid., pp. 114, 116.

25. Ibid., p. 114.

26. Ibid., p. 129. Of course, the term 'totalitarianism' was then unknown.

27. It is now obvious that Marxism as a scientific method, that is, as historical materialism, does not involve commitment to Marxism as communist utopia. Some of the best Marxologists (J.Y. Calvez in France, Stanley Moore in the United States) have rightly pointed out that there is a tension between Marxism as an all-embracing theory of communism and Marxism as historical materialism. The latter deals with historical processes as made by humans but not designed by them—in other words, it is a theory of the unintended results of human action, of creating history within the structure of alienation, without the possibility of controlling its course. In contrast with this, Marx's theory of communism presupposes conscious steering of historical processes, assuming, therefore, that consciousness would no longer be determined by life, that men would be not only actors in but also authors of their history. For an elaboration of this distinction, see J.Y. Calvez, *La pensée de Karl Marx* (Paris: Editions du Seuil, 1956), pp. 533–34; and Stanley Moore, *Marx on the Choice Between Socialism and Communism* (Cambridge, MA, and London: Harvard University Press, 1980), pp. 18, 90.

28. The most notable exception to this was, of course, Rosa Luxemburg.

29. Berdiaev, "Socialism as Religion," pp. 112–13.

30. Ibid., pp. 122–23.

31. Marx, *Selected Writings*, p. 89.

32. Ibid., p. 92.

33. L. Trotsky, *Literature and Revolution* (Ann Arbor, MI: The University of Michigan Press, 1966), p. 256.

34. L. Trotsky, *Terrorism and Communism* (Westport, CT: Greenwood Press, 1986), p. 170.

35. Berdiaev, "Socialism as Religion," pp. 128–29.

36. Ibid., p. 112.

37. S. Bulgakov, *Ot marksizma k idealizmu: Sbornik statei (1896–1903)* (St. Petersburg: Obshchestvennaia pol'za, 1903), p. ix.

38. Ibid., p. 122.

39. Ibid., pp. ix-x. By Marxist eschatology Bulgakov meant the belief in the inevitable collapse of capitalism (the so-called *Zusammenbruchstheorie*).

40. Ibid., p. xiv.

41. Ibid., pp. 140–41.

42. The titles of these articles are "Ivan Karamazov kak filosofskii tip" (1901) and "Dushevnaia drama Gertsena" (1902).

43. Bulgakov, *Ot marksizma k idealizmu*, p. 105.

44. Ibid., p. 109.

45. Ibid., p. 108.

46. Ibid., pp. 105–6.

47. Ibid., p. 98.

48. See G.F. Putnam, *Russian Alternatives to Marxism: Christian Socialism and Idealistic Liberalism in Twentieth-Century Russia* (Knoxville, TN: University of Tennessee Press, 1977).

49. In *Moskovskii ezhenedel'nik*, 1906, nos. 22–25. It was published as a separate pamphlet in St. Petersburg in 1907. Reprinted in S.N. Bulgakov, *Filosofiia khoziaistva* (Moscow: Nauka, 1990), pp. 310–42.

50. See Bulgakov, *Filosofiia khoziaistva*, p. 311.

51. Ibid., pp. 313–14.

52. Ibid., p. 317.

53. See *Auf dem literarischen Nachlass von K. Marx, F. Engels und F. Lassalle*, ed. F. Mehring, 4 vols. (Stuttgart, 1902). The first two volumes of this publication contained Marx's and Engels's works of 1841–47.

54. Bulgakov, *Filosofiia khoziaistva*, p. 336.

55. Ibid., p. 338.

56. Ibid., p. 326.

57. Ibid., pp. 331–32.

58. Moore, *Marx on the Choice*, p. 9.

59. The only book that dealt with this problem was Thomas G. Masaryk's *Die Philosophischen und Sociologischen Grundlagen des Marxismus*, published in 1899. Bulgakov referred to chapter 9 of this book ("Die religiose Frage"), containing an analysis of Marx's essay "On the Jewish Question." See Bulgakov, *Filosofiia khoziaistva*, p. 318.

60. See A. Walicki, "Karl Marx as Philosopher of Freedom," *Critical Review*, vol. 2, no. 4 (Fall 1988), pp. 10–58.

61. Bulgakov, *Filosofiia khoziaistva*, p. 341.

62. Ibid., pp. 341–42.

63. N.K. Berdiaev, "K istorii i psikhologii russkogo marksizma" (1906), in *Sub specie aeternitatis* (St. Petersburg: M.V. Pirozhkov, 1907), p. 390.

64. Berdiaev, "Pravda sotsializma," pp. 113 and 122–29.

65. He devoted to this problem a series of articles in *Voprosy filosofii i psikhologii* over the years 1911–17, collected in book form as *Ob obshchestvennom ideale* (Moscow, 1917; revised ed. Berlin: Slovo, 1922).

66. For an excellent formulation of the programmatically antichiliastic and anti-utopian tendency in Kant's philosophy, see G.A. Kelly, *Idealism, Politics, and History. Sources of Hegelian Thought* (Cambridge: Cambridge University Press, 1969), pp. 114–15 and 127–31.

67. See E. Trubetskoi, *Mirosozertsanie V.S. Solov'eva*, 2 vols. (Moscow: A.I. Mamontov, 1913), vol. 1, pp. 111, 564–84.

68. Cf., E. Voegelin, *The New Science of Politics* (Chicago, IL: University of Chicago Press, 1987), pp. 119–20.

69. See P.I. Novgorodtsev, *Ob obshchestvennom ideale*, ed. A.V. Sobolev (Moscow: Pressa, 1991), pp. 146, 214–18, 228. Novgorodtsev was even more consistent than Bulgakov in interpreting Marxism as a further development of Feuerbachianism;

he criticized Bulgakov for his statement that Marx took up only the "critical side" of Feuerbach's philosophy, claiming that in fact Marx embraced also Feuerbach's "anthropotheism." See ibid., p. 146, fn. 1.

70. See ibid., pp. 272–79.

71. Ibid., p. 271.

72. Marx and Engels, *Selected Works*, vol. 3, p. 18.

73. Ibid.

74. Ibid., p. 19.

75. Novgorodtsev, *Ob obshchestvennom ideale*, pp. 313–14.

76. This was emphasized also by Berdiaev, who pointed out that Marx wanted everything to be arranged rationally, so that life would be completely rationalized. See Berdiaev, "Socialism as Religion," p. 124.

77. Novgorodtsev, *Ob obshchestvennom ideale*, p. 315.

78. Engels's words from his pamphlet *Socialism: Utopian and Scientific* (see Marx and Engels, *Selected Works*, vol. 3, p. 150).

79. Novgorodtsev, *Ob obshchestvennom ideale*, p. 321.

80. See ibid., pp. 302–3, fn. 3.

81. See ibid., p. 271, fn. 1.

82. Two other books mentioned in this context were F. Mauthner, *Der Bolschevismus, seines Verhältnisses zum Marxismus* (Berlin, 1920), and H. Cunow, *Die Marxische Geschichts-gesellschafts- und Staatstheorie* (Berlin, 1920); see ibid., p. 271.

83. Ibid.

84. Ibid., p. 419.

85. Ibid., p. 522.

86. Ibid., p. 521.

87. Ibid., p. 522.

88. Ibid., p. 237.

89. See ibid., pp. 221–22. In pointing out the contrast between historical materialism as the explanation of the reified "kingdom of necessity" and communism as the "kingdom of freedom," Novgorodtsev anticipated, to a certain extent, the views of young Lukacs (in his *Geschichte und Bewusstsein*) and the interpretations of some contemporary Marxologists (see note 27 above).

90. Ibid., p. 395.

PIAMA P. GAIDENKO

5 | The Philosophy of Freedom of Nikolai Berdiaev

Russian philosophy, as well as Russian culture in general, is now faced with a historic task—to put the time back into joint. The revolution of 1917, followed by the civil war and many decades of "barracks communism," broke the natural chain of spiritual development in the country, tearing us away from our tradition. This situation was especially onerous for philosophy: the burden of ideological dogmas allowed for no freedom of thought. Now, at last, we have the right to speak freely, and we must rediscover and reconsider what was accomplished during this period, both by world philosophical thought and by the Russian philosophy that continued its life in emigration. And we must reconsider it in the light of our own experience —the experience of living "under the rubble" of a totalitarian regime.

Nikolai Berdiaev is without question one of the most brilliant and influential thinkers of the Russian Silver Age. In Russia, intellectuals and scholars rediscovered Berdiaev's works long ago; as far back as the end of the fifties, his works (not easily obtained) were read, retyped, and passed on to others. The interest in his writings was prompted by the fact that Berdiaev dealt as a rule with critical social and political topics, and his aphoristic style, his ability to express his ideas clearly and graphically, and his stance as a social commentator permitted him to be read with almost no special preparation. That is why it was Berdiaev's works that helped many of us, born and raised in a "closed" society, to understand what was going on in our country and to find our way not only in philosophy but in life—which for the most part amounts to the same thing.

It was a great event in my intellectual life, in particular, to open in 1959 the journal *Put'* (The Way), which Berdiaev published in Paris beginning in 1925. All the issues of that journal were preserved in the "special archives" of the Lenin Library, and for three months, putting aside my dissertation on Heidegger, I read one issue after another. There I found answers to many painful questions: for me the journal *Put'* proved to be more than a university.

Berdiaev's thought reflected the spiritual atmosphere of the two pre-revolutionary decades. Banished from the country in 1922 together with other independent philosophers, Berdiaev had the opportunity to think over what had taken place in Russia before his eyes and with his participation. This living testimony has great value for us today. But in order to understand his testimony adequately, it is necessary to grasp his philosophical position, which determined the "angle of refraction" from which he viewed what transpired. For if we wish to recover our philosophical heritage, we must not treat it as a dead museum piece to be carefully preserved as it is. It is a living heritage, and everything living is characterized by further development. Everything true and enduring in it should become our own possession, and our task is to separate, by means of sober critical analysis, what is enduring from those features that bear the stamp of their epoch and thus are finite and transient.

Man was always at the center of Berdiaev's philosophical interest: no matter how his political sympathies and philosophical enthusiasms changed, no matter what influences he experienced in the course of his development, his thought was centered on human beings, their freedom, their fate, the meaning and goal of their existence. In this sense Berdiaev is a deeply Russian thinker; in this lies his kinship with Russian literature and Russian art. "The entire world is nothing in comparison with human personality, with the unique person of a man, with his unique fate."[1]

According to Berdiaev, each human personality is something unique and unrepeatable; it cannot be explained in terms of any other sort of reality, either natural or social, and cannot be reduced to it. "Personality," he writes, "is not a part and cannot be a part in relation to any kind of whole, not even to an immense whole, or to the entire world."[2]

Berdiaev distinguishes the notion of personality from the notion of an empirical human being, who is on the one hand a part of nature and on the other an element of the social whole. The empirically existing human being, considered from the natural point of view as having a certain bodily and spiritual organization, is, according to Berdiaev, not a *personality* but an *individual*. As an individual he has sociocultural peculiarities of his own, which distinguish him from other individuals belonging to other social organisms. Thus an individual is determined both by society and by nature and is, in Berdiaev's words, a particle of the universe. Personality, according to Berdiaev, is a spiritual reality, and therefore "no law at all is applicable to it."[3] It cannot be made an object of scientific research—that is the thesis that links Berdiaev's existential philosophy with the conceptions of man of Kierkegaard, Jaspers, Heidegger, and Sartre. The fundamental characteristic of personality is its *freedom*: personality, according to Berdiaev, does not merely *possess* freedom, it *is* freedom.

Thus Berdiaev rejects the definitions of man offered by traditional philosophy. He does not accept the notion of substance as a feature of man's being, though in his early period, under the influence of Russian neo-Leibnizian ideas, he was inclined to regard man as a spiritual substance—a monad. However, in the thirties he gave up thinking in terms of such traditional categories as substance and even being. Personality, according to Berdiaev, is not substance but a creative act; it is resistance, rebellion, struggle, "victory over the dragging burden of the world, the triumph of freedom over the world's slavery."[4]

Berdiaev does not agree with the definition of man, going back to ancient philosophy, as a being whose possession of reason distinguishes him from other animals. Of course man is a rational being, but for Berdiaev this is not his chief distinction. To reduce man to reason would mean, according to Berdiaev, to deprive him of his uniqueness, of his unrepeatability, and hence of his personality. "Reason in itself is not personal, but universal, common, impersonal reason. . . . The Greek understanding of man as a rational being, does not fit in with personalist philosophy."[5]

This reveals the very core of Berdiaev's personalism or existentialism: the philosopher fears above all the dissolution of personality into some impersonal element, its loss of self-sufficiency, of independence—in a word, of freedom. In whatever way this impersonal element is conceived —whether as natural-cosmic, as social, or even (strange to say) as moral-rational—it is in any case, Berdiaev is deeply convinced, dangerous for personality; it threatens personality with slavery. In his mature years as well as in his early period, Berdiaev rejects the moral reason of Kantian idealism as the supreme law for man, for every law is a limitation, whereas personality, according to Berdiaev, must be free. "The moral and rational nature of man with Kant is an impersonal common nature."[6] Thus the philosopher rejects not only the law of necessity but the law of the good, the law of rational action, because the latter is also universal.

Berdiaev is especially opposed to the universal as it appears in the social sphere, as the power of the state, the nation, the people, the collective, over personality. Here he touches upon one of the most acute and painful problems of our age, which is the age of totalitarian regimes, of mass types of community that are despotic and intolerant of individual freedom. Here lies the profound truth of Berdiaev's rejection of the impersonal element, the enduring significance of his proclaimed principle of freedom of personality, the value of personalism. Perhaps for the twentieth century there is no topic more important than the topic of "man and the collective," and this is the pivot of Berdiaev's thought.[7]

A distinguishing feature of Berdiaev's philosophy of man is a consciously adopted *paradoxicalism*, a stress on the incompatibility of man's basic characteristics.

> The superhuman principle is a constituent element of man's nature. . . . The very fact of the existence of man is a break in the natural world and proves that nature cannot be self-sufficient but rests upon a supernatural reality. As an entity belonging to two worlds and capable of outgrowing himself man is a self-contradictory and paradoxical being, combining opposite poles within himself. With equal justice he may be said to be base and lofty, weak and strong, free and slavish.[8]

Christian anthropology in general regards man as a natural-supernatural being combining bodily and spiritual principles; as for Berdiaev, his anthropology is oriented rather toward the teaching of the German mystics, and therefore man for him is "the child of God and of non-being, of meonic freedom. His roots are in heaven, in God, and also in nethermost depths."[9]

Thus Berdiaev regards man as a denizen of three worlds—the divine, the natural, and the diabolical ("meonic"). It is the task of Berdiaev's doctrine of freedom—the most important subject of the Russian philosopher's reflections—to explain in what paradoxical way these worlds are combined in man.

As a philosopher Berdiaev was influenced on the one hand by Russian religious thought—above all by Fedor Dostoevskii and Vladimir Solov'ev—and on the other hand by German idealism and mysticism. In his youth he read Kant's *Critique of Pure Reason* and Hegel's *Phenomenology of Mind*. However, Kant's transcendentalism came to Berdiaev first in the interpretation of Schopenhauer. Both Kant and Schopenhauer proceed by counterposing two worlds—nature, or the phenomenal world ("representation," to use Schopenhauer's term); and freedom, or the noumenal world ("the world as will," according to Schopenhauer). The former is revealed to us from the outside, through the senses, and the latter is revealed from within. Whereas in the realm of nature man is subordinated to the law of necessity and is included, as a physical being, in the causal nexus of phenomena, in the realm of freedom he is a "thing in itself," a cause initiating a chain of phenomena.

These principles are common to Kant and Schopenhauer. The latter, however, interprets the noumenal world as the realm of a will that is a law unto itself—an irrational will, the essence of which is the insatiable tendency to *desire*. Will, as Schopenhauer understands it, is close to the concept of *passion*: it is ardent desiring, longing, and at the same time suffering, because of the impossibility of satisfaction. Satisfaction is always temporary and finite, whereas the striving and longing of the will are constant and infinite. Therefore, for will the world is a vale of sorrow and suffering.

Will, according to Schopenhauer, underlies all its objectivizations, which are in fact what comprise the world of "representation," subject to necessity and comprehended by means of the understanding. Will itself is given to each of us from within and is apprehended by intuition. Rejection of the world of the objectivization of will (that is, of the empirical world) as not true reality—this principle of Schopenhauer's was especially dear to Berdiaev.

There is a great difference between Kant's and Schopenhauer's understanding of free will. For Kant free will is practical reason subordinated to the law of the good—the Categorical Imperative—which is universal and which reads as follows: act so that the maxim of your will could be a principle of universal legislation. Expressed otherwise, the Categorical Imperative is a demand addressed to each individual to treat another person not merely as a means but as an end as well. Evil, according to Kant, is the result of man's subjection to his selfish inclinations, the inability to follow the law of the good because of his weak nature. For Schopenhauer, on the contrary, *will is beyond good and evil*: it is an irrational element precisely because it does not know this distinction, which is valid only on the plane of representation—the plane of the phenomenal not the real world. Will is not subject to the law of reason, including practical reason—such is Schopenhauer's conclusion.

On this point Berdiaev is closer to Schopenhauer. He rejects the interpretation of freedom as *subjection to the universal moral law*: subjection in general, regardless of its content, but especially subjection to a *universal* principle, is for the Russian philosopher the locus of slavery, unfreedom. Freedom means not to be subject to anyone or anything—that is Berdiaev's deep conviction. In one of his earlier articles he writes:

> The moral law demands above all that man should never be a slave, even if it be a slave to others' suffering and weakness and to his own pity for them; that man should never stifle his spirit, never give up his right to a vigorous life, to infinite development and perfection, even if it be for the sake of the well-being of others and the whole of society. The human self should never bend its proud head to anything but its own ideal of perfection, to its God, to whom alone it is answerable.[10]

No wonder that Berdiaev appears as an antagonist not only of Kant but also of the general European ethical and religious tradition—a tradition that has two sources, Christianity and ancient thought, and is based on the distinction between good and evil. Berdiaev, attempting to deepen and develop Nietzsche's amoralism, wants to create an ethics that is "beyond good and evil": "The highest value lies beyond good and evil. The force of the question is not often seen; as a rule, ethics is entirely on this side of good and evil, and the good is not a problem for it. Nietzsche did see the full force of it. He said that the will to truth is the death of morality."[11]

However, in Berdiaev's opinion even Nietzsche was not consistent enough; he preserved moral valuations by putting what is "beyond good" above what is "on this side":

> And, of course, Nietzsche was a moralist, he preached a new morality. . . . "Beyond" there should be neither good nor evil. . . . We shall reach a more satisfactory result when we grasp that our valuations relating to good and evil are symbolic and not real. "Good" and "evil," the "moral" and the "immoral," the "high" and the "low" do not express any real existent. . . . In its inmost being reality is neither good nor evil, neither moral nor immoral, but it is symbolized in this way.[12]

Berdiaev inherited from Kant the idea of the *autonomy of the will*, according to which nothing external, no authority, can be a law for my will; the will is free only when it imposes on itself a law to obey. "The human self," writes Berdiaev, "is above the judgment of other people, the judgment of society and even of the whole of being, because the only judge is that moral law which is the true essence of the self and which this self freely acknowledges."[13] Paradoxically, however, having accepted Kant's principle of autonomy, of the free acceptance of a self-imposed moral law, Berdiaev rejected the moral law itself, the requirement to subordinate the individual's willfulness to *duty*, which requires us to be guided by the rule: do not do unto others as you would not have them do unto you. Kantian autonomy of will does not rule out but presupposes subordination of individual inclinations and selfish aims to the welfare of other people. In this sense Kantian ethics is altruistic. As for Berdiaev, he thinks that subjection to any law, including a moral law, is slavery. But voluntary slavery is no better than compulsory slavery. "To cripple one's self, one's human individuality for the sake of duty: these words make no sense to us."[14]

Berdiaev replaces Kant's rational will with Schopenhauer's will, which was artistically portrayed in Nietzsche's *The Birth of Tragedy from the Spirit of Music* and which enchanted Russian as well as other philosophers and poets with its ecstatic, bacchanalian Dionysianism. In the light of the Dionysian outburst, Kantian ethics appears particularly banal, even vulgar. "Kant," writes Berdiaev, "interpreted in too old-fashioned a way the idea that human nature is sinful and spoiled, and arrived at a number of false ethical postulates that in essence negated the Dionysian principle of life."[15] The Dionysian principle of life is something that old Europe knew well: it is the very passion[16] that since the eighteenth century had continually been crowding out traditional *virtue*, which finally appeared unattractive and ludicrous, especially in the eyes of the romantically minded part of educated society. In the nineteenth century the romantics *demonized passion*, thereby imparting to it the halo of a theomachist principle, and in this tragic-demonic form it was aesthetically irresistible. It was through this prism that Berdiaev, who in his youth loved the demonic characters of Byron, Lermontov, Dostoevskii (especially Ivan Karamazov and Stavrogin), and Ibsen, perceived the idea of freedom.

Thus freedom for Berdiaev is the absence of any restraint, either from without or from within: self-restraint for him is as unfree as externally imposed prohibition. No wonder that the Russian philosopher writes that freedom is "divine life"; in the sense in which Berdiaev interprets freedom, only God can be free. But divine life of this sort is not given to man, for he is a finite, imperfect, and sinful creature, and with this Christian understanding of man Berdiaev cannot agree. On this point he agrees with the critique of Christianity and Christian ethics that Friedrich Nietzsche made the main task of his life.

Berdiaev also differs here, incidentally, from such representatives of German existentialism as Heidegger and Jaspers and from Soren Kierkegaard, the father of existentialism.

> Melancholy, gloomy, tragic Kierkegaard rules the minds of modern central Europe. The most interesting and important trend in theological and religious thought is Barthianism, which is permeated with an acute feeling of the sinfulness of man and the world and which interprets Christianity exclusively from the eschatological standpoint. This trend is a religious reaction against the liberal, humanistic, and romantic Protestantism of the nineteenth century. A similar reaction in Catholicism is neo-Thomism. But both *Barthianism and Thomism humiliate man*. Western Christianity is marked by *a weakened faith in man*, in his creative power, in his work in the world.[17]

Berdiaev does not share the Christian belief that the source of evil in the world is man—to be more precise, man's Fall[18]—and it is no accident that for him anthropology is Christology: for Berdiaev, in every man lives not merely God's image but God Himself, that is, Jesus Christ. According to Berdiaev Christ is Absolute man, and since Christ is the Son of God, so man, too, is a Son and not a creature.

It is characteristic that Berdiaev, even before writing *The Meaning of the Creative Act*, voiced the following maxim, as if he were arguing with

Dostoevskii: "In Christ all things are in a sense permitted."[19] But the question arises: How does one achieve "being in Christ"? This question, which so troubled the Christian ascetics, was apparently a simple matter for Berdiaev to resolve: man is already in Christ from the very beginning, but this truth is revealed to very few, and it is the task of a new religious consciousness to proclaim it. No wonder that the Russian philosopher also ascribes divine omnipotence to man: he is convinced that man, like God, is capable of creating out of nothing. That is why Berdiaev places human creativity above all else, seeing in it the road to man's self-salvation. "The creative act is not determined; it is always creation out of nothing, that is, out of freedom."[20] Berdiaev eliminates the medieval distinction between a finite and an infinite creator: he is convinced that the human spirit is infinite and in essence differs in no way from the divine spirit. It is understandable that V.V. Zen'kovskii characterized Berdiaev's doctrine of man as *anthropolatry*.[21]

Berdiaev's interpretation of man continues the romantic tradition that goes back to the Renaissance critique of medieval Christianity as an ascetic religion that humiliates man. Berdiaev regarded man not only as the creator of the world but, in a sense, as the creator of himself: "The creative act in a religious-cosmic sense is equal to redemption."[22] Man must make a kind of leap from the kingdom of necessity to the kingdom of freedom, creating a new, previously unknown world. The creative act becomes for Berdiaev a theurgic act, although in the last period of his life it acquires eschatological coloring: by his creative acts man must hasten the end of the world.

It is a premise of Berdiaev's utopian activism that at bottom the world is evil. Evil must have its source; if it is not of man, as Christianity teaches, it must be rooted in the very being of the world. Here we come to the most essential aspect of Berdiaev's concept of freedom—a concept that also, incidentally, goes back to Schopenhauer: "The source of slavery is objectivization."[23] Objectivization is opposed to the subject, to personality, to the human self in its freedom; born of will, objectivization becomes chains that bind the will. The object as such, objectivity, that which exists in itself, independently of the subject, is considered by the Russian philosopher to be the source of man's unfreedom. On this point Berdiaev bases himself not only on Schopenhauer but on Fichte as well.

> Consciousness which exteriorizes and alienates is always slavish consciousness. God the Master, man the slave; the church the master, man the slave; the state the master, man the slave; society the master, man the slave; the family the master, man the slave; Nature the master, man the slave; object the master, man-subject the slave. The source of slavery is always objectivization, that is to say exteriorization, alienation. . . . Putting an end to slavery is putting an end to objectivization.[24]

Thus slavery threatens man from every side, for each of his activities inevitably acquires the form of a certain product that is external to the actor himself. Consciousness itself is also an activity of objectivization, for an act of consciousness is directed toward something that is an object for it.

However, if not only society but also nature and even God are to be viewed as forms of the objectivization of subjectivity, it is evident that the subject must be understood not as an individual "self" but as an Absolute "Self," as was the case with Fichte. Our philosopher is interested in personality; as we know he does not accept the universal "Self" of Kantian–Fichtean philosophy. It is not surprising, then, that human personality gradually becomes divine and that anthropology becomes Christology. Such a person is no longer God's creature but God's Son, as Berdiaev says. And in respect to personality, to the man-God, the whole world of creatures is objectivization, unauthentic being, or simply evil. Therefore the only justified relation to the world and all its manifestations is negation, revolution, rebellion. Berdiaev wrote in his autobiography:

> But I have throughout sympathized with all the great rebels recorded in the annals of history: with the revolt of Luther against ecclesiastical tyranny, and of the Enlightenment against authority; with Rousseau's revolt of "nature" against "civilization," and the revolt of the French revolution against oppression; with the revolt of Idealism against the power of the objective, and Marx's revolt against capitalism; with Belinskii's revolt against the Hegelian world-spirit and world harmony, and the anarchistic revolt of Bakunin; with Leo Tolstoi's revolt against history and civilization, Nietzsche's rebellion against reason and morality, and Ibsen's revolt against society. Christianity itself is to me the embodiment of the revolt against the world and its laws and fashions.[25]

As we can see, in his late years Berdiaev remained the same revolutionary anarchist that he was in his youth. *Metaphysical anarchism is a characteristic feature of Berdiaev's philosophical position, of his personalism.* The overthrow of every objective regulation, of all objective order, is the heart of his philosophy of freedom.

The idea of a social revolution that is summoned to eliminate capitalism and the "power of the bourgeoisie," which Berdiaev hates as an aristocrat and as a representative of artistic bohemia,[26] unites him with Marxism, as does the ardent striving "not to explain the world but to change it." At the end of the nineteenth century, moving away from Marxism and criticizing materialism and the theory of class struggle, Berdiaev calls for a revolution in morals, religion, and the family and for the rejection of "historical Orthodoxy" with its asceticism and conservatism in the governmental and sexual spheres.

Berdiaev does move away from his former convictions for a time when, in 1909, he joins the other authors of the collection *Vekhi* (Landmarks) in criticizing the utopian revolutionarism of left-radical intellectuals. But in the twenties and thirties he returns to those convictions, conscious of the global character of his revolutionary ideas: to be negated now, he proclaims, are not only all forms of objectivization but being itself.

> The hierarchical order of being from God down to a beetle is a crushing order of things and abstractions. It is crushing and enslaving and there is no room for personality in it either as an ideal order or as a real order. Personality is outside all being. It stands in opposition to being.[27]

Earlier, when he regarded ontology as monadology, sharing the views of Aleksei Kozlov and Lev Lopatin, Berdiaev wrote: "We spontaneously comprehend and then cognize ourselves as being, as spiritual substance, as an 'I'."[28] As far back as 1916, in *The Meaning of the Creative Act*, the notion of being has a positive connotation. But the logic of his own thinking leads Berdiaev steadily to the rejection of being as such. He deeply sympathizes with ancient Gnosticism, with Marcion and Basilides, who rejected the world on the ground that it was created by an evil god, by the Old Testament Yahweh.[29] Berdiaev's reasoning is fully in the spirit of Marcion's; he does not doubt that the world is created by Satan: " 'The world' is evil, it is without God and not created by Him. We must go out of the world, overcome it completely: the world must be consumed, it is of the nature of Ariman. Freedom from the world is the *pathos* of this book."[30]

Already evident here is the main theme of Berdiaev's later works—the theme of the opposition of freedom and being. The rebellion against everything that is not the "self" is expressed by Berdiaev in the form of an aphorism: "Slavery to being is indeed the primary slavery of man."[31] No wonder that Berdiaev's book *The Divine and the Human* begins with the words of Max Stirner, a German philosopher who denied any sort of reality except the personal "I": "Max Stirner said, *'Ich habe meine Sache auf Nichts gestellt,'* 'I have based my case on Nothing.' I for my part say that I have based my case upon Freedom. Freedom is Nothing, in the sense that it is not one of the realities of the natural world, it is not a certain thing."[32]

In the attempt to base freedom on "nothing," Berdiaev turns to the doctrine, advanced by the German mystics (especially Jacob Boehme), of the Nothing—the *Ungrund* or "abyss" that is the source of the being of God Himself. According to Boehme, at the basis of the divine being is an unconscious, irrational "nature"—God's potency, which precedes His actual being.

> For the first time perhaps in the history of human thought, Boehme saw that at the basis of being and superior to being lies groundless freedom, the passionate desire of nothing to become something. . . . He is the founder of metaphysical voluntarism which was unknown alike to medieval thought and to the thought of the ancient world.[33]

For Boehme, Berdiaev goes on, freedom—that is, the irrational element, chaos, the "abyss"—is, thus, the root of everything existing, including God. "Primary passion lies in the depth of the world"[34]—this is how Berdiaev sums up Boehme's conception, returning thus to Schopenhauer and the romantic sources of his youth. German mysticism—Meister Eckhart, Angelus Silesius, Jacob Boehme—indeed provided the basis for German idealism and especially for Fichte's doctrine of the developing God, Schelling's theory of the "irrational nature" in God Himself, and Schopenhauer's conception of dark, irrational will as the principle of the world.

So, freedom for Berdiaev is nothing, potency, chaos, sheer possibility. And as such it is not simply prior to everything real, actual, or formed—prior to cosmos and logos. Not only is freedom prior to being, according to Berdiaev, it determines the path of being. "Consent to world creation is heard from the freedom of nothing, it is heard from the mysterious depths of potency."[35]

However, Berdiaev does not find Boehme's interpretation of the Nothing altogether satisfactory. He thinks that Boehme's Nothing, which is the "ground" or "groundlessness" in God, cannot guarantee man complete freedom, for it is the *divine* Nothing! And if man's freedom is rooted there, it means that man again falls into dependence upon God, albeit in an extremely weakened form. Therefore our philosopher makes a correction in the conception of the German mystics: the primordial Nothing should be treated as independent of God, as an entirely self-sufficient source—to be more precise, sourcelessness—and only thus can man's freedom be "saved."

In our opinion, this is a purely *Luciferian freedom* that differs in no way from sheer arbitrariness, though Berdiaev did not want to be understood in this way. Interpreting the beginning of the world as pure potency and seeing in the latter the source and mystery of man's freedom, the Russian philosopher rightly points out that in ancient Greece (in medieval Christian theology as well, we may add) pure potency was conceived as matter, chaos, nonbeing. But freedom, as Berdiaev conceives it, is precisely this chaos or matter, and Berdiaev not only sees this very well but insists on it. "The world is not created out of matter," writes the philosopher, "but out of freedom, for the nothing is not matter but freedom."[36]

But *renaming* matter as freedom changes nothing! If at the ground of everything existing lies chaos and nonbeing, then the world is evil. But this evil comes not from a God who created it but from that same freedom that in the beginning, like the matter of the Greeks, was beyond God and from which comes Berdiaev's freedom, valued more highly than any being.[37] Berdiaev thinks that this irrational element of freedom was discovered only in the Christian era, for "the Greeks feared infinity, whereas freedom as an irrational element contains infinity, the possibility of the triumph of chaos. This freedom for the Greeks is the triumph of matter. True freedom is the triumph of form."[38] In the Christian era irrational freedom was discovered, and the dogma of the Fall, Berdiaev points out, is connected with it. "Acceptance of the idea of the Fall," he continues, "is acceptance of the truth that at the base of the world process lies primordial, irrational freedom."[39]

It might seem that Berdiaev is right here—that man is created free and that God has never encroached upon his freedom. But this reasoning contains another assumption. To say that the world process began with the Fall means to put the latter in the place of divine creation as that from which the world process took its start. What is more, it means to ascribe to Satan— for the sources of the Fall include not only man's freedom but also the temptation by the Serpent—the act of world creation that rightly belongs to the Other. There is a certain logic in this. To insist on freedom that is a law unto itself, freedom that at bottom is Nothing and is opposed to Being, means to insist not simply on human but rather on Luciferian freedom—the freedom of Cain, to which the young romantic Berdiaev so often appealed, enthralled by the character of the super-romantic Stavrogin.[40] Two central ideas in Berdiaev's thought meet here: the negation of "this world" as the handiwork of an "evil God," and the conviction that man is above all creatures and *above God*: for as a personification of freedom—that is, of *nonbeing*—he is not only *prior to God*, he is above God. The primacy of freedom over being means, finally, the primacy of man not only over the world but over God.

In this light it is no surprise that rebellion, negation, and revolution are the final word of Berdiaev's personalism: this is the consequence of the attitude of "mystic Gnosticism" that was always characteristic of the philosopher and that remained the basic theme of his thought despite some particular shifts of emphasis.

Berdiaev can be called a philosophical representative of neoromanticism, a frame of mind that was very characteristic of the Russian Silver Age and was represented especially vividly in poetry by a pleiad of symbolists who revived the spirit of mysticism that never died in romanticism.

Mysticism is a striving beyond the boundaries of the world, a detachment from its riches and diversity. Often the rejection of the world is fraught with a mood of rebellion; it is no mere chance that the spirit of revolution was brought to Europe by Protestantism, one of the sources of which was the antitraditionalism of mystical currents and sects that broke with the past and sought God in the depths of the individual self. In this sense Berdiaev is not far from the truth when he speaks of the "revolutionary-mystical mood" characteristic of people with "the new religious consciousness": "New religious people, people of a future religion of freedom, must do away with hypocritical moralism, must challenge the state-family improvement associations and yield to the revolutionary-mystical mood in which the problem of sex and love is posed and resolved religiously, rather than positively, socially, or morally."[41]

In the Russian Silver Age, everything connected with hatred of "improvements in living," of the philistinism connected with such living, of bourgeois vulgarity and banality, invariably had a "revolutionary-mystical" coloring; such was Blok's "world conflagration," Ivanov's "Dionysian orgy," Berdiaev's craving for "the end of this world." Ecstatism is the name of this mood. Tragism is its keynote. Utopianism is its approach to ontological, epistemological, and social problems. Chiliasm is its last word, the summing up of this mood.

What an astonishing thing is human consciousness! Berdiaev was among those people of tender conscience who, along with Dostoevskii's characters, would give back to God their "ticket of admission" if the price of "world harmony" was one tear of an innocent child. But then millions of lives, including the lives of children and innocents, were sacrificed to the Moloch of revolution and civil war. And what did we see? Did Berdiaev turn away in anger and disgust from his beloved theme of revolution? Not at all! Petulantly answering those who reproached him with utopianism, our philosopher writes: "Hypocritical and false is the argument of conservative and bourgeois Christianity that it is impossible to transform society because of the sinfulness of human nature."[42] As in his youth, Berdiaev in the thirties and forties is still convinced that it is the world that is sinful and spoiled, not man, and he continues to expose the "evil of the world": "I do not accept God's world," Berdiaev says, repeating the words of Ivan Karamazov, for they give him the right to say: "Communism is right when it puts an end to the sin found in society."[43]

Berdiaev was one of those who in our cruel age exposed the false and inhuman character of totalitarian regimes, including the Stalinist regime. His works helped many of us in the fifties and sixties to open our eyes to what was going on in our society. He sternly condemned violence and terror, which had become the everyday practice of totalitarian states, and he defended the person's inalienable right to freedom. The quest for spiritual freedom is the keynote of Berdiaev's thought. And he was often very insightful in this regard. Denouncing fanaticism as alien to spiritual freedom, the philosopher writes: "No fanaticism of any kind must ever be allowed. We must struggle for spiritual freedom and spiritual liberation in the realm of thought, in the state, in the family, in social life."[44] The enduring significance of Berdiaev's philosophy, its innermost truth, lies in its defense of spiritual freedom.

But being an advocate of the abolition of every kind of state, every "external establishment," Berdiaev as a maximalist and extremist proved blind to the distinction among *forms of the state*: he saw no essential difference between a liberal-constitutional, law-based state system and an authoritarian system, because *any kind of state* was for him a Leviathan that subordinates personality to the collective and deprives it of freedom. It is characteristic that among the "truths of communism" Berdiaev lists "criticism of formal democracy,"[45] since he cannot accept the "bourgeois state" in any form. As G.P. Fedotov points out,

> Berdiaev . . . was never an orthodox Marxist, if only because he was never a materialist. But even his break with Marx was not complete or final. In emigration he was gradually returning to the teacher of his youth. He valued Marx first and foremost as a critic of the capitalist system who mercilessly stripped away its masks and fictions. But he also saw in him earmarks of the humanist, struggling against the dehumanization of the worker by the machine and the impersonal economic order.[46]

It is not only the criticism of formal democracy that allies Berdiaev with Marxism. Inwardly close to him is the spirit of Marx's theomachism or Prometheanism. In his article "The Truth and Falsity of Communism" Berdiaev likewise approves the political organization and regulation of the economy, the centralization of economic policy—that is, in essence what we today call the command-administrative, bureaucratic system. And this is understandable, for Berdiaev identifies economic freedom with the capitalism he hates.

Underlying these (unexpectedly totalitarian) tendencies in the philosopher's attitude toward the law-based state is, in the end, his disdain not only for the state as such but, what is more, for any sort of givenness, for any "objectivization"—in the final analysis, for being in general.

Today, exiled Russian philosophy is returning to its native soil. We are recovering our historical memory, which will help us to comprehend our fate and, by tying together the broken threads of history, consciously to build our future. Near and dear to us is the main theme of Berdiaev's thought—the theme of personality, freedom, man's search for the meaning of his existence, his conviction that man cannot "establish himself on the Earth without God." But if we do not want a repetition of what happened to Russia in the twentieth century, we must read Berdiaev soberly and realistically, without succumbing to the temptations of utopianism, maximalism, and extremism; without being seduced into deifying man; without forgetting that although man is created in the image and likeness of God, still he is not God, he is a finite being. And being—the being both of the world and of man himself—is *granted* to him, *not created* by him. The negation and destruction of being as such is an evil path that we must not take. The proud romantic attitude of "rejection of God's world" should, I believe, give way to the awareness that it is not nature and not God but man that is the source of evil and sin in the world. This awareness is not the humiliation but the sobering and subduing of man, and in the final analysis it is the source of his true and creative power, not his imaginary, destructive power.

Notes

1. N. Berdyaev, *Slavery and Freedom*, trans. R.M. French (New York: Scribner's, 1944), p. 20.
2. Ibid., p. 21.
3. Ibid., p. 24.
4. Ibid.
5. Ibid., pp. 24–25.
6. Ibid.
7. "Of all the forms of slavery to which man is liable," writes the philosopher, "the greatest importance attaches to the slavery of man to society. Man has been a socialized creature all through the long millennia of civilized life. And the sociological doctrine of man would persuade us that it is precisely that socialization which has created man. Man lives, as it were, in a social hypnosis. And it is difficult for him to set his freedom in opposition to the despotic claims of society, because the social hypnosis, through the lips of sociologists of various schools of thought, convinces him that he has received his very freedom from society and from society alone. Society, so to speak, says to man: You are my creation; everything that is best in you has been put there by me, and therefore you belong to me and you ought to give your whole self back to me" (ibid., p. 102).
8. N. Berdyaev, *The Destiny of Man*, trans. Natalie Duddington (New York: Harper and Bros., 1960), pp. 45–46.
9. Ibid., p. 46.
10. N. Berdyaev, *Sub specie aeternitatis* (St. Petersburg: M.V. Pirozhkov, 1907), p. 88. The article, "Eticheskaia problema v svete filosofskogo idealizma," was first published in *Problemy idealizma*, ed. P.I. Novgorodtsev (St. Petersburg: Moscow Psychological Society, 1902).
11. Berdyaev, *The Destiny of Man*, p. 17.
12. Ibid., pp. 17–18 (the words "he preached a new morality" were omitted by the

translator and have been added to this quotation—Ed.). Here Berdiaev goes further than Schopenhauer, since the latter postulated "beyond good and evil" an unconscious vital element—will—which he considered to be a source of evil and suffering, and it is in *overcoming* will that he saw the moral principle.

13. Berdiaev, *Sub specie aeternitatis*, p. 88.

14. Ibid., p. 93.

15. Ibid., p. 94.

16. "People, and particularly philosophers, who are engaged in intellectual pursuits, are apt to believe that the world consists exclusively of the figments of their intellect and is the embodiment of their rationalizations. In point of fact, the world is both torn and held together by passions, which alone make it worth the knowing, while the extinction of passion brings the commonplace, with its unmeaning and unreality, into being" (N. Berdiaev, *Dream and Reality: An Essay in Autobiography*, trans. Katharine Lampert [New York: Collier Books, 1962], p. 92).

17. N. Berdiaev, "Dukhovnoe sostoianie sovremennogo mira," *Put'*, 1932, no. 35, p. 21 (italics added).

18. For Berdiaev the Fall proves man's power and exaltation: "The idea of the Fall is at bottom a proud idea, and through it man escapes from the sense of humiliation. If man fell away from God, he must have been an exalted creature, endowed with great freedom and power" (*The Destiny of Man*, p. 26).

19. Here the paradoxical ethics of "beyond good and evil" is already outlined.

20. N. Berdiaev, "Metafizicheskaia problema svobody," *Put'*, 1928, no. 9, p. 59.

21. V.V. Zenkovsky, *A History of Russian Philosophy*, trans. George L. Kline, 2 vols. (London: Routledge and Kegan Paul, 1953), vol. 2, p. 767.

22. Berdiaev, "Metafizicheskaia problema svobody," p. 59.

23. Berdyaev, *Slavery and Freedom*, p. 59.

24. Ibid., p. 61.

25. Berdyaev, *Dream and Reality,* pp. 63–64 (the words "Nietzsche's rebellion against reason and morality" were omitted by the translator and have been added to this quotation—Ed.).

26. The philistine, the shopkeeper, the bourgeois are objects of the philosopher's profound scorn. "Besides the social bourgeoisie we must acknowledge the deep spiritual and cultural bourgeoisie of the nineteenth century," wrote Berdiaev in 1901 (*Sub specie aeternitatis*, p. 10).

27. Berdyaev, *Slavery and Freedom*, p. 80.

28. Berdiaev, *Sub specie aeternitatis*, p. 174. The quotation is from the 1904 article "O novom russkom idealizme."

29. See N. Berdyaev, *The Meaning of the Creative Act*, trans. Donald A. Lowrie (New York: Harper and Bros., 1955), pp. 128–29.

30. Ibid., pp. 15–16.

31. Berdyaev, *Slavery and Freedom*, p. 78.

32. N. Berdyaev, *The Divine and the Human*, trans. R.M. French (London: Geoffrey Bles, 1949), p. v.

33. N. Berdyaev, *The Beginning and the End*, trans. R.M. French (New York: Harper and Bros., 1957), p. 107.

34. Ibid., p. 112.

35. Berdiaev, "Metafizicheskaia problema svobody," p. 57.

36. Ibid., p. 59.

37. It is no wonder that V.N. Losskii said that Berdiaev was obsessed by the "obscurantism of freedom": in Berdiaev's interpretation freedom is demonism; it is evil, prior to and above good.

38. Berdiaev, "Metafizicheskaia problema svobody," p. 58.

39. Ibid.

40. It is noteworthy that D.S. Merezhkovskii paid attention to this point, seeing in Berdiaev's doctrine of freedom the possibility of its turning into "diabolical chaos": "One must love in order to be free. Freedom is not prior to love, but love is prior to freedom. Be free and you shall know the truth—that is a delusion of Mangodhood. Know the truth—that is, love—and you shall be free—that is the truth of Godmanhood. What is called anarchy vacillates between this delusion and this truth. . . . Anarchy in the name of freedom *without love* is the road not to divine order but to diabolical chaos" (D.S. Merezhkovskii, "O novom religioznom deistvii [Otkrytoe pis'mo N.A. Berdiaevu]," in *Bol'naia Rossiia* [Leningrad: Leningrad University, 1991], p. 99).

41. Berdiaev, *Sub specie aeternitatis*, p. 357.

42. N. Berdiaev, "Pravda i lozh' kommunizma," *Put'*, 1931, no. 30, p. 23.

43. Ibid.

44. Berdyaev, *The Destiny of Man*, p. 173.

45. Berdiaev, "Pravda i lozh' kommunizma," p. 28.

46. G.P. Fedotov, *Novyi grad*, ed. Iu.P. Ivask (New York: Chekhov Press, 1952), pp. 309–10.

6 | Merezhkovskii's Readings of Tolstoi: Their Contemporary Relevance

> *The ancient Greeks had Homer's Iliad and Odyssey, the Arabs*
> *have the Koran, we have the novels of Tolstoi and Dostoevskii.*
>
> Iurii Davydov, 1982[1]

Dmitrii Merezhkovskii's *L. Tolstoi and Dostoevskii, Life and Art. A Study* (1900–1901) opens with a prediction—the choices of his generation of Russians will "determine the future, not only of Russia, but of the entire world."[2] Merezhkovskii was referring to the religious choices of persons who matured in the 1870s and 1880s. He believed that the apocalypse was imminent, that Russians must choose between Christ and Anti-Christ, and that literature should guide them. The life and work of great writers served as a text from which to proselytize his own ideas. The very first work to treat Tolstoi and Dostoevskii as religious writers, Merezhkovskii's study contrasted the life, work, and religion of one with the other, and with Nietzsche. Partly because of Merezhkovskii's prominence as the initiator and chief proselytizer of God-seeking, his study became the point of departure for early twentieth-century discussions of the two literary giants.[3] He was a cofounder of the Religious-Philosophical Society of St. Petersburg and of the review *Novyi put'* (New path, 1903–4), and his historical novels were international best-sellers.

Merezhkovskii's prediction came true. The choices made by his generation, to which Gor'kii and Lenin also belonged, did shape the course of Russian and world history. From Merezhkovskii's point of view, Russians opted for the Anti-Christ.

The writings of the God-seekers were banned in the early 1920s, but in the 1970s and 1980s they were rediscovered by Soviet intellectuals, who circulated them illegally in samizdat. In response, official publications attempted to expose God-seeking's class-based and reactionary nature.[4] In

1988, however, Gorbachev sanctioned their publication as part of his call for "new thinking." A veritable explosion of interest in the God-seekers followed, as Russians sought to fill in the "blank spots" of their history, reconnect with their lost cultural roots, and taste long-forbidden fruit. But it is not only these factors. The God-seekers' rejection of positivism speaks directly to contemporary Russians disillusioned with communism.

Merezhkovskii's prediction may have a second life. The choices made by the present generation of Russians may also "determine the future, not only of Russia, but of the entire world."

Literary criticism has extraliterary significance everywhere, but it was especially important in nineteenth- and twentieth-century Russia, where conditions of censorship led to the creation of an "aesopian language" in which writers' names served as symbols or codewords for ideas that could not be spelled out. The complexities, ambiguities, and contradictions in the life and work of Tolstoi and Dostoevskii permitted critics of different ideological schools to make them into positive or negative symbols, in accord with their own views. Merezhkovskii did both. In *Tolstoi and Dostoevskii*, he praised Dostoevskii and debunked, or, more accurately, "deconstructed," Tolstoi. As his views changed and as new issues arose, Merezhkovskii's treatment of them shifted accordingly, but far more drastically with respect to Tolstoi, whom he "reconstructed" as a freedom fighter, prophet, and saint—however, always with qualifications.

The issues that concern a particular generation vary, and this is reflected in their readings of great writers. Merezhkovskii helped define the issues of Tolstoi and Dostoevskii criticism for his generation. Even people who disagreed with him, such as Lenin and Gor'kii, were concerned with some of the same issues and reacted to Tolstoi in similar fashion, as we will see.

Merezhkovskii was officially rehabilitated at an international conference devoted to him at the Gor'kii Institute in Moscow (March 1990), and his plays *Paul I* and *Tsarevich Aleksei* were staged at the Moscow Art Theater.[5] Since his rehabilitation, his historical novels and some of his essays have been reprinted, a complete scholarly edition of his works is planned, and articles about him have appeared in both academic journals and the popular press. So far interest is greatest in his historical novels and in his activities in the Religious-Philosophical Society.[6] *Tolstoi and Dostoevskii* has not yet had a major impact on contemporary Russian thought. But I believe that it will, because since the 1980s discussions of Tolstoi and Dostoevskii have revolved around the issues that Merezhkovskii treated—morality, religion, and national/cultural identity. We will return to the contemporary scene briefly later on. Now let us turn to Merezhkovskii. We will concentrate on his views on Tolstoi, because his views on Dostoevskii have been treated elsewhere and are well known.[7]

Merezhkovskii's Deconstruction of Tolstoi

In *Tolstoi and Dostoevskii,* Merezhkovskii presented a reading of Tolstoi and Dostoevskii that was at once Christian (as Merezhkovskii defined the term; see below) and Nietzschean. He had written about Dostoevskii before, but this was his first extensive treatment of Tolstoi. In the 1890s, he rejected the "slave morality" that Tolstoi preached but did not puzzle over whether or not Tolstoi's Christianity was authentic. And when he mentioned Tolstoi it was to contrast him with Turgenev or Pushkin, not with Dostoevskii. In "Pushkin" (1896), several pages are devoted to denigrating Tolstoi as Pushkin's antipode.[8] This section of the essay, though relatively brief (five pages out of eighty-six), contained the seeds of his future writings on Tolstoi.

Pushkin was Merezhkovskii's ideal, the perfect union of Apollo and Dionysus, a superhuman figure who reconciled the Christian "truth of heaven" and the pagan "truth of the earth" (cf., Zarathustra's dictum "Be true to the earth my brothers"), a Russian counterpart to Goethe. Tolstoi epitomized the slave morality of Christianity. Working out this idea in a series of polar oppositions, Merezhkovskii stated that Pushkin symbolized harmony; Tolstoi, rupture. Pushkin's peace and quiet stem from his sense of the fullness of life; Tolstoi tries to deaden himself to the world. In Pushkin, the thinker and the artist merge; in Tolstoi, the thinker has contempt for the artist. Pushkin belonged to world culture, but did not deny his Russianness; Tolstoi rejects love for the homeland in favor of an abstract cosmopolitanism. Pushkin expresses the aristocratic spirit; Tolstoi, the utilitarianism and banality of the crowd. Pushkin is the bard of The Bronze Horseman; Tolstoi denies the heroic spirit in history. Pushkin subordinates sensuality to beauty; Tolstoi rejects the pleasures of the flesh. Unconsciously, Tolstoi is a pagan, not a shining heroic type (like Pushkin) but "a dark barbarian," "a son of ancient chaos," "a *blind Titan* digging to get away from the physical power of death to the quietude of the Kingdom of God" (18:169). Merezhkovskii juxtaposed the "mad pagan, Friedrich Nietzsche" with the "no less mad Galilean, Lev Tolstoi" and bewailed the loss, or, more accurately, "murder," of the Pushkinian spirit in Russian literature (18:161, 171). The same charges, especially "madness" and related concepts such as "wildness," recur in Merezhkovskii's subsequent writings on Tolstoi, as does the image of a "blind Titan." The 1896 version of the essay has a stronger conclusion. Merezhkovskii linked the "murder" to "the hopeless twilight of democratic equality and utilitarian virtues, with sad tears of repentance, humility, and pity," and then stated:

> If sometime the spirit of Pushkin were to rise from the dead [*voskresnet*] it would overcome the contemporary disorder. The genius of a higher harmony who saw the sun of the Renaissance, he would say to those dead shades that hover over us as a mute and awesome storm cloud, to the pagan madness of Nietzsche, to the Galillean madness of Lev Tolstoi: Enough [!]. (P. 86)

Merezhkovskii set about trying to discover Pushkin's "secret"—that which enabled the great writer to harmonize the two truths in an all-encompassing higher truth. In the course of this search, he turned to Christ. Around 1900, he concluded that "historical Christianity" (Christianity as preached by the churches) was obsolete and that the apocalypse was imminent. Merezhkovskii's apocalyptic Christianity constituted his answer to Nietzsche. God is not dead; He lives and will return to earth. The world is not meaningless chaos, endless Dionysian flux, eternal recurrence: it has a definite beginning, a middle, and an end. Nietzsche's critique of Christian asceticism, humility, and self-abnegation applies only to "historical Christianity." Real Christianity is not a slave morality but a new and higher supramoral phenomenon, a revaluation of all values that trespasses all limits and boundaries of the moral law; it is a phenomenon of the greatest freedom beyond good and evil. Christianity is not life denying; on the contrary, personal immortality is the supreme affirmation of life. Jesus Christ is the Superman that Nietzsche sought in vain. He Himself would grant humankind a New Revelation, a Third Testament, that would reconcile Christianity and paganism and accomplish a complete revaluation of all Christian values. Preaching the need for a "new religious consciousness," Merezhkovskii embarked on his quest for a new interpretation of Christianity that would allow Christians to enjoy the pleasures of this world. It was this religious quest that led Merezhkovskii to the issue of whether Tolstoi's Christianity was authentic.

Tolstoi and Dostoevskii was written in the first flush of Merezhkovskii's "religious quest." The study continues his attack on Tolstoi but in a different context. Merezhkovskii reformulated the "two truths" as polarities *within* Christianity, or, more accurately, a set of polarities that stemmed from an overarching eschatological dualism. Tolstoi and Dostoevskii, he said, represented the main trends in Russian thought, which are "incompletely and superficially known as Westernism and Slavophilism" (9:5), but these are actually expressions of fundamental, different, and hitherto incompatible religious world views—Christianity and paganism, spirit and flesh, Russia and Europe, God-man and man-god, Christ and Anti-Christ. Merezhkovskii's generation had to reconcile them. In his view, Dostoevskii represented the "spirit" and Tolstoi, despite the asceticism he preached, the "flesh." Merezhkovskii clearly favored Dostoevskii, perhaps hoping to be seen as his successor.

In a sense, Merezhkovskii was Tolstoi's rival for the mantle of prophet. For Tolstoi also rejected "historical Christianity" (though he did not use that term) but in favor of a return to the Gospels, as he interpreted them, rather than a New Revelation, which he did not expect. Many Russians regarded Tolstoi as an exemplar of Christian idealism, frequently contrasting his views with those of the "amoral" Nietzsche. Promoting his own interpretation of Christianity necessitated distinguishing it from Tolstoi's and unmasking the latter's as not Christian at all. Accordingly, Merezhkovskii deconstructed Tolstoi's Christian persona. As an artist, Merezhkovskii argued, Tolstoi is an unconscious pagan, but as a preacher or prophet he is really a Buddhist, and the unconscious pagan is preferable to the professed Christian. Merezhkovskii's deconstruction featured the following four charges.

Hypocrisy

Tolstoi is a hypocrite; he does not live the Christianity he preaches. Merezhkovskii's "unmasking" of Tolstoi's moral pretensions exudes the deconstructive spirit of Nietzsche's *On The Genealogy of Morals*—the basic text for Foucault's "Nietzsche, Archaeology, History." Tolstoi's indifference to his own wife and children indicates his incapacity for love. His vaunted asceticism is a mask for comfort and convenience. Actually, his simple cabin with its sparse furniture and distance from the main house provides ideal working conditions. It is cozy and comfortable; no extraneous decorations distract him, and everything he needs is there. The window opens onto a garden; not one sound from outside is heard. The air is pure; the temperature warm enough. "What could be better?" Tolstoi's peasant garb is more comfortable than the fashions of Paris and London. His eschewal of alcohol and tobacco is wholesome. He has achieved not "American comfort [*komfort*] but true luxury," the "luxury of simplicity." His vegetarianism is not self-denial but a special kind of Epicureanism. He is very demanding; his *kvas* must be just right. The vegetarian dishes that his wife prepares for him are just as tasty, nourishing, and varied as meat— indeed, more luxurious and more refined, because they demand greater resourcefulness and attention on the part of the cook. The result is a new creative art—vegetarian cookery (9:63–65).

Animality and Obsession with Death

The root of Tolstoi's professed asceticism is his preoccupation with the
flesh. Nietzsche's physiologism and his attacks on "the despisers of the
body" are indirectly reflected here, for they sensitized Merezhkovskii to
the importance of the bodily, the physical, and the animal in man. In all of
world literature, Merezhkovskii claimed, there is no writer comparable to
Tolstoi in the depiction of the human body (10:13). It is as if Tolstoi the
artist seeks to reach the limits of nature—the supernatural in its ultimate
bodily limits—the "superbodily" (*sverkhtelesnoe*). His writings exude a
"demonic surplus of the *fleshly*, strength, health" (9:112), the force of life
itself, its surplus and intoxication, which gives his characters a striking,
almost repulsive and frightening vitality (note the Dionysian subtext).
Tolstoi is the "seer of the flesh" (10:15), but only in part of the human
soul. Like the sun shining on the dark surface of the sea but not penetrating the depths, Tolstoi focuses on externals but leaves the character's
inner depths unexplored. He describes each character in terms of minute
physical characteristics that become his leitmotif: Lise Bolkonskii's upper
lip (10:5), the "little white hands of Napoleon," the "energetic small
hands" of Anna, Platon Karataev's "roundness." Tolstoi speaks of the
latter's "round" body, "round" head, "round" movements, "round" speech;
there is something "round" even in his soul. Roundness, however, is a
geometric not a human concept. Platon Karataev does not emerge as a real
person; he does not exist for himself but is only a molecule, a part of ALL,
a drop in the ocean of all-rational, all-human, universal life.

   As an artist Tolstoi plunged into this abyss of animality and at its
ultimate limit met a second principle, consciousness of death, the very
foundation of his Christianity. Tolstoi's fear of death is so profound that it
"approaches religious impotence," transcends the physical and becomes
metaphysical. Merezhkovskii attributed Tolstoi's fear of death to the loss
of his mother in infancy. Tolstoi's physical-fleshly orientation stems, not
from Christianity, but from an authentic pagan religiosity, "from the endless depths of the mystery of the flesh, this divine animalness, I say divine
in order to express, from a definitely religious perspective, that the animal
in man is just as holy and heavenly as the spiritual, and is in essence one"
(9:12). The Nietzschean element here is the animal part of man, symbolized to the ancient Greeks by the satyr—half man, half goat. Pauline
Christianity, said Merezhkovskii, mistakenly separated spirit and flesh,
exalted the spirit at the expense of the flesh as even nonbelievers do.

   Tolstoi's "flesh," however, is not the healthy pagan flesh that loves life
and the world but the result of his own morbid preoccupation with death

and dying. Not free dispassionate loving but the horror felt by the Cossack, Uncle Eroshka, at a naked corpse permeates Tolstoi's works (11:204). His writings describe the dying flesh, but not its resurrection. He rises against the Church in the name of fleshless spirituality (11:20). For Tolstoi death is not the beginning of some new superanimal but only the end of the old.

Merezhkovskii, too, was obsessed with death. One reason he turned to Christ is that Nietzscheanism did not enable him to overcome his fear of death. Another was his hope of being reunited in heaven with his beloved mother. Maxim Gor'kii, another popularizer of Nietzsche, found Tolstoianism repulsive and also claimed that Tolstoi was preoccupied with death. Tolstoi's attitude, said Gor'kii, was: "Go away! Love God or your neighbor and go away! Curse God, love everyone and—go away! Leave me, because I am a man and therefore condemned to death."[9] He condemned Tolstoi's obsession with death as an irresponsible self-indulgence and was as critical of Tolstoi's rejection of culture as Merezhkovskii, but on democratic grounds. Reason and science, Gor'kii believed, were what the people needed.

Buddhistic Negation

Tolstoi's religion is not Christianity but Buddhism, for he denies the very heart of Christianity, the divinity of Christ. He ignores the personal aspect of Christianity, the human soul, the inner spirit, living feelings, submerges them into "one white flower of cosmological abstraction" (12:208). Tolstoi proclaims "an eternal no without an eternal yes" (11:198), Nirvana, eternal nothingness (12:198–200), what Nietzsche called the "will to nothingness" (12:52). Tolstoi is just as anti-Christian as Nietzsche and just as much a nihilist as Turgenev's Bazarov. There is no affirmation in Tolstoi's works, only negation. There is no appreciation of the divine principle of beauty, which in Dostoevskii's words is "a strange and terrible thing, a riddle posed by God" (11:83). Tolstoi flees from culture, stands outside it, denies its essence. Merezhkovskii could not forgive Tolstoi for *What is Art?* (1897). Tolstoi's negativism, he said, precludes his being a true spiritual leader in the full sense of the word. Merezhkovskii coveted that role.

Tolstoi's characters are not even living persons, only contemplators. His novels present no heroes, only victims who display a Christian or, better, a Buddhist rejection of personal will. They are "heroes of inactivity," passively submitting to nature's dictates, giving themselves over to the torrent of elemental animal life. Their lives are a series of meaningless events devoid of causal significance, purpose, and meaning. Reality itself is an illusion unpunctuated by landmarks. Platon Karataev, the only wise man in all of Tolstoi's novels, recognizes the futility of planning; he stands outside history and culture. And when there are no true heroes, there is no tragedy: "There is no unifying denouement, that which the ancient Greeks called catastrophe. On this ocean of shoreless epos all is agitated, in motion, like sparkles and glimmers of separate waves. Everything is born, lives, dies, and is again born—without end, without purpose" (10:66). The subtext is the meaningless universe of Schopenhauer and Nietzsche. "And just as there is no liberating horror, there is no liberating laughter" (cf., Zarathustra, "Learn to Laugh!"). "Not once, reading Tolstoi, does one even laugh, nor even smile." The heart becomes heavy, there is nothing to breathe, no air (10:66). The implicit comparison is to Pushkin's "lightness"—one of Merezhkovskii's favorite adjectives for Pushkin. Tolstoi believed, said Merezhkovskii, that to love God means to love nothing, to submerge oneself in Nirvana, in nonexistence (11:198). The dying Prince Andrei, for example, ceases to love other people, gazes at them in a "cold, almost hostile" manner, curses the living in order to die with God (11:203). But the "cold white light" Andrei sees is not truly Resurrection.

Merezhkovskii's Christianity was mythologically and psychologically oriented, for he wanted to overcome the harmful effects of Socratic rationalism, the "theoretical blight" that, according to Nietzsche, hovers over contemporary culture. A myth requires a concrete visible image, a personal God. Particularly obnoxious to Merezhkovskii, therefore, was Tolstoi's rational Christianity, Tolstoi's claim that there is nothing supernatural, miraculous, mysterious, or mystical in Christianity at all, that it is only a doctrine that teaches people how to live (11:192, 204). He attacked Tolstoi's religion as impersonal, will-less, and inhuman, a religion without God the Father or God the Divine Son, a cerebral Christianity without Christ, and pointed out that Tolstoi went so far as to change the word 'son' (*syn*) to 'lad' (*otrok*) in his translation of the Gospels in order to demystify Jesus (11:213). Tolstoi's God, Merezhkovskii asserted, is an 'It' not a 'He'. One cannot love an 'It'; one can only fear it as a dying hare fears the hunter. In Tolstoi's religion, man is the hare and God is the hunter; man is the criminal sentenced to death and God is the executioner (11:191). And like a dying hare, Tolstoi ultimately submits: "Thy will be done." Tolstoi's Christian love has no daring (a Nietzschean virtue); it does not cast out fear.

Merezhkovskii also objected to Tolstoi's moralism, claiming that moralism debases religion, reduces all the dangerous barren heights and depths (note the Nietzschean imagery) to one practical, useful, village-economy flatness. Such Christianity is one of the most insipid of all insipid things, salt that has ceased to be salt. Tolstoi reduces God to a dead abstract formula, a convenient and conditional mathematical sign, 'x' in the moral equation; when the equation is solved, 'x' is known and no longer necessary. God equals good. Tolstoi's religion is like a machine. A machine has no living soul, no living body, no mystery. Everything is clear, shameless, and naked. Tolstoi's religion is naked, fleshless, soulless, devoid of ritual. Merezhkovskii considered ritual the steps by which, for centuries, millions of people approached God. To him, Christianity was a supramoral phenomenon beyond ordinary conceptions of good and evil.

Ahistoricism

Tolstoi has no sense of history. He is not interested in the first cause of the world. Merezhkovskii's opposition to Tolstoi's ahistoricism reflected his mythologizing orientation. Myths need origins, a divine scheme of the world that pervades an entire culture. To Christians, history is God's plan; it has a beginning, a middle, and an end. Tolstoi, however, regards history as meaningless and purposeless. Unconsciously he fears it, as if he feels that he cannot cope with it, and thus distances himself from the natural historical paths of humanity to the area of the abstract, the contrary to nature, the antihistorical. "The living tie of the past with the future, the living chain of religious succession, that 'procession of torch bearers' who from century to century, from people to people, transmitted the flaming torch of universal historical Christian culture—Tolstoi destroys in the name of the present, only the present." He ignores the links between history and culture. It is as if "his Christianity did not grow from Russian or West European soil but fell from the heavens already prepared." He skips over centuries of Christian culture—Sergei of Radonezh, Nils Sorskii, and Francis Assisi. "There was Socrates, there was Confucius, Buddha, Christ, and now there is L. Tolstoi." "All the superstructure of man on nature, everything cultural—for Tolstoi is only conditional, only artificial, and consequently false, uninteresting, insignificant. With a light heart he passes them by. This part of elemental human life is inaccessible to him" (10:34–35). Tolstoi is a colossal egoist, who thinks only of himself.

  War and Peace ignores the titanic nature of the struggle against Napoleon and, more importantly, its religious aspect. The Russian people considered Napoleon Anti-Christ, but to Tolstoi he was just a "little man with white hands," "human all too human." The issue of Napoleon, as posed by both Nietzsche and Dostoevskii, is the issue of the man-god, the summit of the basic ideals of West European culture. Napoleon was not just a "hero of contemplation" like Dante or Michelangelo but an "artist of activity" like Caesar or Alexander the Great. He loved power as an artist; in his own words: "I love power as a musician loves his violin, for the sounds, chords, and harmonies he can elicit from it" (11:72, 184–88). The hero and artist have their own tradition. Napoleon united and lived them. He said of himself, "I am divine. I am God," and even considered founding a new religion (11:118). An entire century of philosophic thought from Goethe's Prometheus to Nietzsche's Anti-Christ was needed to recognize Napoleon's significance: the revaluation of all values, self-affirmation versus self-renunciation, revolt against the old, against the new, against any social order or social contract at all. Dostoevskii was right to regard Napoleon as a demonic man-god, Merezhkovskii declared; the great force of the Napoleonic idea is not political or even moral but religious—the meeting of the Russian spirit with the great incarnation of the spirit of Western Europe, of Christ with the Anti-Christ. But to Tolstoi, Napoleon is just the man with the "little white hands."[10]

Tolstoi's true significance was not as a Christian preacher or prophet at all but as the "great pagan." Tolstoi did not fall away from Christianity, because he never was a Christian. It is not that he did not want to be one, quite the contrary. He tried all his life, but when he speaks of Christianity, one feels that he speaks somehow "not of that" (11:33). Tolstoi's tragedy is that all his life he tried not to believe in his own unconscious insights into the "mystery of the flesh" and tried to stifle his pagan love of life on this earth. Tolstoi's paganism is something primordial, unbaptized, elemental, and unconscious. Once again, Merezhkovskii called Tolstoi a "blind Titan," digging in the earth without a conscious direction. Note the change from "Pushkin," where Tolstoi's digging was seen as an attempt to escape death. The authentic Tolstoi is the Cossack, Uncle Eroshka, the avatar of a pre-Christian sensibility. Like a child, like Adam in paradise, Eroshka does not know good and evil. Drunk with the living joy of life, he smells of homemade wine and clotted blood (note the Dionysian allusions). Truly puzzled by the Christian preacher Akim's views on sex, Eroshka says "Sin? where? love is not sin but salvation?" (2:27). Eroshka asserts that the beast is smarter than man, that "the beast knows all." He considers the beast a divine creature and is himself one with nature, with elemental life (12:174–75). But Akim destroys Eroshka's paradise with consciousness of death and suffering, chases the stubborn pagan onto the path of Christian love, and the secret of the beast becomes more and more terrible, until the beast becomes a monster. In "Critique of Dogmatic Theology," Tolstoi claimed that God is half man, half monster; Merezhkovskii considered this a blasphemous inversion of one of the deepest dogmas of Christianity. In Christianity, God is love, not a monster who evokes fear and horror. But Tolstoi sees no joy in Christ, no gaiety

(12:38). In his conscious religion, Tolstoi rises against the Church in the name of fleshless Christianity.

Merezhkovskii considered *Anna Karenina* Tolstoi's best work because of its treatment of sexual passion, an aspect of the "mystery of the flesh." Anna perished, said Merezhkovskii, not by her own fault but because of the religious mistake of the entire (Christian) world concerning sex. Her thoughts on divine truth, on holiness, on her love for Vronskii stem from Tolstoi's unconscious religious depths as expressed by Eroshka—the blind but clairvoyant pagan. After *Anna Karenina*, Tolstoi retreated from authentic life into a life of abstraction, denied his real prophetic insights into "the mystery of the flesh." Still, here and there one finds glimmers of the real Tolstoi; for example, Nekhliudov's cry in *Resurrection*—"I want to live!" Tolstoi's unconscious religion is paganism. His "religious truth" is "the truth of paganism," the "truth of the flesh," which "historical Christianity" disdained. But Tolstoi's unconscious paganism, his "pagan holiness," is the sole path to Dostoevskii's Christianity (11:35).

The mission of his generation, Merezhkovskii concluded, was to combine Tolstoi's unconscious insights, his "pagan holiness," with Dostoevskii's "Christian holiness," for, as the two summits of Russian literature, they were the first to see the rays of the setting sun, the end of the old world and the beginning of the new—the Kingdom of God on Earth.

Merezhkovskii's Reconstruction of Tolstoi

Merezhkovskii's "reconstruction" of Tolstoi began shortly after Tolstoi's excommunication by the Holy Synod (1901), continued steadily thereafter, and reflected changes in his own religious and political views. During the Revolution of 1905, he became an advocate of "religious revolution" and reinterpreted Tolstoi and Dostoevskii accordingly to stress their political ideas. He hailed Tolstoi as a prophet of Christian anarchism but faulted him for condemning the revolution. He praised Dostoevskii as the prophet of the Russian Revolution[11] but criticized his concept of theocracy. After the Revolution of 1905, Merezhkovskii denied the equal validity of Christianity and paganism as a dangerous heresy and distanced himself from Nietzsche, whose ideas continued to shape his thought nevertheless. Dismayed by the unelevated state of postrevolutionary Russian society and culture, he found Tolstoi's moralism less obnoxious and began to make him a cult figure, though with qualifications. He even wrote: "St. Leo, pray to God for us." Merezhkovskii still used Tolstoi's life and work to promote his own views, but his growing esteem for Tolstoi as a man (he had always esteemed him as an artist), and as a *de facto* Christian, was sincere.

Tolstoi's Excommunication and the Revolution of 1905

In the summer of 1904, Merezhkovskii and Gippius visited Tolstoi at his estate and discussed religious questions. "I already felt," Merezhkovskii later recalled, "that my book was not just to him, and that despite the deepest intellectual differences, Tolstoi was nevertheless nearer to me, more native to me, than Dostoevskii" (24:115). In *Eternal Companions* (1897), he had stated explicitly that he felt closest to Dostoevskii (18:6).

Tolstoi's excommunication was a catalyst for this reversal. Not only was Merezhkovskii profoundly impressed with Tolstoi's defiance of the Church, he believed that the Holy Synod had violated the Christian principle of freedom and realized that its action could jeopardize his own "religious quest" as well.[12] Mindful of these considerations, he supported Tolstoi against the Holy Synod but distinguished Tolstoi's interpretation of Christianity from his own. At the third session of the Religious-Philosophical Society, Merezhkovskii spoke on "Lev Tolstoi and the Russian Church"; the entire fourth session was devoted to a discussion of his talk. Retreating slightly from his charge that Tolstoi was not a Christian, he stated that "it is impossible to speak of Tolstoi's Christianity," but it is also "impossible not to speak of it."[13] Once again, he stated that Tolstoi's negativism precluded him from true spiritual leadership. Educated Russians support Tolstoi's rebellion against Church dogmatism and scholasticism, but his denial of culture, science, and art and his Buddhist quietism are entirely alien to them. Theirs is "a common no, but not a common yes." Still favoring Dostoevskii, Merezhkovskii counterposed Elder Zossima, seeker of a Christian "truth of the earth," with preacher Akim, acolyte of "historical Christianity."[14] Quoting Dostoevskii's deathbed statement, "the Russian Church has been paralyzed since the time of Peter the Great," he claimed that Dostoevskii was referring to Peter's Spiritual Reglement (1721), which established the Holy Synod and subordinated the Church to the state and the spirit to the flesh. Wishing to reopen the issue of Church–state relations, Merezhkovskii asked four questions: (1) Is the Holy Synod the lawful representative of the Universal Church of Christ? Must there be a civil sword behind the spiritual iron? (2) Is the decision of the Synod simple testimony of Tolstoi's falling away from the Church or is it "anathema"? (This was somewhat ingenuous.) (3) Does not Tolstoi's artistic creativity testify to his search for God? (4) Is the "anathema" over Tolstoi also an anathema over all educated Russian society, even though it diverges from Tolstoi in his unbelief and in other forms of negation? And what will be the consequences to the Church of this anathema?[15] The abolition of the Holy Synod became a tenet of the

Church reform movement that arose during the Revolution of 1905; many of its leaders had attended the meetings of the Religious-Philosophical Society.

Until 1904, Merezhkovskii's primary interests were what he called the "inner man" (the soul or the psyche), art, cultural creativity, and finding higher spiritual truths. But the closing down of the Religious-Philosophical Society made him realize that his religious quest required political freedom. In 1904, he proclaimed that autocracy is from Anti-Christ. After some initial hesitation, he interpreted the Revolution of 1905 as the first stage of a far greater religious revolution yet to come. In his own words: "The events of 1905–1906 made me understand, not abstractly but in life, the tie of Orthodoxy with the old order [autocracy] in Russia and with a new understanding of Christianity that negates both. . . . The end of autocracy means the end of Orthodoxy" and vice versa (24:115). In "Revolution and Religion" (1907), Merezhkovskii argued that the two were once united but became separated in the nineteenth century and are now in the process of being reunited (13:36–96). From this point of view, he reinterpreted Russian literature and thought from the time of Catherine the Great to the present, including Tolstoi's and Dostoevskii's "religious-revolutionary significance." Each was a prophet who saw only one part of a whole and hence required the insights of the other.

Tolstoi was the prophet of religious anarchism. He rejected the state as an ungodly kingdom, but he had no concept of a church, or even of a community, at all. The very title of Tolstoi's book, *The Kingdom of God Is Within You*, signals the incompleteness of his conception.

> [Tolstoi] was first to show what immeasurable strength can be acquired by the rejection of the State Church, by making the political religious. He showed the place where the lever that can destroy any State Church was located. But he himself did not know how to take hold of this lever.
> For Tolstoi, "the Kingdom of God" is only "within us," within each human person, solitary and isolated; for him the business of salvation is an exclusively internal, individual, and noncommunal one. Here he follows the same unconscious deviation as the whole of Christianity. He replaces the mysticism of the Gospels, the last union of spirit and flesh, partly with a superficial philosophical rationalism, abolishing all mysticism as a superstition, and partly with a deep, not Christian, but Buddhist metaphysics—the absolute absorption of one principle by another, of the fleshly by the spiritual. In this sense, Tolstoi, strange to say, is more churchly than the church itself, more Orthodox than Orthodoxy itself, to the great detriment, of course, of his religious truth. Again, strange to say, Tolstoi is an anarchist, but not a revolutionary. He rejects the political revolution as he does any social activity. Having repudiated the state, the false community, he repudiates the true religious community as well;

having repudiated the State Church, he repudiates, or rather does not see, the true church at all. (13:61–62)

On leaving Orthodoxy, Merezhkovskii continued, Tolstoi fell into a terrible emptiness, which he confused with true Christianity. He is a "blind Titan," who does not see the soil he is displacing nor the earthquake that could be created if only he knew where to dig.

Dostoevskii was the prophet of the Russian Revolution and of an autocratic theocracy. His heroes were "atheist-mystics," not simply godless but theomachists. Their revolt against the human order led them to revolt against the divine order. He hated the atheistic revolutionaries but had a premonition of a religious revolution, of a final conflict between Church and state. Elder Zossima states that "the triumph of the Church is the absolute negation of the state." Dostoevskii himself said that "the Church is truly the kingdom and appointed to reign" over the entire earth. Dostoevskii propagated the true idea of the Church as the Kingdom of Godmanhood. But he regarded the autocracy as holy and was suspicious of freedom (13:58–61).

Their "truths" must be reconciled. Anarchy without theocracy is rejection without affirmation. Either it remains an empty abstraction or leads to pure destructiveness. But theocracy without anarchy, affirmation without rejection, also either remains an ineffectual abstraction or leads to reaction as it did with Dostoevskii.

And yet, Merezhkovskii continued, Dostoevskii expressed doubts about Orthodoxy and autocracy, while Tolstoi also believed in the holiness of the Russian autocracy. In his deathbed delirium, Dostoevskii urged the tsar to put his trust in the people. Almost immediately after, Tsar Alexander II was assassinated. Tolstoi begged Alexander III to pardon his father's killers, but in vain. Alexander did not even reply to Tolstoi's letter. But Pobedonostsev told Tolstoi that Christ would not have forgiven the murderers of the Russian tsar. At that point, according to Merezhkovskii, Tolstoi became a Christian anarchist.

This was the last call of the future preacher of anarchy to the false theocracy. This means that even Tolstoi believed in the most secret depths of his heart, believed, perhaps, no less than Dostoevskii, in the holiness of the Russian autocracy. It means there is some kind of terrible temptation in this most Russian of all Russian madnesses, where the tsar is "God's anointed," where the tsar is "Christ," but Christ means precisely, "God's anointed" . . . the Orthodox autocracy has always meant: the Russian tsar is another Christ. (13:64)

Merezhkovskii's point was that even Tolstoi succumbed to the "terrible temptation" of autocracy, the idea that the tsar is God's anointed. Power cannot be divided (into Church and state). Christ Himself and not another pretender must rule Russia. The constitutional monarch would fail because the secular intelligentsia cannot answer to the question that the people will surely ask—is the tsar God's anointed or not? (13:95-96).

"Revolution and Religion" was reprinted in *Not Peace but a Sword* (1908). The title, of course, is an allusion to Jesus' statement, "I came not to send peace, but a sword" (Matt. 10:34). It announces Merezhkovskii's rejection of Christian pacifism, including Tolstoi's, for he considered pacifism a slavish quality and valorized activism, rebelliousness, and daring.[16]

Maxim Gor'kii was then propagating a Marxist surrogate religion, which he called "God-building." Apotheosizing the rebellious and daring proletariat, Gor'kii hoped to co-opt religious idealism for the revolution, or, to put it somewhat differently, to inspire a religious revolution on behalf of socialism. In "Notes on Philistinism" (1905), he denounced Tolstoi's doctrines of self-perfection and nonresistance as benefiting the possessing classes, to which Tolstoi belonged. Several years later, he excoriated Dostoevskii's neurotic heroes and his cult of suffering as bad influences on the workers.[17]

The Tolstoi Festival of 1908

In 1908, liberals and some radicals tried to make Tolstoi's eightieth birthday into a festival of Russian liberation. Merezhkovskii was among them. Government and Church opposition blunted their plans, but Tolstoi's birthday was celebrated widely nonetheless. Congratulatory telegrams poured in from all over the country, and tributes to Tolstoi as the "great writer of the Russian land" and the "voice of civilized mankind" filled the press.[18] Even Lenin wrote an article on Tolstoi, who had many proletarian admirers, partly to clarify the Bolshevik position. In "Lev Tolstoi, Mirror of the Russian Revolution," Lenin castigated bourgeois hypocrisy and emphasized the contradictions in Tolstoi's views: "On the one hand, the remarkably powerful, forthright and sincere protest against social falsehood and hypocrisy; and on the other, the Tolstoian . . . who publicly beats his breast and wails: 'I am a bad, wicked man, but I am practising moral self-perfection; I don't eat meat anymore, I now eat rice cutlets.' "[19] These contradictions, Lenin explained, stemmed from Tolstoi's position as a member of the landholding aristocracy, hostile to encroaching capitalism on the one hand and to the workers' revolution on the other. Lenin lambasted Tolstoi's doctrine of nonviolence, even blaming it for the failure of the Revolution of 1905.

Merezhkovskii wrote two articles for the Tolstoi festival, "Lev Tolstoi and the Church" (not to be confused with his speech to the Religious-Philosophical Society) and "Lev Tolstoi and Revolution" (both 1908). In "Lev Tolstoi and the Church," he denounced the "antijubilee" campaign and noted the irony that Tolstoi's birthday was being celebrated, not in " 'God-bearing Russia'," but in " 'godless France'," where Church and state are separate. Even if Tolstoi is a heretic as the Church claims, he is a great writer, and genius is a gift from God. And Christianity is greater than its dogma. Tolstoi acts as a Christian. With his head, Tolstoi denies that Christ is the Son of God, but with his heart, he affirms Him. Tolstoi's paganism is actually a "religious paganism," which "at its highest limits is Christianity before Christ" and was so regarded by the Church Fathers. On the icons of the most ancient Russian churches, together with the saints and martyrs are depictions of the sibyls, wise men, and poets of pagan antiquity, those who did not know the name of the Lord but expected His advent. Tolstoi is one of these "Christian-pagans," not as a religious teacher but as a great artist (16:149). In the ancient world, paganism prepared the way for Christianity. Tolstoi's "religious paganism" will lead to a new Christianity. The way is being prepared for the Second Advent. The miracle will occur in Russia, where the godless intelligentsia celebrates Tolstoi's birthday. The blind will see. The universal festival of Tolstoi, a "non-Christian," is a festival of universal Christianity. Tolstoi is the "greatest man in Russia today." When the Church expelled him, it "expelled us as well, because we are with him, and we are with him because we believe that Christ is with him" (16:150).

In "Lev Tolstoi and Revolution," Merezhkovskii exalted the Tolstoi festival as unique, as the first universal festival of peace and goodwill, the first to be devoted to a hero of the spirit rather than a world conqueror. But there is a thorn in the crown—Tolstoi's condemnation of the Russian revolution—which stems from his failure to recognize the "ultimate divine truth of human personality." That self-affirmation is the religious principle of every revolution simply escapes him. As an artist Tolstoi sees the flesh and "the mystery of the flesh," and through the latter, he sees "the mystery of the vital-elemental, the faceless" (that which Nietzsche described as Dionysian deindividuation). But he only touches on the "mystery of human personality." That is why Tolstoi hates Shakespeare. Tolstoi denounced Shakespeare in an essay, "On Shakespeare and on Drama" (c. 1904), mostly about *King Lear*. Shakespeare fathomed the "mystery of the other," the existence of separate human personalities. His characters are different from one another and from the author. In Tolstoi, "an almost elemental animal-god I envelops everything that is not-I." His heroes, or,

more accurately, anti-heroes, are really one person, himself. "Without Tolstoi there is no Levin," but there is a Hamlet without Shakespeare. With
respect to the religious revelation of human personality, Shakespeare was
closer to Christ than was Tolstoi, the professed Christian (16:153–54).
Tolstoi hates and rejects European culture because it is "not Christian," but
"the authentic revelation of Christ is the revelation of the absoluteness of
the person" (16:155). Prometheus, Faust, Cain, and Zarathustra represent
the highest points of the European genius, the genius of the person, affirm-
ing himself in revolt, struggling with God, but in the last analysis, sons of
God.[20] Ultimate negation as the path to victorious affirmation, paganism as
the path to Christianity—this Tolstoi does not see. Therefore, Tolstoi rejects the Russian revolution.

Yet Tolstoi's personal life has been an eternal inner revolt, an eternal
inner revolution. Bifurcating Tolstoi in much the same way that Lenin did,
though for different reasons, Merezhkovskii wanted Tolstoi to merge his
"internal revolt" with an "external" one against Church and state. "The
revelation of the human personality, the revelation of Christ, is being realized in all human affairs, but now especially in Russia . . . in the Russian
liberation movement . . . [we see] the revolt of absolute personality in the
face of the enslaved and reviled People." Either the Russian people will not
carry the cross or its cross is freedom. And Tolstoi, not alone but only with
the entire Russian people, will be able to raise his cross. Merezhkovskii
perceived Tolstoi as a great and solitary figure, battling the Church, the
state, and his own family; he identified with Tolstoi's "aloneness" and
wanted him to overcome it. "Today, the enemies of Russian freedom are
Tolstoi's enemies, and its friends are his friends. Today he and they are
one. Whether they desire it or not, the Tolstoi festival is a festival of the
Russian Revolution. . . . As a prophet of Russian and universal liberation,
as long as humanity lives, Tolstoi will live" (16:156).

Tolstoi's Death

Tolstoi's death (November 1910) inspired another round of tributes. All
sorts of people rushed to claim his heritage. Tolstoi's admirers exalted him
as a Russian saint. Gor'kii condemned their attempts to "create a legend"
as self-serving, hypocritical, and downright harmful, because the people do
not need a holy saint. Tolstoi is "great and holy because he is a man, a
madly agonizing fine man, a man of all mankind."[21] Lenin praised Tolstoi
as an artist of genius and appropriated his heritage for the proletariat. By
studying Tolstoi's literary works, he said, the Russian proletariat "will
learn to know its enemies better," while in examining his doctrine the

entire Russian people "will have to understand where their own weakness lies." He described "Tolstoi-anism in its real historical context [as] an ideology of an Oriental, an Asiatic order"—what Merezhkovskii had called Buddhism.[22]

Merezhkovskii wrote: "Who is he? Artist, teacher, prophet? No, more. His face is the face of humanity. If inhabitants of other worlds were to ask our world, Who are you?—humanity would answer by pointing to Tolstoi." He described Tolstoi as a Christian and even as a kind of martyr. "Outcast, excommunicated, impenitent, not with words but with his entire life and death, he confessed to Christ. Russians must pray for him even if the Church is silent" ("The Death of Tolstoi," 1910).[23]

From here on, Merezhkovskii propounded the religious significance of Tolstoi's "deed" not his "word," specifically excluding his doctrine. He claimed that Tolstoi's death was not an end but an achievement, a fulfillment of life, and extolled Tolstoi's "life and death, especially his death, as phenomena of holiness," partly because he believed that Tolstoi overcame his fear of death at last.[24] Perhaps now that Tolstoi was dead, Merezhkovskii hoped to be seen as his successor. The essays of this period (1910-1921) were often simplistic and far more sermonlike than the previous ones, and his polarities seem mechanical and forced. Still using Tolstoi as a symbol, exactly what he symbolized kept shifting, reflecting Merezhkovskii's own anguish at the state of Russia and the world and his hope for a religious revolution and a new order.

Several other entries in *It Was and Will Be: Diary, 1910–14* (1915) are devoted to Tolstoi. In "Unsalty Salt" (pp. 285–93), Merezhkovskii asserted that Tolstoi has not been forgotten, but he has been abandoned, and bewailed the popularity of novels such as Anastasiia Verbitskaia's *The Keys to Happiness* and Artsybashev's *Sanin,* whose protagonists preach a vulgar Nietzscheanism of selfishness and promiscuity. "Two Russias" opens with the words, "St. Leo, pray to God for us!" penned by Countess Aleksandra Tolstaia to her nephew in 1858. Although she wrote this half in jest, her words are becoming prophecy as Tolstoi's image recedes. Tolstoi represents the rift between the Russia of the past and the Russia of the future. Just as Rousseau was the precursor of the French Revolution, Tolstoi is the precursor of the Russian Revolution yet to come.[25] The rift that he represents is the first sign of the earthquake (the apocalypse) that will change the face of the world. Tolstoi, therefore, has great religious significance. It turns out that Tolstoi's "wild" (i.e., "mad") devaluation of the intellect will have positive results. In turning from culture (Merezhkovskii means secular culture), Tolstoi turned to Christ, to the new Christianity, which will lead to a new Christian culture. For this reason, "for the Russia of the future, Tolstoi is holy; for the Russia of the past, he is anathema" (p. 43).

In "St. Helena" (pp. 103–23), first published in 1913, Merezhkovskii returned to the theme of Napoleon's religious significance. Napoleon was the "iron barrier to revolution," the force that defeated chaos. "Here is the obscure command by which he was sent into the world" (p. 121). People need freedom, but they also need order and obedience, for without them freedom becomes chaos. Napoleon defeated chaos; he introduced a new iron into the world—will, power, order, obedience. Order means reason. Napoleon conquered Europe in the name of the universal principle of reason. In "human only human reason," there is something demonic or divine. This "only human reason" was embodied in Napoleon (p. 122). The overcoming of Napoleon, therefore, is the overcoming of rationalism. Merezhkovskii wanted "another order," based on the Christian principle of love. Napoleon had too much contempt for people, too much self-love. But "it is not for us to judge him. He did what he was sent into the world to do" (p. 123). After the Bolshevik Revolution, Merezhkovskii yearned for a "new Napoleon," who would curb the "red terror."[26]

Tolstoi is the subject of two essays in *From War to Revolution, An Unmilitary Diary* (1914–17)—"Unholy Russia" (1916) and "A Day Laborer for Christ" (n.d.).[27] The first sentence of "Unholy Russia" is: "Where is Russia's path?" The greatest Russian writers were eternal signposts. Tolstoi was the last. "After Tolstoi there is no one—or Gor'kii." Tolstoi and Dostoevskii expressed the "truth of the individual," the "truth of personality," the aristocracy in a higher sense (note Merezhkovskii's reversal on Tolstoi). Gor'kii does not have his own "face" (*Gesicht*—the word also means vision); his is the collective face of the entire folk (*narod*), democracy in the true religious meaning of the word. With Gor'kii, Russia stands before an entirely new religious world. The question is which religion will prevail: Gor'kii's dogmatic atheism or the faith of Gor'kii's grandmother. The latter exemplifies the elementary religious power of the Russian people, which nourished Tolstoi and Dostoevskii and lives on in Gor'kii's unconscious. Some years before, Merezhkovskii had stated that Tolstoi and Dostoevskii express the deepest folk elements and the highest cultural consciousness, while Chekhov and Gor'kii speak for the philistine middle layers of society (14:60). Previously he had called Dostoevskii "The Prophet of the Russian Revolution," but in this essay he wrote that Tolstoi and Dostoevskii both counseled humility, endurance, and inaction, and he postulated a new polar opposition, Tolstoi and Dostoevskii versus Gor'kii, advocate of resistance, rebellion, uprising, action. "In this sense, 'sinful' Russia is holier than 'Holy Russia'. . . . Gor'kii does not believe in

Holy slavish Russia but in the sinful, awakening, self-liberating Russia. He knows there is no Holy Russia, but he believes there will be one." The atheist Gor´kii is actually doing God's work. In counseling rebellion and resistance, Gor´kii "is closer to us than Tolstoi and Dostoevskii. In this sense we are not with them, but with Gor´kii" (pp. 19–20).

In "A Day Laborer for Christ," however, Merezhkovskii wrote that "Tolstoi grows before our eyes" (p. 34). Praising Tolstoi's desire to abolish poverty and inequality, he vaunted Tolstoi's Christianity as ancient and eternal but also new, because Christian holiness ignored the pain of slavery and poverty. Tolstoi felt this pain. Where Christian holiness ends, Tolstoi's begins. Pain belongs to the cursed flesh. Tolstoi worked all his life for a new holy flesh, without pain. He was neither a saint, nor a prophet, nor a teacher, but a simple worker, a day laborer for Christ (p. 44). This reading of Tolstoi contradicts the unabashed elitism of Merezhkovskii's previous works, but it is compatible, in a rough sort of way, with his contempt for the middle class. In another essay, "The Spirit Is Not Extinguished," he deplored the brutalizing effects of the war on society and culture and compared his contemporaries to drunken bacchantes. He stated that the wish of Rousseau and Tolstoi is now being fulfilled—"back to nature, simplicity"—though in a different way than they intended. "Human nature is wide, far too wide," they thought; they wished to make it narrower. People have indeed become narrower and poorer. Merezhkovskii was echoing Dmitrii Karamazov's statement "Yes, man is broad, too broad, indeed I'd have him narrower" and Zarathustra's observation "*Everything* has become smaller." But he trusted that the Word of Christ would prevail (pp. 161–64).

Tolstoi and the Bolshevik Revolution

Merezhkovskii hailed the February Revolution but vehemently opposed bolshevism. He fled Soviet Russia, which he called "the realm of the Anti-Christ," in December 1919. "Lev Tolstoi and Bolshevism"[28] addresses the issue of whether or not Tolstoi was with the Bolsheviks, an issue "not so easy" to resolve (p. 191). In ethics, aesthetics, politics, and metaphysics Tolstoi is "not with us," but in ethics he is not with the Bolsheviks either. At best, he is between or above both camps. He is a simplifier, like the Bolsheviks and like Bakunin, Stenka Razin, Pugachev, and Rousseau. His "wild wisdom" is reactionary and destructive, as is his flight from culture. Tolstoi's "will to simplicity" is a "will to wildness," and the "will to wildness" is a "will to impersonality." Tolstoi negates Napoleon and darkens the sun of personality (Nietzsche's Apollonian principle). Instead of the sun, Tolstoi offers the goalless, small, and round Platon Karataev. "The sun of Napoleon banished the first flood" (the French Revolution). "Who will banish the second?" The flood levels all heights and depths. That was the wish of Tolstoi and Lenin. Bolshevism is barbarism, animalization. In this context, Merezhkovskii quoted Voltaire's famous quip, after reading Rousseau's "Discourse on the Origins of Inequality," that he was too old to get down on all fours and romp in the woods. "Bolshevism is the suicide of Europe. Tolstoi began it. Lenin completed it" (p. 195).

Nevertheless, Merezhkovskii continued, Tolstoi is not with the Bolsheviks, because religion was his highest value. Metaphysically, Tolstoi's "will to wildness" is the end of culture, but metaphysics is not the same as religion. Religion is not yet culture, but there is no culture without religion. In religion, the end of the old culture is the beginning of the new. The childhood of the world is not in the past but in the future. (In *Tolstoi and Dostoevskii*, he had called Tolstoi's heroes naive, eternal children.) Tolstoi was not a reactionary but a religious revolutionary, the greatest of all revolutionaries. Lenin's politics incarnates the steel sword of endless destruction; Tolstoi's politics is a green rod, a branch of the tree of life. It is blasphemy to link him with Lenin. Moreover, in Tolstoi's metaphysics there is an open "will to facelessness, to impersonality," but in Tolstoi's religion there is a "special will to one countenance" (Jesus). Tolstoi is with Him. With whom are we? The answer determines whether Tolstoi is with us or not (p. 198).

Repeating Countess Tolstaia's statement "St. Leo, pray to God for us," Merezhkovskii cautioned that Tolstoi is not yet a saint. "Despite his greatness he is as sinful as we are. Perhaps that is why we love him more than we love the saints." When saints die, they go straight to heaven; sinners must first go through the cleansing fire of purgatory. Bolshevism is Tolstoi's purgatory. All Russia is burning in the fire of Tolstoi's sins but will not be consumed. The green rod will save her. "Only the sins will be consumed, and then Holy Russia—St. Leo—will emerge. 'St. Leo, pray to God for us.' As long as we do not say this, Russia will not be saved" (p. 198). In other words, his generation still had the opportunity to choose Christ.

Conclusion

We have seen how Merezhkovskii's deconstruction and subsequent reconstruction of Tolstoi stemmed from his own needs at different times. Gor'kii's view of Tolstoi evolved similarly. In his essay on Tolstoi, Gor'kii admitted that he did not know whether to love or hate Tolstoi but then stated "this man is godlike."[29] Saintlike but not a saint, godlike but not a god, Tolstoi had become an iconic figure for both of them.

Tolstoi remained an iconic figure in the Soviet period, partly because of Lenin's and Gor'kii's esteem for him. But literary discussions revolved around new issues: the nature of the new Soviet art, the best way to disseminate communist ideals to an unsophisticated public, the role, if any, of the Russian classics, and how to present them to Soviet readers. Particular emphasis was placed on literary form, style, and language. Tolstoi's simple language, clear plots, and well-defined characters made him into a model for Soviet writers. His hostility to capitalism was stressed, but its grounding in Christianity was downplayed or ignored. As for Dostoevskii, Soviet critics tended to alternate between praising his sympathy for the poor and condemning his reactionary views. Merezhkovskii's writings were not particularly relevant to these issues; moreover, as an active enemy of the Soviet regime, his name could be mentioned only pejoratively, if at all. Even in the 1920s, when Tolstoi's physiologism was a trope of Soviet literary criticism, Merezhkovskii's study was not given due credit.

In post-Stalinist Russia, another set of issues emerged. The search for a specifically socialist morality that began in the 1960s led to new readings of Tolstoi and Dostoevskii, which emphasized their moral teachings.[30] In the 1970s literary critics began to contrast Nietzsche and Dostoevskii, to Nietzsche's detriment, making the German into a symbol of traits deemed undesirable in Soviet society, such as hedonism and individualism. Dostoevskii and Tolstoi were described as humanists and democratists. In the 1980s some philosophers tried to apply their moral teachings to a "humanist correction of Marxism."[31]

Iurii Davydov's book *An Ethic of Love and a Metaphysic of Self-Will* (1982), subtitled *Problems of Moral Philosophy*, argues the need for a morality based on the Russian classics. "It is impossible," Davydov asserted, "to find another path to the pithy understanding of moral-philosophic problems than the one that passes through the Russian classics" (p. 7). Tolstoi and Dostoevskii espoused a truly Russian "ethic of love," while Nietzsche, Camus, and Sartre espoused the "metaphysic of self-will" that characterizes the contemporary West.

In the course of his argument, Davydov specifically takes issue with Merezhkovskii's *Tolstoi and Dostoevskii*. Rather than regard Tolstoi and Dostoevskii as polar opposites, Davydov stresses their common Russian morality, using 'Russian' as a codeword for 'Christian'. The (Christian) principle of love, he claims, enabled Tolstoi to overcome Schopenhauer's "metaphysics of horror" (and Nietzsche's Dionysian principle). (When I asked Davydov, in 1988, if he was a Christian, he answered, "It is no secret. My son is a priest.")[32] He faults Merezhkovskii for viewing Tolstoi and Dostoevskii through the eyes of Nietzsche but ignores Merezhkovskii's charge that Tolstoi was unable to love. Merezhkovskii had stressed Dostoevskii's and Nietzsche's affinities. Davydov argues that Nietzsche utilized Dostoevskii's psychological insights to crystallize his own world view, which was the polar opposite of Dostoevskii's.[33] Though reprimanded by the journal *Kommunist* for a nonmaterialistic interpretation of ethics, which indeed it was, Davydov was able to publish a second edition of the book in 1989. He did not change the chapters on Tolstoi but added a chapter on Shatov's religious nationalism (Shatov is a character in *The Possessed*), in which he denied that Dostoevskii was a national chauvinist. In the preface to the second edition, he emphasized the need for absolute moral principles of good and evil and the relevance of Tolstoi and Dostoevskii to the tasks of perestroika. Here, too, Davydov diverges from Merezhkovskii, who sought a spirituality without moralism. Merezhkovskii's subsequent writings on Tolstoi are not discussed, either because Davydov did not know about them, or because he deemed them irrelevant to his argument. His book can be regarded as an intergenerational dialogue and as a continuation of the God-seekers' attempt to articulate what Viacheslav Ivanov called "the Russian idea," in a 1909 article to which Merezhkovskii responded. The details of the Merezhkovskii–Ivanov polemic need not concern us here.[34] My point is that Merezhkovskii's thought is relevant to contemporary issues and, more broadly, that in Russia ideological reorientations are accompanied by new readings of Tolstoi and Dostoevskii.

Since the collapse of the Soviet Union, much has been written about "the Russian idea." Subsumed under this term are the very issues—moral, religious, and national/cultural—that Merezhkovskii treated in the works we have discussed. In a replay of the *fin de siècle*, Russians are again discussing how to make Christianity relevant to life in this world, Christian attitudes toward sex, Christian art, and the proper relation of Church and state. They are trying to define a postcommunist Russian identity and to find the organizing principles by which they can reconstruct their world. Surely Merezhkovskii's writings will figure in these discussions, as the full corpus of his works becomes available. How his works will be interpreted and applied to current problems remains to be seen, but we can be fairly confident that just as Merezhkovskii used Tolstoi and Dostoevskii to promote his own views, contemporary Russian readers will interpret Merezhkovskii in the light of their own agenda. So far, they have paid

144 BERNICE GLATZER ROSENTHAL

virtually no attention to his discussion of Tolstoi's religious anarchism or to his hagiographic writings on Tolstoi. Neither Merezhkovskii's warnings on the terrible temptation that autocracy holds for Russians nor his exaltation of Napoleon as the restorer of order have attracted their attention, even though they are chillingly relevant today.

Notes

1. Iurii Davydov, *Etika liubvi i metafizika svoevoliia* (Moscow: Molodaia gvardiia, 1982), p. 7.
2. Dmitrii S. Merezhkovskii, *Issledovanie—L. Tolstoi i Dostoevskii. Zhizn' i tvorchestvo*, vols. 9–12, in *Pol'noe sobranie sochinenii*, 24 vols. (Moscow: Sytin, 1914), 9:iii–v. Volume and page references to this edition of Merezhkovskii's writings (identified below as PSS) are henceforth given parenthetically in the text. The work on Tolstoi and Dostoevskii appeared first in serial form in *Mir iskusstva* (The world of art) from 1900 to 1902. The sharply abridged English translation, *Tolstoy as Man and Artist, With an Essay on Dostoievsky* (New York and London: Putnam, 1902), comprises mainly volume one of the original.
3. To give but one of many possible examples, the symposium *O religii L'va Tolstogo* (Moscow, 1912), is filled with references to Merezhkovskii's study. The contributors were Sergei Bulgakov, V.V. Zen'kovskii, Evgenii Trubetskoi, V.I. Ekzempliarskii, Andrei Belyi, Nikolai Berdiaev, A.S. Volzhskii, and Vladimir Ern. Virtually all of them had been regular attendees at the meetings of the Religious-Philosophical Society.
4. See, for example, S. Povartsov, "Traektoriia padeniia (O literarno-esteticheskikh kontseptiiakh D. Merezhkovskogo), *Voprosy literatury*, 1986, no. 11, pp. 153–90; and S.N. Savel'ev, *Ideinoe bankrotstvo bogoiskatel'stva v Rossii v nachale XX veka* (Leningrad: Izdatel'stvo Leningradskogo universiteta, 1987).
5. A volume containing the revised conference papers will be published by the Institute; it is currently in press.
6. See, for example, "Vstrecha," about the Religious-Philosophical Society, by the late, very popular priest Aleksandr Men', *Nauki i religiia*, 1991, no. 1, pp. 7–12. The article includes a discussion of Merezhkovskii's speech to the third session, "Lev Tolstoi and the Russian Church." I am indebted to Kristi Groberg for this reference.
7. Bernice Glatzer Rosenthal, *D.S. Merezhkovsky and the Silver Age* (The Hague: Martinus Nijhoff, 1975); C.H. Bedford, *The Seeker* (Lawrence, KS: University of Kansas Press, 1975); and "Stages of Nietzscheanism," in *Nietzsche in Russia*, ed. Bernice Glatzer Rosenthal (Princeton, NJ: Princeton University Press, 1986); Edith Clowes, *The Revolution of Moral Consciousness* (DeKalb, IL: Northern Illinois University Press, 1988).
8. The essay was published in P.P. Pertstov, ed., *Filosofskie techeniia russkoi poezii* (St. Petersburg: Merkushev, 1896), pp. 1–86, and reprinted with some revisions in *Vechnye sputniki* (1897) and in PSS, 18:89–171. Unless otherwise specified, citations are from the PSS.
9. Maksim Gor'kii, "Lev Tolstoi" (1919), in *M. Gor'kii. Sobranie sochinenii v vosemnadtsati tomakh*, 18 vols. (Moscow: Gosudarstvennoe izdatel'stvo khudozhestvennoi literatury, 1960–63), vol. 18, pp. 77–79. This essay is composed of fragments written at different times. Gor'kii's interest in Nikolai Fedorov suggests that he may also have been obsessed with death; see Irene Masing-Delic, *Abolishing Death* (Stanford, CA: Stanford University Press, 1992), pp. 123–54.

10. Merezhkovskii had small delicate hands and may have been sensitive on the subject.

11. In *Dostoevskii, prorok russkoi revoliutsii* (1906, PSS vol. 14), Merezhkovskii interpreted the revolution as the peasants' demand for a Christian "truth of the earth," symbolized, to Merezhkovskii, by a scene in *The Brothers Karamazov* in which Elder Zossima's disciple, Alesha, kisses the earth.

12. To open the Religious-Philosophical Society, Merezhkovskii and Gippius needed the permission of Konstantin Pobedonostsev, overprocurator of the Holy Synod. The minutes were published in *Novyi put'*. Each issue had to be passed by a political and a religious censor. Tiresome haggling over the content and language of every issue resulted. Publication of the minutes of the fifth, sixth, twenty-first, and twenty-second sessions was not permitted at all. In April 1903 Pobedonostsev closed down the Society because it offered a forum for heresy. Recent research indicates that the Holy Synod was considering excommunicating Merezhkovskii as well.

13. "Lev Tolstoi i Tserkov'. Referat D.S. Merezhkovskogo," *Zapiski Peterburgskago Religiozno-Filosofskago Obshchestva, 1901–1902* (St. Petersburg, 1906), p. 64. This was first published in *Novyi put'*, 1903, no. 2 (February), pp. 57–64 (second pagination —the minutes of the Society). The same issue contained an article "Al'bom Iasnaia poliana," pp. 135–43, with seven drawings of Tolstoi by Il'ia Repin. The literary section included letters by Tolstoi.

14. In his study of Gogol', written around this time, Merezhkovskii blamed Gogol''s nervous breakdown on his confessor's condemnation of worldly art. At the eleventh session of the Religious-Philosophical Society, he read the portions of *Tolstoi and Dostoevskii* that dealt with Christian attitudes to art. The topic of the twelfth session was Christian marriage and included a discussion of Tolstoi's "The Kreutzer Sonata."

15. *Zapiski*, p. 74.

16. Terrorists referred to the "propaganda of the deed," by which they meant political assassination. Merezhkovskii stopped short of endorsing the latter, but he and Gippius were friendly with the terrorist Boris Savinkov. In his drama *Paul I* (1907), Merezhkovskii raised the issue of whether murder for a higher ideal was justified. The government prohibited the production.

17. "Zametki o meshchanstve" (1905), in *M. Gork'ii, Sobranie sochinenii v tridtsati tomakh*, 30 vols. (Moscow: Gosudarstvennoe izdatel'stvo khudozhestvennoi literatury, 1953), vol. 23, pp. 341–67. In 1913 Gor'kii waged a newspaper campaign against the staging of Dostoevskii's plays by the Moscow Art Theater, because he considered Dostoevskii's neurotic, tormented heroes and his cult of suffering harmful influences on the workers. See "O 'karamazovshchine'," and "Eshche o 'karamazovshchine'," ibid., vol. 24, pp. 146–72. In the latter article he stated that his objection was not to Dostoevskii but to stage productions of his works that sensationalized the characters.

18. Tolstoi himself asked that his birthday be ignored. See Jeffrey Brooks, "Russian Nationalism and Russian Literature: The Canonization of the Classics," in *Nation and Ideology. Essays Dedicated to Wayne Vucinich* (Boulder, CO: East European Monographs, 1981), p. 323.

19. Vladimir I. Lenin, "Leo Tolstoi as Mirror of the Russian Revolution," *Collected Works*, 45 vols. (Moscow: Foreign Language Publishing House, 1963), vol. 15, p. 205.

20. Viacheslav Ivanov praised *bogoborchestvo* in a 1904 essay "On the Nonacceptance of the World." Taking his cue from Ivan Karamazov's refusal to "accept the ticket of admission" to a world where innocent children suffer, Ivanov refused to accept the constraints of the natural order, the laws of nature. The concept became a tenet of Georgii Chulkov's doctrine, mystical anarchism, which Ivanov supported.

Merezhkovskiii opposed mystical anarchism for reasons that cannot be entered into here but polemicized with Ivanov on it and related subjects.

21. Gor'kii, "Lev Tolstoi," p. 79. His first reaction to Tolstoi's flight was anger at what he considered Tolstoi's desire for suffering and martyrdom, as a way of forcing people—"you understand, to force!"—to obey his despotic rules of life (pp. 75–76).

22. "L.N. Tolstoi" (PSS, 16:327); "Tolstoi and the Proletarian Struggle" (PSS, 16:353–54); "Lev Tolstoi and His Epoch" (PSS, 17:51); "L.N. Tolstoi and the Modern Labor Movement" (PSS, 16:330–32).

23. "Smert' Tolstogo" (1910), "*Bylo i budet; dnevnik 1910–14* (Petrograd: Trud, 1915), pp. 17–19; pages henceforth cited parenthetically in text. Merezhkovskii did not provide the date of the diary entries. When available, date of first publication is given parenthetically in the text.

24. Ibid., and p. 43. See also his praise of the "wisdom" of Tolstoi's diary. "It is a book about death. Man is the creator of his life and death" (*Vom Krieg zur Revolution. Ein unkriegerisches Tagebuch* [Munich: R. Piper, 1919], p. 42).

25. On Tolstoi's admiration for Rousseau, see Thomas Barran, "Rousseau's Political Vision and Tolstoy's *What Is Art?*" *Tolstoi Studies Journal*, vol. 5 (1992), pp. 1–14.

26. D. Merezhkovsky, *Life of Napoleon* (New York: E.P. Dutton, 1929), and *Napoleon the Man* (New York: E.P. Dutton, 1928).

27. "Das Unheilige Russland," "Ein Tagloehner Christi," *Vom Krieg zur Revolution*, pp. 1–20 and 33–44, respectively. Dates of entries not provided.

28. "Lev Tolstoi und der Bolschewismus," in Dmitrij Mereschkowskij, Zinaida Hippius, Dmitrij Philossofow, and Wladimir Slobin, *Das Reich des Antichrist. Der Bolschewismus, Europa und Russland* (Munich: Drei Masken Verlag, 1921), pp. 189–98 (pages henceforth cited parenthetically in text).

29. Gor'kii, "Lev Tolstoi," p. 93.

30. See James P. Scanlan, "Philosophy of Morality," chap. 7 in *Marxism in the USSR: A Critical Survey of Current Soviet Thought* (Ithaca, NY: Cornell University Press, 1985), pp. 265–92.

31. Ivan T. Frolov, the chief "philosopher of perestroika" according to Evert van der Zweerde, attempted to use Dostoevskii and Tolstoi for a "humanist correction of Marxism." See, for example, Frolov's "O zhizni, smerti i bessmertii (Etiudy novogo [real'nogo] gumanizma)," in *Voprosy filosofii*, 1983, no. 1, pp. 83–98, and no. 2, pp. 52–64. I am indebted to Evert van der Zweerde for this reference.

32. This was at the conference on Nietzsche and Soviet Culture, in which Davydov participated, held at Fordham University, June 1988.

33. For details, see B.G. Rosenthal, "Current Soviet Thought on Nietzsche," in *Nietzsche Heute*, ed. Sigrid Bauschinger, Susan Cocalis, and Sara Lennox (Bern and Stuttgart: Franke Verlag, 1988), pp. 195–210.

34. See "From Decadence to Christian Renewal: The Parallel Paths of Merezhkovsky and Ivanov," *Slavic and East European Arts*, vol. 6, no. 2 (Winter 1990), pp. 43–45. "The Russian Idea" was the title of a lecture Solov'ev gave in Paris in 1888; it was published in Russian in *Put'* in 1911. Berdiaev borrowed the title for his famous book, *The Russian Idea* (New York: Macmillan, 1948).

IV

Russian Émigré
Thought Reclaimed

For the greater part of the twentieth century, the best works by Russian philosophers were written and published outside Russia and had little if any impact in the homeland. A prime cause of this situation, of course, was the mass exodus of Russia's philosophical elite that followed the Bolshevik revolution. Some prominent non-Marxist thinkers fled communist rule voluntarily, taking refuge in various European cities—Lev Shestov in Paris after a short sojourn in Berlin; Vasilii Zen'kovskii first in Belgrade, then Prague, and finally Paris; Dmitrii Merezhkovskii in Warsaw briefly, followed again by Paris. The greatest dislocation, however, was created by the forcible expulsion of scholars in 1922 that was described by Dzhimbinov in his essay in section I—an event that amounted to the wholesale exportation of the Bolsheviks' philosophical opposition. Nikolai Berdiaev, Sergei Bulgakov, Semen Frank, Nikolai Losskii, Ivan Il'in, and many other philosophers, most still in their prime, were among the roughly 160 prominent intellectuals and social figures compelled by the Bolshevik government in that year to leave Russia forever.[1]

Virtually all the exiled philosophers remained active and productive in their new locations, continuing to write in Russian and enjoying a receptive audience, if not in their native land, then certainly among the large, literate Russian community abroad and, through translations of their works, among the public in their adopted countries and around the world. Berdiaev, Losskii, and Shestov in particular were widely translated into the major European languages and developed considerable reputations abroad.

For the continuing dissemination of their Russian-language writings, these reluctant émigrés were indebted above all to an unlikely organization—the Young Men's Christian Association (YMCA) of North America. This ecumenically minded group resolved not long after the Russian Revolution to establish in Paris, which had become the intellectual center of the emigration, a press to publish Christian literature in the Russian language. Within a year of his expulsion from Russia, Nikolai Berdiaev had been named editor-in-chief of the YMCA Press, a position he retained until his death some twenty-five years later. During this time (and continuing after it) the press published hundreds of volumes, including works by virtually every major philosopher in the Russian emigration, most of whom had a strong Christian orientation. Berdiaev presided over the press with a hand that was remarkably even, considering the strength of his own philosophical convictions; he published manuscripts of high philosophical quality even if they were written by his severest critics.

Through the activity of the YMCA Press and other publishing houses and institutions such as the Russian Orthodox Institute in Paris, Russian philosophy flourished in the émigré community for decades after the revolution. Needless to say, the works thus produced were carefully kept from the hands and minds of Soviet citizens, most of whom had no knowledge of the very existence of these works—or of their authors, for that matter. At the same time, the Iron Curtain was not an impermeable barrier. As Piama Gaidenko relates in her essay above, works by Berdiaev found their way into the "special collections" (*spetskhrany*) of major Soviet libraries, where by the 1950s some privileged scholars, at least, could gain access to them. Two particular works by other émigré philosophers were deemed important enough by Soviet authorities to warrant the production of limited, carefully restricted Soviet editions, as we saw in Dzhimbinov's essay: Losskii's *History of Russian Philosophy*, translated into Russian in 1954 from an English-language edition published in the West in 1952; and Zenkov'skii's two-volume *History of Russian Philosophy*, published in Moscow in 1956 after its original publication by the YMCA Press in 1948–50.

Only with the coming of glasnost in the late 1980s, however, did the entire philosophical wealth of the emigration became potentially accessible to the Soviet public, and this potential was exploited with remarkable speed and enthusiasm. It is interesting to note that, many years before, those responsible for the operation of the YMCA Press were confident that the philosophical works they were keeping alive would one day reach a far greater audience within Russia itself. Donald A. Lowrie, the YMCA associate who was Berdiaev's principal American collaborator throughout his tenure as editor-in-chief of the press, wrote the following in 1960 concerning the press:

> Its present importance as the sole source of books in Russian with a Christian background . . . fades beside the possibilities of distribution in a future

Russia. Many of these books are of lasting interest; Berdyaev, Bulgakov, and Zenkovsky will be as pertinent later as now, and in a land where books are published in hundreds of thousands instead of the standard YMCA Press edition of three or four thousand, their influence will be greatly multiplied.[2]

Lowrie's prophecy of the enduring attraction of these writers has been amply fulfilled in recent years, and their books are indeed being widely distributed in the new Russia—if not in editions of hundreds of thousands, like the old communist classics, then certainly by the tens of thousands.

Because some of the principal émigré philosophers who were already prominent and influential before the revolution, such as Berdiaev, Bulgakov, and Merezhkovskii, have been treated in previous sections of this book, the present section will concentrate on two other thinkers who were major figures in the emigration: the highly original Russian-Jewish religious existentialist Lev Shestov (born Lev Isaakovich Shvartsman) (1866–1938), discussed here by Taras D. Zakydalsky; and one of the most controversial of the émigrés, the ardent anti-Bolshevik and monarchist Ivan Aleksandrovich Il'in (1883–1954), discussed by Philip T. Grier.

Although the two thinkers are both beneficiaries of the current Russian philosophical revival, they could scarcely be more different. Il'in directly continued the Russian religious-philosophical tradition; he was firmly committed to Russian Orthodox Christianity and imbued with the spirit of Slavophilism. Shestov, on the other hand, subscribed neither to Russian Orthodoxy nor to any other religious or philosophical position that could be called "orthodox"; his was a searching, skeptical spiritual quest of the existentialist variety, which rejected all dogma in the attempt to capture the true faith of the Old and New Testaments. Il'in's concerns were strongly social, national, and corporatist; Shestov focused insistently on the individual, with almost no attention to social or political issues. Il'in was a Russian patriot with utopian ideas of a transfigured holy Russia of the future; Shestov essentially ignored the issue of Russia and its national fate in his concern with the tragic fate of the individual everywhere, and utopian dreams were incompatible with his despairing rejection of all forms of rational world order. In all of these respects, Il'in was much closer to the dominant pattern of a "Russian thinker" than was Shestov.

Shestov, born into the family of a wealthy merchant in Kiev in 1866, was educated as a lawyer at Moscow and Kiev universities but never practiced that profession. Increasingly occupied with philosophical questions, he spent many years studying and writing philosophy between 1895 and 1914, living alternately in St. Petersburg and Western Europe, principally Switzerland. Two of his important philosophical works were published during that prewar period—*Dostoevskii i Nitshe* (Dostoevskii and Nietzsche) (1903) and *Apofeoz bespochvennosti* (The apotheosis of groundlessness) (1905). With the outbreak of World War I in 1914, Shestov settled in Moscow; after the Bolshevik revolution he left Moscow for Kiev, and from 1918 to 1920 he taught philosophy at Kiev University and at Simferopol' University in the Crimea. Emigrating in 1920, he settled in Paris, where he produced the remainder of his uniquely probing, aphoristic, critical philosophical studies; between 1922 and 1937 he also lectured frequently at the University of Paris. Although he was a friend of Edmund Husserl and other mainstream European philosophers of the day, Shestov was intellectually most attuned to the irrationalism of Pascal, Dostoevskii, and Nietzsche—not to mention Kierkegaard, whose thought he found especially congenial when he discovered it late in life.[3]

Despite what Zakydalsky calls the "un-Russian" character of Shestov's thought, the renewed availability of his writings has provoked much interest among Russians today. His current popularity is not as great as that of the more traditional religious philosophers, however—a fact that Zakydalsky attributes to Shestov's avoidance of the social and political questions now so much in the forefront and to his opposition to any sort of system building, whether it be Marxist or religious-idealist. Zakydalsky nonetheless finds a wide range of critical approaches to Shestov in current and recent Russian philosophical literature; with some reservations, Zakydalsky believes that each of these diverse approaches, provided it makes no claim to completeness or finality, offers a useful perspective from which to view this exceptionally multifaceted thinker. He also suggests that by their very "un-Russianness," Shestov's skepticism and tolerance of uncertainty can have a beneficial effect on the Russian mentality in the difficult days at hand by counteracting the epistemological overconfidence that has wreaked such havoc in Russian history before.

From Philip Grier's account below of Ivan Il'in's life and work, it is evident that although both Il'in and Shestov studied law at Moscow University and shared a common fate in exile, their philosophical interests were poles apart. Il'in's work in the Law Faculty was both serious and formative, leading to a lifelong interest in legal, social, and political themes. He became a follower of one of the principal professors in the Law Faculty, the liberal legal theorist Pavel Novgorodtsev (another Russian philosopher who is being rediscovered in the present day, as we saw in section II above), and Novgorodtsev's respect for the rule of law as a critical constituent of social order became a cardinal feature of Il'in's outlook as well, albeit in somewhat uneasy combination with his Slavophile convictions. The Slavophile convictions themselves, of course, tied in with Il'in's Orthodoxy and his ardent Russian patriotism, also separated him from Shestov. Finally, despite his Slavophile proclivities, Il'in admired, and developed original interpretations of, the philosophy of Hegel— the very archrationalist whose thinking, to intellectual rebels like Shestov and Kierkegaard, epitomized the ills of modern philosophy.

Grier examines in some detail the features of Il'in's thought that have made him perhaps the most controversial of Russia's once forgotten philosophers. What first drew attention was Il'in's uncannily accurate prophecy of the dismemberment of the Soviet Union and of the ethnic tensions and breakdown of social order that it would create. The controversy, however, arose not from the prophecy itself but from Il'in's prescription for dealing with what he predicted—that is, from his call for a Russian national dictatorship to restore order. This stance, taken together with Il'in's outspoken patriotism, his Orthodoxy, and his theoretical arguments to justify not simply monarchy but a monarchy that is in some sense "autocratic," was virtually guaranteed to turn Il'in into the darling of the ultra–right-wing religious nationalists in present-day Russia, who conveniently ignore the liberal elements in Il'in's overall social and political philosophy. In the nationalists' hands, to Grier's regret, Il'in is made out to be not only an authoritarian but a purveyor of the doctrine of Western "Russophobia," or the view that the West fears and seeks to destroy Russia.

A striking example of the appropriation of Il'in by the extreme religious patriots is provided by the work of Evgenii Troitskii, the contemporary neo-Slavophile whose ideas are discussed in James P. Scanlan's essay in section I above. Understandably, Troitskii is captivated by Il'in's expressions of devotion to his homeland; in the introduction to a book of selections from Il'in's writings that Troitskii published in 1992, he uses as an epigraph the following words of Il'in—words that are, in fact, remarkably relevant given the current Il'in revival: "If Russia needs my books, the Lord will save them from destruction; but if neither God nor Russia needs them, then I myself don't need them. For I live only for Russia."[4] As a heartfelt expression of love of one's country, such words might come from any writer who is a sincere patriot. But as Troitskii goes on, his enthusiasm for Il'in's patriotism takes on darker significance, and by the end of his introduction he identifies Il'in—favorably, of course—with the most extreme anti-Westernism and illiberalism. Here is a portion of Troitskii's peroration:

> Now there is an immediate danger that Russia will be turned into a semicolony. For that reason, particularly salutary is the legacy of the great scholar-patriot [Il'in] who showed that Western Europe is striving to convert Russia

to Catholicism, to colonize her, to keep her from access to the open seas, to partition her into small states, to weaken her . . . by stubbornly thrusting upon the Russian nation West European forms of republicanism, democracy, and federalism that are impossible for it to adopt. . . . These words [of Il'in's] are the profound unmasking of a Russophobia that is demagogically covered up with the fig leaf of anticommunism.[5]

Grier calls into question this interpretation of Il'in's legacy and defends the philosopher against related charges of fascism and anti-Semitism. The postcommunist "dictatorship" that Il'in calls for, Grier argues, should be construed as a temporary emergency measure only, and in general Il'in's "authoritarianism" should be understood as only one aspect of a comprehensive political theory in which the rule of law is paramount. Il'in's ultimate political ideal, on Grier's interpretation, is a state in which popular self-government has been made possible by the development of legal consciousness (which for Il'in includes the acknowledgement of natural law), as well as moral and religious consciousness, on the part of the citizens. Grier also admits, however, that interpreting Il'in's political philosophy, with its unique mixture of Slavophile and liberal elements, is a daunting task. Given the complexity of that task, the question of Il'in's place in present-day Russian thought is clouded by a double uncertainty: despite the noisy attention already paid to some aspects of Il'in's legacy, it is still unclear what Il'in himself intended the exact contours of his political philosophy to be, and it is unclear what role, if any, that philosophy will play in deciding Russia's future.

Notes

1. For a detailed recent account of the forced deportation, see L.A. Kogan, " 'Vyslat' za granitsu bezzhalostno' (Novoe ob izgnanii dukhovnoi elity)," *Voprosy filosofii*, 1993, no. 9, pp. 61–84.

2. Donald A. Lowrie, *Rebellious Prophet: A Life of Nicolai Berdyaev* (New York: Harper and Bros., 1960), p. 201.

3. For further discussion of the life and thought of Shestov, see two works by George L. Kline: "Shestov, Leon," in *The Encyclopedia of Philosophy*, ed. Paul Edwards, 8 vols. (New York: Macmillan, and Free Press, 1967), vol. 7, pp. 432–33; and *Religious and Anti-Religious Thought in Russia* (Chicago, IL: The University of Chicago Press, 1968), pp. 73–102. For a recent Russian perspective on Shestov's philosophy, published after the completion of Zakydalsky's essay, see Valery A. Kuvakin, "Lev Shestov," in *A History of Russian Philosophy*, ed. Valery A. Kuvakin, 2 vols. (Buffalo, NY: Prometheus Books, 1994), pp. 594–620.

4. Ivan Il'in, *Rodina. Russkaia filosofiia. Pravoslavnaia kul'tura*, compiled with an introduction by E.S. Troitskii (Moscow: Assotsiatsiia po kompleksnomu izucheniiu russkoi natsii, 1992), p. 3.

5. Ibid., p. 15.

TARAS D. ZAKYDALSKY

7 | Lev Shestov and the Revival of Religious Thought in Russia

Among the outstanding Russian philosophers of this century, Lev Shestov was the most isolated and "un-Russian" thinker. His exclusive and stead-fast concentration on the tragic fate of the individual in this world as well as his skeptical and "adogmatic" style of philosophizing placed him outside the main trends of Russian philosophy.[1] Unlike Marxists and positivists, he showed no interest in political and social issues and denied the relevance of science to the ultimate questions in philosophy; and unlike religious think-ers, he rejected any rational basis for faith and denied even the compatibil-ity of faith and reason. Estranged from the philosophical life of his own country, particularly after the Bolshevik revolution, Shestov attracted more attention abroad than at home and received greater recognition from Euro-pean than from Russian thinkers.

The short-lived liberalization of the Soviet regime under Nikita Khrushchev's rule led to a partial lifting of the curtain on Russia's intellec-tual history. The five-volume *Filosofskaia entsiklopediia* (Philosophical Encyclopedia), which came out from 1960 to 1970, published for the first time reliable information about many Russian thinkers of the late nine-teenth and early twentieth centuries whose names had been banned from Soviet publications for at least three decades. The regime had regarded them as its enemies and their ideas as politically subversive. Among them were thinkers who had emigrated or had been expelled from Russia in the early 1920s or who had been persecuted by the Stalinist regime in the 1930s. The first three volumes were typically Soviet in tone: they left no doubt as to who was a hero or villain. The fourth volume was more schol-arly, and the fifth volume was even better: its coverage of ideologically unacceptable thinkers and subjects was not only impartial but also deeper and more comprehensive. The full-page Shestov entry, which appeared in the last volume, gave a clear and balanced outline of the two stages of Shestov's philosophical development—his negative, nihilist outlook (up to 1911–14) and his positive, fideist world view.[2] It placed Shestov in the antirationalist current in Western and Russian thought and pointed out his influence on existentialism.

In the 1970s, although political discussion was stifled and dissent was harshly suppressed, research in the history of Russian thought was allowed to continue and some scholarly work was published. Very little was written on Shestov, but what did appear was original and perceptive. Two articles, one by the prominent philosopher Valentin Asmus and the other by Viktor Erofeev, deserve to be singled out.

In his tightly knit article, Asmus shows that there is a contradiction at the core of Shestov's philosophy and concludes from this that at bottom "L. Shestov is the greatest skeptic."[3] Asmus's argument begins with the observation that Shestov was not only a champion of existentialism but also its critic. As an existentialist Shestov rejected a rational world order accessible to reason (irrationalism) and rational morality (amoralism) and defended individualism and ethical solipsism. Shestov attacked such defenders of rational knowledge as Socrates, Plato, Aristotle, Anselm, Spinoza, Leibniz, Kant, Hegel, and Husserl. His philosophy was born out of despair, not wonder, and was pessimistic. But at the same time Shestov examined the history of existential thought and showed that not one of its great representatives—neither Plato, Plotinus, Duns Scotus, William of Occam, Luther, Pascal, Nietzsche, Kierkegaard, nor Dostoevskii— maintained his position against reason to the end. Hence, Shestov arrived at the paradoxical conclusion that existentialism as a permanent philosophical outlook is impossible.[4] While he rejected reason for faith, he did not believe in the power and victory of faith, according to Asmus. He believed that there is something in human nature or in existence that makes it impossible for man to surrender reason and determinism for faith and freedom. Thus, "L. Shestov is a champion of existentialism, who does not believe in the victory of existentialism, not only in the past, but also in the future."[5] This implies that in the final analysis Shestov was a nihilist throughout his philosophical career and never overcame his all-consuming doubt.[6]

I think Asmus's interpretation of Shestov is correct, but his argument leaves something to be desired. His point that Shestov exposed the breakdown of existential thought in the past is well substantiated, but this point does not entail that Shestov believed the breakdown to be inescapable. Asmus does not support his claim that existentialism was not a viable philosophical option for Shestov by either directly quoting Shestov or producing the logical grounds for the claim. It can be justified, however, by adducing Shestov's admission that neither despair nor the faith to which it leads can be chosen: they simply happen to men. But beliefs that are simply induced causally, not accepted or rejected on the basis of argument, have no philosophical relevance.

Erofeev rejects the view, expressed by Asmus and held also by Semen Frank, that Shestov's philosophy did not undergo any major changes. Although the "idea of salvation in all its different variations permeates all of Shestov's work,"[7] his thought can only be understood if it is grasped in its contradictory evolution. Erofeev delineates in considerable detail what I would call the moral, tragic, and religious stages of Shestov's development.

The first stage was articulated in Shestov's first book *Shekspir i ego kritik Brandes* (Shakespeare and his critic Brandes) (1898), and then criticized in his *Dobro v uchenii gr. Tolstogo i F. Nitshe* (The good in the teaching of Count Tolstoi and F. Nietzsche) (1900). In Shakespeare, whom he called his first teacher of philosophy, Shestov discovered that chance is the chief threat to human existence. It is chance that afflicts men with senseless suffering and mutilation. In Shakespeare's works men overcome chance by endowing its horrors with moral purpose. The purpose of tragic events is to give birth to personality, to the moral hero.[8] Thus morality gives life meaning. But Shestov soon found this solution unconvincing, according to Erofeev. He realized that there are too many horrors that do not lead to the sufferer's moral growth but simply, as in Ophelia's case, to her destruction. Nor can individual suffering be justified by its contribution to universal progress, enlightenment, or happiness.[9] Shestov considered Nietzsche's solution—the *amor fati*—but could not reconcile himself to the horrors of existence and decided to seek God beyond morality. Thus he entered the realm of tragedy.[10]

The philosophy of tragedy, Erofeev explains, was first articulated in *Dostoevskii i Nitshe* (Dostoevskii and Nietzsche) (1903). Its hero is the Underground Man who bangs his head against the wall rather than accept false ideals. For him nothing can overcome the absurdity of individual existence. In *Apofeoz bespochvennosti* (The apotheosis of groundlessness) (1905), Shestov was torn by two contradictory inclinations—exultation in his despair and openness to the possibility of salvation. From despair he moved to a struggle against the laws of nature and tried to break down the barrier between this world and the other.[11] But there was no conclusion to the struggle, observes Erofeev.

Thereafter, Shestov began to search for salvation not in this world but in another world; he wanted a salvation that was different from what he had sought at the beginning.[12] During the war period Shestov reconstructed his world view: he sacrificed everything—reason, morality, free will, sensibility, everyday life, communication with others—to find God, or rather to invent, without acknowledging this, his own God.[13] In his earliest works published abroad he already spoke as a believer. Because of his skepticism, his religious life was never peaceful and happy. At the end of the 1920s he discovered Kierkegaard, who had a great impact on him. In particular, he adopted Kierkegaard's idea of repetition and interpreted it in his own way as the alteration of the past. Since only the injustices of the past are to be undone by God, the idea of justice is implicit in Shestov's concepts of repetition and God. But this concept of God is incompatible with his notion of God as arbitrariness and undermines his whole religious philosophy.[14]

I have presented only the skeleton of Erofeev's complex outline. Since Shestov is an "experimental" rather than a dialectical thinker, his thought does not develop according to a regular pattern. This makes it difficult, if not impossible, to decide which of his moves are significant developments and which are inconsequential trials or aberrations. Erofeev's account seems to be overloaded with details and is difficult to follow. In any case it is only one of any number of possible accounts. Erofeev's critical comments, most of which I have left out, are always on the mark. Most investigators of Shestov's philosophy, whether Russian or Western, agree in distinguishing at least two different stages in his development.

Besides the two articles I have discussed, chapters devoted to Shestov appeared in A.I. Novikov's *Nigilizm i nigilisty: Opyt kriticheskoi kharakteristiki* (Nihilism and nihilists: An attempt at a critical description) (1972) and in V.A. Kuvakin's *Religioznaia filosofiia v Rossii: Nachalo XX veka* (Religious philosophy in Russia: The beginning of the twentieth century) (1980). Understandably, both authors deal with Shestov from the specific perspective and within the special limitations imposed by their works as a whole. Novikov detects in Shestov a "pure philosophical nihilism" that is more consistent than either Nietzsche's or Dostoevskii's nihilism. It consists of denying the intelligibility of the world, any absolute or relative truth, and the possibility of communication.[15] Novikov bases his interpretation on Shestov's early works, in which the dominant attitude is skeptical and stoical. Kuvakin, on the other hand, is interested in Shestov's religious period, which begins, according to him, with Shestov's work on the book *Sola Fide* in 1911–14. Shestov represents for Kuvakin the nihilist tendency of the God-seeking movement in Russian philosophy, a tendency that is expressed on the one hand in his rejection of knowledge, art, morality, culture, and social life for the sake of personal salvation, and on the other in his adogmatic, content-free religious faith. The most that can be said about his religious beliefs, according to Kuvakin, is that he was attached to the ideas and spirit of the Old Testament.[16]

The most obvious and important change in the area of Shestov studies since the beginning of perestroika has been the publication of Shestov's own works. Not all his works, but a good and representative sample of them, have for the first time become available to the scholarly community and the reading public in Russia. The amount of his writings and the sources in which they have been reprinted indicate that there is a wide and growing interest in Shestov's ideas in Russia. Since 1989 his writings have appeared in various portions—as fragments, articles, and books—in popular and scholarly periodicals, article collections, and collections of his works.[17] A volume of selected works published in 1993 includes the texts of three of Shestov's books: *Dobro v uchenii gr. Tolstogo i F. Nitshe* (also published earlier in *Voprosy filosofii*), *Dostoevskii i Nitshe*, and *Apofeoz bespochvennosti* (also published separately in Leningrad in 1991).[18] Two more books are included in the first volume of the two-volume collection of Shestov's works included in the *Voprosy filosofii* appendix series: *Potestas Clavium* and *Afiny i Ierusalim* (Athens and Jerusalem).[19] A sixth book, *Kirgegard i ekzistentsial'naia filosofiia* (Kierkegaard and existential philosophy), was reprinted separately in Moscow in 1992.[20] These works, which represent the substance of Shestov's thought, belong to different periods of his philosophical career and provide a pretty accurate, if not a full, idea of his intellectual development. His other works can be expected to appear in Russia soon.

In the past few years there has been a noticeable increase in the quantity of interesting work on Shestov's philosophy. Some of it consists of introductory essays, the purpose of which is to introduce a selection from Shestov's works, and some consists of imaginative, synthesizing interpretations of this thought. The format of the articles in the first group is similar: they contain some biographical information, a brief sketch of Shestov's main ideas, and a few comments about the history or contents of the particular selection that follows. They cannot be judged by the same standards as the longer, independently written studies belonging to the second group, although they often contain original insights and criticisms. The best articles of the introductory genre are those of N.V. Motroshilova, V.L. Kurabtsev, and A.V. Akhutin.

Introducing Shestov's article on Husserl, Motroshilova examines Shestov's treatment of other philosophers such as Schelling, Hegel, and Solov'ev and admits that it is one-sided and extreme.[21] She tries to justify this kind of treatment and comes uncomfortably close to contradicting herself. As to Shestov's treatment of Husserl, she points out that his idea of phenomenology is derived from Husserl's early works. Hence he ignores Husserl's transcendentalism and transforms Husserl into some kind of "super-Plato or super-Hegel."[22]

Kurabtsev's introduction to a chapter from Shestov's *Kirgegard i ekzistentsial'naia filosofiia* is focused on Shestov's religious thought.[23] After distinguishing four stages in Shestov's intellectual development— the prephilosophical (up to 1895), the God-seeking (up to 1911), the religious-existential (to the early 1930s), and the religious with some concession to reason[24]—he dwells on Shestov's belief in the power of faith to transform man into a being equal to God—into an earthly being who is daring and free and cherishes his spirit, reason, body, and senses—and to change the world into paradise.[25] Faith for Shestov is unlimited divine power that God granted Adam.

In his introduction to the new two-volume edition of Shestov's works, Akhutin tries to define Shestov's place in Russian and European philosophy. He points out that Shestov stands outside the religious and the secular traditions of Russian philosophy. The source of Shestov's philosophical searching is Russian literature: according to Shestov, the freest philosophers in Russia were Pushkin, Lermontov, Gogol', Dostoevskii, Tolstoi, and Chekhov. Armed with questions and doubts aroused by these writers, Shestov wandered among the world philosophers looking for answers. Thus, Akhutin adroitly sums up Shestov's life work as "an attempt to reexamine classical West European philosophy in light of the revelations with which Russian literature impressed him and much later also Western thought itself."[26]

Each of the studies in the second group presents a very different interpretation of Shestov's work as a whole. All of the interpretations, in my opinion, are equally valid; they concentrate on different themes in Shestov and highlight different aspects, strengths, and weaknesses of his philosophy. Other interpretations from other viewpoints are no doubt possible and welcome, for Shestov's asystematic thought is like a many-faceted gem: to be appreciated it has to be viewed from many different angles. There is no privileged perspective for viewing it, and there is no perspective from which all the facets can be seen at the same time. As long as one does not attempt the impossible—to give a complete and definitive interpretation of Shestov—one can construct an interpretation that is both consistent and illuminating.

Renata Gal'tseva discusses Shestov in her recently published book *Ocherki russkoi utopicheskoi mysli XX veka* (Outlines of Russian utopian thought of the twentieth century).[27] With its quick pace, its clear and concise language, and its sharp critical thrusts, her style of writing is reminiscent of Shestov's. She views Shestov as an "existentialist who appeared long before existentialism."[28] The main theme of his writings in both his early atheistic period and the later religious one was the inescapable tragedy of human existence.[29] Taking up Nietzsche's struggle against rationalism, he rejected the German philosopher's immoralism and remained faithful to the Russian tradition of compassion for the defeated and the suffering. His hero was not the master and creator but the "drowning man," the "living dead," who had been abandoned and forgotten by idealist philosophers.[30] Renouncing every consolation, he beat his head against the wall in hopeless despair until he discovered faith in an omnipotent God whose arbitrary will is restricted by neither ontological nor moral laws.

Gal'tseva is right in pointing out that Shestov's concept of the divine and human will as "objectless volition" is a purely negative one.[31] It expresses his antirationalism and cannot, without contradiction, serve as the basis of a positive faith in man's salvation. She detects another contradiction in Shestov's doctrine of salvation: if individual liberation consists merely in attaining faith—that is, in changing one's attitude to things—then contrary to his attack on idealism, Shestov has to accept it.[32] This difficulty can be overcome, I think, by distinguishing several senses of 'idealism'. Shestov rejects not idealism per se but what might be called the idealism of reason, and this form of idealism differs from the idealism of faith that he defends. Gal'tseva's third criticism of Shestov's idea of salvation is both perceptive and irrefutable. If salvation consists in undoing the past, then not only the horrors of the past but also the moral victories, by which at least some individuals overcame tragedy and gave meaning to their lives, will be revoked. This salvation is even more oppressive to the individual than the self-renunciation proposed by the rationalist tradition.[33] In pushing his critique of rationalism to the extreme, Shestov leaves the individual more vulnerable than before: instead of the slave of necessity he becomes the plaything of caprice.

In her short monograph *Lev Shestov*, L.M. Moreva emphasizes the religious and mystical character of Shestov's philosophy and downplays the significance of his irrationalism, utopianism, and existentialism.[34] The most comprehensive and accurate way to describe his thought is to call it a "transcendent metaphysics of man," for his central idea is that man is a creator created in God's image.[35] The transcendent element in man manifests itself in his infinite striving, audacity, and inconsolability and gives him the power to do even the impossible. Creation, according to Shestov, is a mystical act in which thought is not dependent on being, as in the case of knowledge, but being is dependent on thought.[36] To participate with God in creation, man has to break through necessity and the self-evident to faith, the "second dimension of thought."[37] The idea of man as creator is already present in Shestov's early philosophy; hence the transition from his philosophy of tragedy to his philosophy of faith was not a linear but a circular movement.[38]

To me, Moreva's account of this transition is not at all clear, and I doubt that Shestov's early and later concepts of creation are similar. Shestov's philosophy of tragedy was greatly influenced by Nietzsche. In this context human creativity is the power to create ideas, ideals, and values. When in his early works Shestov raised the question whether man can create out of nothing, he meant whether, recognizing the groundlessness of his existence, man could still give value or meaning to his life. In the context of Shestov's religious philosophy, creation means something very different: it means bringing into being not ideal but sensible objects. Although this kind of creation is an act of thought, the thought here is very different from what ordinary men and philosophers mean by thought. This kind of creative thought is faith. Moreva is right to call it a mystical or supernatural power, but she fails to explain the purpose of this power for Shestov: namely, to undo the Fall and all the subsequent horrors of existence. As a result, she leaves the reader with the mistaken impression that man's destiny, according to Shestov, lies in a transcendent, mystical realm, not in the natural world we see around us. She also fails to notice how paradoxical it is for Shestov to invoke supernatural powers in order to create paradise for man not in another but in the natural world.

Kuvakin begins his article "Oproverzhenie i predpolozhenie L'va Shestova" (Lev Shestov's refutation and supposition) by pointing out that Shestov's thought calls for and at the same time resists interpretation. It is expressed in aphorisms, paradoxes, sarcastic comments, and criticisms of other thinkers; hence to be comprehended it must be reconstructed.[39] But, because of its complexity, ambiguities, and inconsistencies, it is not only difficult but also dangerous to interpret him: it is easy to oversimplify and vulgarize him.[40] Shestov tried to construct a philosophy that would be quite different from the coercive, antihuman systems of the past, a philosophy that would immunize people to systems of thought or world views and give them "freedom from convictions."[41] To safeguard individual freedom, Shestov proposed a pluralist concept of existential truth, according to which the truth that matters is individual, nonobligatory, easily changed, and incommunicable. But philosophy cannot give this kind of truth; hence it must be adogmatic. The most philosophy can do is to clear away the obstacles to salvation, such as the confusion of existential truth with rational knowledge, and to prepare people to face the horrors of existence.[42] Obviously, this concept of philosophy rules out any positive doctrine for Shestov. Kuvakin admits that this is a most difficult problem, and he tries to work around it by claiming that Shestov's doctrines are very different from the usual philosophical doctrines: they are sketchy, conditional, and open.[43] Then he gives an outline of Shestov's basic doctrines by analyzing concepts such as truth, life, soul, man, nature, and God.

For Kuvakin what is most striking about Shestov's philosophy is its contradictory nature and religious coloring.[44] Some contradictions arise because of the different senses in which Shestov uses key concepts. Other contradictions are programmed to undermine rationalism or to express the irrational nature of reality and the incommunicable nature of the truth. The religious aspect of Shestov's thought consists of the struggle for faith. But his religiousness is problematic. It is a matter of controversy whether he accepts another world beyond this one.[45] For him God's transcendence, for example, does not exclude equality with man. Transcendence in his philosophy can be interpreted as that which is beyond not the natural world but merely the ordinary (commonplace) world.[46]

Kuvakin's account suggests to me that in his writings Shestov tried to do a number of different jobs without drawing a clear line between them: (1) to construct a metaphilosophy defining the nature and limits of existential thought; (2) to express his own existential philosophy, which is in principle incommunicable and constantly changing; and (3) to encourage others to prepare themselves for the horrors of life by developing their own philosophy. The statements that come under the first and last tasks could be called adogmatic to distinguish them from Shestov's philosophy proper, his personal world view. The statements that belong to his own philosophy cannot be said to be adogmatic or content free, but, since they are only approximate expressions of the author's personal beliefs without any truth claims for others, they can be treated lightly.

Although in the past few years interest in Shestov has grown rapidly among Russian intellectuals and some fresh and valuable studies of his thought have been produced, there is a certain continuity with the earlier scholarship on Shestov. This is evident not only in the strengths but also in the weaknesses of Russian research on Shestov. A Western reader, accustomed to a less dogmatic, more analytical style of writing, is struck immediately with the dearth of analysis and debate in the Russian literature. Interpretations and criticisms of Shestov's teachings are rarely accompanied by even a cursory analysis of his key concepts. The views of other researchers, if mentioned at all, are used usually to bolster one's authority, not to clarify through contrast the position one is trying to develop.

The revival of Russian philosophical traditions in recent years has favored some thinkers more than others. Judging by the number of studies about them and the number of reprinted titles, much more attention has been devoted to religious thinkers such as Vladimir Solov'ev, Nikolai Berdiaev, and Pavel Florenskii than to Shestov.[47] One reason for this situation is that Shestov wrote next to nothing on historical, social, or political issues, which for understandable reasons are widely and heatedly discussed today in Russia. No other Russian philosopher focused his attention as intensely and narrowly on the individual and the individual's tragic fate. As early as 1905 Berdiaev pointed out that his friend Shestov did not get the attention he deserved because his writings did not serve the march of history and/or any other general good.[48] This explanation is valid also today. Another, deeper reason for Shestov's lower rating in public attention is the dogmatic mind-set that has been cultivated in Soviet society. The underlying principles of the Marxist world view—that reality is law governed, that the laws of nature are knowable, that salvation is attainable through knowledge, that the universal is more important than the individual —are precisely the truths Shestov struggled against. But these are also the principles on which most idealist and religious systems are built. People raised on one system of thought naturally feel at home in another system and disoriented in "asystemic" thought.[49] This observation points to Shestov's potential usefulness for Russia's intellectual culture.

As Shestov's works become generally available in postcommunist Russia, one can expect them to play an important role in breaking down old habits of thought and stimulating critical and creative thinking. Judging from the Russian press, more and more Russian intellectuals are coming to realize that the roots of their country's tragic history lie in dogmatism, suppression of individuality, and intolerance of doubt. Learning to live in uncertainty may be necessary today for the very survival of society, and there is no finer teacher of this than Shestov.

Notes

1. In the subtitle of his book *Apofeoz bespochvennosti*, Shestov describes his work as an "Experiment in Adogmatic Thought."
2. R. Gal'tseva, "Shestov, Lev," in *Filosofskaia entsiklopediia*, ed. F.V. Konstantinov, 5 vols. (Moscow: Sovetskaia entsiklopediia, 1960–70), vol. 5, pp. 505–6.
3. V. Asmus, "Lev Shestov i K'erkegor (ob otnoshenii L'va Shestova k zachinateliu zapadnoevropeiskogo ekzistentsializma)," *Filosofskie nauki*, 1972, no. 4, p. 77. An expanded and improved version of this article appeared as "Ekzistentsial'-naia filosofiia: ee zamysly i rezul'taty (Lev Shestov kak ee adept i kritik)" in *Chelovek i ego bytie kak problema sovremennoi filosofii: Kriticheskii analiz nekotorykh burzhuaznykh kontseptsii*, ed. T.A. Kuz'mina (Moscow, 1978), pp. 222–51.
4. Asmus, "Ekzistentsial'naia filosofiia," p. 223.
5. Ibid., p. 246.
6. Ironically, Asmus's assertion about the stability of Shestov's outlook plays a part in his argument that Shestov's philosophy reflects the position of the Russian bourgeois defeated by the revolution ("Lev Shestov i K'erkegor," p. 80). But Shestov's nihilism reached its clearest expression in 1905, when the class he allegedly represented was far from defeated.

7. V. Erofeev, " 'Ostaetsia odno: proizvol' (Filosofiia odinochestva i literaturno-esteticheskoe kredo L'va Shestova)," *Istoriia literatury*, 1975, no. 10, p. 157. This article was reprinted as a preface to Lev Shestov, *Izbrannye sochineniia* (Moscow, 1993). For Frank's view, see his *Iz istorii russkoi filosofskoi mysli kontsa XIX i nachala XX veka: Antologiia* (Washington–New York: Inter-Language Literary Associates, 1965), p. 157.

8. Erofeev, " 'Ostaetsia odno: proizvol,' " p. 159.

9. Ibid., p. 162.

10. Ibid., p. 168.

11. Ibid., p. 175.

12. Ibid., p. 177.

13. Ibid., p. 180.

14. Ibid., pp. 184–85.

15. A.I. Novikov, *Nigilizm i nigilisty: Opyt kriticheskoi kharakteristiki* (Leningrad: Lenizdat, 1972), p. 134.

16. V.A. Kuvakin, *Religioznaia filosofiia v Rossii: Nachalo XX veka* (Moscow: Mysl', 1980), pp. 252–53. A similar claim about Shestov's empty faith was made by Sergei Bulgakov in "Nekotorye cherty religioznogo mirovozzreniia L.I. Shestova," *Sovremennye zapiski*, 1939, no. 68, p. 312.

17. Excerpts from *Afiny i Ierusalim* were printed in *Dialog* (1991, no. 5) and in the almanac *Silentium* (St. Petersburg, 1991), and fragments from *Apofeoz bespochvennosti* were published in *Iskusstvo kino* (1991, nos. 1 and 2). Shestov's article on Alexander Pushkin was reprinted in the collection *Pushkin v russkoi filosofskoi kritike: Konets XIX–pervaia polovina XX veka* (Moscow: Kniga, 1990), and his article on Dostoevskii, "Prorocheskii dar," was reprinted in *O Dostoevskom: Tvorchestvo Dostoevskogo v russkoi mysli 1881–1931 godov* (Moscow: Kniga, 1990). A number of Shestov's articles or book chapters have appeared in journals: "Pamiati velikogo filosofa (Edmund Gusserl')," in *Voprosy filosofii*, 1989, no. 1; " 'Iulii Tsezar' Shekspira," in *Inostrannaia literatura*, 1990, no. 6, and as an addendum to *Apofeoz bespochvennosti*; "Gefsimanskaia noch'. Filosofiia Paskalia" in *Filosofskaia i sotsiologicheskaia mysl'*, 1991, nos. 1 and 2; "Kirkegard—religioznyi filosof" in *Obshchestvennye nauki i sovremennost'*, 1991, nos. 2 and 3; "O 'pererozhdenii ubezhdenii' u Dostoevskogo" and "V.V. Rozanov," in *Russkaia literatura*, 1991, no. 3; "Otchaianie i nichto" (a chapter from *Kirgegard i ekzistentsial'naia filosofiia*), in *Vestnik Moskovskogo universiteta. Seriia 7. Filosofiia*, 1991, no. 5; and "Chto takoe russkii bol'shevizm?" in *Strannik: literatura, iskusstvo, politika*, 1992, no. 1. The last article, printed as a brochure in 1920 but destroyed by the Russian publisher, was one of only two that Shestov ever wrote on a political theme; a French translation appeared in *Mercure de France*, 1920, no. 142.

18. Lev Shestov, *Izbrannye sochineniia* (Moscow, 1993). For the earlier publications, see *Voprosy filosofii*, 1990, no. 7, pp. 59–132, and L. Shestov, *Apofeoz bespochvennosti* (Leningrad: Izdatel'stvo Leningradskogo universiteta, 1991).

19. Lev Shestov, *Sochineniia v 2-kh tomakh*, 2 vols. (Moscow: Nauka, 1993), vol. 1.

20. Lev Shestov, *Kirgegard i ekzistentsial'naia filosofiia* (Moscow: Progress-Gnozis, 1992).

21. Lev Shestov, "Pamiati velikogo filosofa (Edmund Gusserl')," *Voprosy filosofii*, 1989, no. 1, pp. 144–62. Motroshilova's introduction is "Parabola zhiznennoi sud'by L'va Shestova," pp. 129–43.

22. Ibid., p. 142.

23. The Russian-language edition of Shestov's book, which was originally published in French in 1936, came out in 1939; the selection consists of pp. 157–64.

Kurabtsev's introduction to the selection is "Ierusalim L'va Shestova," *Vestnik Moskovskogo universiteta. Seriia 7. Filosofiia,* 1991, no. 5, pp. 56–75.

24. This is an idea that is original with Kurabtsev ("Ierusalim L'va Shestova," p. 62). He bases it on what he takes to be Shestov's admission in "Sine effusione sanguinis" (*Put'*, 1937, no. 54) that reason can protect men from fanaticism, superstition, and beastly arbitrariness.

25. Kurabtsev, "Ierusalim L'va Shestova," pp. 64, 70.

26. A.V. Akhutin, "Odinokii myslitel'," in Shestov, *Sochineniia v 2-kh tomakh,* vol. 1, p. 5.

27. R.A. Gal'tseva, *Ocherki russkoi utopicheskoi mysli XX veka* (Moscow: Nauka, 1992). Chapter 2 is titled "Isk k razumu kak delo spaseniia individa (Gnoseologicheskii utopizm L. Shestova)," pp. 77–119. It was written in 1974 and remained unpublished until recently. I am indebted to James P. Scanlan for bringing this work to my attention.

28. Ibid., p. 77.

29. Ibid., p. 78.

30. Ibid., p. 93.

31. Ibid., p. 109.

32. Ibid., p. 111.

33. Ibid., p. 113.

34. L.M. Moreva, *Lev Shestov* (Leningrad: Izdatel'stvo Leningradskogo universiteta, 1991), pp. 58, 72.

35. Ibid., p. 77.

36. Ibid., pp. 52, 54.

37. Ibid., p. 61.

38. Ibid., p. 63.

39. V.A. Kuvakin, "Oproverzhenie i predpolozhenie L'va Shestova," *Filosofskie nauki,* 1992, no. 2, p. 53.

40. Ibid., p. 55.

41. Ibid., p. 57.

42. Ibid., pp. 58, 61.

43. Ibid., no. 3, p. 55.

44. Ibid., no. 2, p. 62.

45. Ibid., p. 63.

46. Ibid., no. 3, p. 54.

47. A. Kolesnikov makes the observation in "Mezhdu Afinami i Ierusalimom," *Dialog,* 1991, no. 5, p. 13, but offers no explanation.

48. "Tragediia i obydennost'," in *Sub specie aeternitatis* (St. Petersburg: M.V. Pirozhkov, 1907), p. 250. The article was first published in *Voprosy zhizni* in March 1905.

49. The affinity between the Russian tradition of religious thought and the philosophic core of the officially sanctioned ideology of Soviet society was discussed by G.A. Wetter in his "Russkaia religioznaia filosofiia i marksizm," in *Russkaia religiozno-filosofskaia mysl' XX veka: Sbornik statei,* ed. N.P. Poltoratzky (Pittsburgh, PA: Department of Slavic Languages and Literatures, University of Pittsburgh, 1975), pp. 99–116.

8 | The Complex Legacy of Ivan Il´in

1

The current massive effort by Russian intellectuals to recover their lost philosophical heritage has been characterized over the past several years by truly impressive numbers of reprintings of previously forbidden and ignored authors, accompanied by very intensive discussion of the merits, defects, and contemporary relevance of their views. Of all the important authors profiting from this "second life," probably none has been rescued from quite such deep obscurity and promises to be placed so firmly among the major stars as has Ivan Aleksandrovich Il´in.

Il´in was born in Moscow in 1883, educated in the Faculty of Law at Moscow University (1901–6), and made a privatdocent there in 1909.[1] After returning from a two-year period of philosophical study abroad in 1912, he taught at Moscow University and simultaneously at a number of other institutions in Moscow (except during periods of arrest) until 1922. Il´in was an adamant, uncompromising foe of the Bolsheviks and was arrested six times by them between 1918 and 1922, eventually being sentenced to execution. The death sentence was commuted to exile for life from Soviet Russia in 1922, and in that year, at age 39, he settled with his wife in Berlin. He taught at the Russian Scientific Institute in Berlin until 1934, when he was removed from the Institute by the Nazis and forbidden all further employment and political activity in Germany.[2] He escaped from Nazi Germany in 1938 with his wife and lived in Switzerland (also forbidden by the Swiss government to engage in overt political activity) until his death in 1954.

Despite the turbulent circumstances of his life, Il´in managed to create an impressively large body of significant writing in a variety of fields, including the interpretation of Hegel; ethics; political and legal theory; extensive proposals for the reconstruction of the Russian state, church, and society in the aftermath of the collapse of the Bolshevik regime; literary and artistic criticism; and religious thought. In addition to his more scholarly work, he kept up a more or less constant stream of journalistic writing on just about every topic of significance to the Russian emigration, including politics, diplomacy, history, religion, economics, literature, and art. In addition to contributing widely to many of the Russian-language newspapers and journals of the emigration in various European capitals as well as America, he published and edited his own journal, *Russkii kolokol* (Russian bell), in Berlin from 1927 to 1930.[3]

During the years 1940–41 in Switzerland, Il'in undertook the private circulation of a series of short articles on the contemporary situation to a list of subscribers he himself compiled. Forbidden by the Swiss to engage in public political activity, he was forced to reproduce these on a ditto machine and circulate them by hand.[4] He took up a similar form of activity beginning in 1948 and continued it until his death in 1954, composing a large number of short reflections on the contemporary situation, anticipating the eventual collapse of the Soviet Union, and describing in extensive detail the tasks that would have to be undertaken by true Russian patriots in order to reconstruct the nation. These short "bulletins," anonymously authored by Il'in, were circulated by an emigrant organization named the "Russian Joint Military Union" (*Russkii obshche-voinskii soiuz*). By the time of Il'in's death, there were 215 such bulletins, and in 1956 the same organization collected and published all of them in two volumes entitled *Nashi zadachi* (Our tasks), this time under Il'in's name. It is this work that first excited great interest in Il'in following the collapse of the Soviet regime.

The author of this enormous outpouring of books, brochures, articles, and lectures was once a figure of considerable importance in Moscow; he remained an important influence in the emigration in his own lifetime, but he has been essentially unknown in recent decades in his native land. As one of the most enduringly vehement, principled, and uncompromising foes of the Bolsheviks, he was consigned to the Soviet memory hole more effectively than most. More curiously, however, by the 1950s he had also been consigned to comparative oblivion by a significant part of the Russian émigré intellectual community, and the various explanations for that development form a much more complex and interesting story.

Part of the answer is surely to be found in certain traits of Il'in's own character and intellect: he seems to have been morally upright to the point of conspicuous rigorism. He repeatedly demonstrated exemplary personal courage.[5] He was strikingly clear headed, objective, and penetrating in his analyses of the historical tragedies and moral evils afflicting the world in his time.[6] He was extraordinarily forceful and outspoken in condemning every sign of wavering or compromise with the Bolshevik evil that he detected over the years among his fellow émigrés, to the point, doubtless, of appearing to many of them as a particularly severe, self-appointed watchdog of the moral and spiritual condition of the emigration.[7] He attacked the Tolstoian doctrine of nonresistance to evil, so dear to many contemporary Russian intellectuals, in the strongest possible terms, as a product of moral weakness and intellectual inadequacy and blamed it in part for helping to undermine resistance to the Bolshevik evil in the years before the October Revolution.[8] He was also scrupulous in assigning blame for the success of the Bolsheviks in significant measure to the failings of the tsarist autocracy, moral and spiritual as well as political. And in one-on-one intellectual debate he conspicuously overmatched many of his opponents.

The moral exactitude that characterized his life seems to have been matched by the intellectual precision reflected in his views; his capacity for making distinctions and the subtlety of his historical and moral judgments doubtless created an impression of extraordinary complexity, or, more likely, paradox, among his contemporaries. He was applauded by many as the principal theorist of the White Idea[9] and a staunch supporter of the monarchical principle. Yet he was scathing in his criticisms of the tsarist autocracy, held the failings of the Romanovs particularly to blame for the emergence of bolshevism, and refused to support the claim of the Romanov pretender in exile. Living in the midst of the White emigration, most of which was devoted to the program of "agrarian restoration" of their appropriated lands and estates, he argued for the utter impossibility of such a program, which could only drive the peasantry into the camp of the Bolsheviks.[10] He rejected the ideology of the extreme right wing of the White Russian camp, declaring a particular contempt for the Black Hundreds.[11] He was scornful of their anti-Semitism in the 1920s and likewise refused to cooperate with the Nazis' anti-Semitism during the 1930s.[12]

A further difference of opinion separating Il'in from some of his contemporaries concerned the issue of the rule of law. Il'in was a singular figure in Russian intellectual history in that he combined the most extreme Slavophilism in general with a strongly held commitment to the rule of law as essential to any future Russian state worthy of the name. These two attitudes had never really been encountered together, certainly not in the clarity and strength with which Il'in defended both, and this combination must have further puzzled at least some of his contemporaries.

In the cause that was dearest to his heart, the future rebirth and reconstruction of a Russia and a Russian state that would be worthy of the highest ideals of the nation, as, among other things, bearer of the eternal values of a pure (and purified) Russian Orthodox Christianity, Il'in was unswerving, uncompromising, and tireless. This ideal vision of a possible future Russian nation and state animating all of Il'in's work was doubtless so far removed from the immediate historical possibilities apparent to his contemporaries that the ultimate source of his views probably remained all but invisible to many of them, despite his most energetic efforts to explain himself and enlist adherents in the cause. Many of the views he advocated are open to almost inevitable misinterpretation if their source is not properly traced to his (in some respects) extrahistorical, mystical vision of an eternal Russia; the misuse of many of his expressed opinions in later years, even when honestly motivated, can be explained to some extent by this circumstance alone.

Finally, one further circumstance should be mentioned as possibly explaining why it was convenient for some of the Russian emigration in the later years to leave Il'in's legacy in something approaching a state of oblivion. As the years of the twentieth century unfolded, eventually revealing the full horror of Bolshevik totalitarianism, there was a natural tendency for the reputations of those intellectuals who had voluntarily cooperated with it in the 1910s and 1920s to suffer some questioning or diminution. A common defense frequently offered for such collaboration held that in the early years of the century no one could have foreseen the brutality and destruction that would be unleashed in the name of bolshevism, and that around the years of the revolution itself sympathy for the radical movement was to be understood as evidence of moral imagination, high intelligence, and/or superior historical understanding. Such a defense of collaboration with the Bolsheviks would tend to be undermined by a vivid recollection of Il'in's well-known views on the nature of the Bolsheviks, his predictions of what victory for the Bolsheviks would mean, and his resolute moral and political opposition to them from the first decade of the twentieth century. As the evidence for the superiority of Il'in's prophetic powers mounted ever higher, the entire subject of Il'in's position among the émigré intellectuals may have grown increasingly burdensome for some.

Il'in's death in 1954 passed almost without notice in the Russian emigration. Writing in the newspaper *Rossiia* in New York a few months later, I. Gorianinov observed: "Since the death of I.A. Il'in many days have passed. How did the Russian emigration respond to the death of this remarkable thinker? With nearly absolute silence."[13] In a sense one does not find this surprising. Il'in's unrelenting hostility to every compromise, however subtle, with the established authority in Russia and his impossibly difficult and demanding prescriptions for the reconstruction of Russia seemed to transcend the bounds of ordinary human resolve. A number of elements of Il'in's life and character that may otherwise be difficult to comprehend come into focus, perhaps, if one thinks of him in some respects as a twentieth-century version of an Old Testament prophet. Such individuals are notoriously inconvenient to have around, and their lack of realism can be positively maddening; a conspiracy of discrete silence may seem the best solution on the whole.

Whatever the full explanation for the obscurity into which his life and work had fallen during recent decades, Russian scholars and publishers have been working overtime in the past few years to remedy the neglect. By one recent count there have been at least 121 republications in Russia of articles or books by Il'in since 1988, plus a significant number of articles and essays discussing his work.[14] Several volumes of a projected fifteen-volume edition of his collected works have already appeared or are currently in press.[15] All of this activity has succeeded in bringing the figure of Il'in rather dramatically back to life. However, as the sketch above is intended to suggest, the power, complexity, and subtlety of his thought are such that a number of additional years will likely be needed before a relatively balanced appreciation of his thought comes to be widely shared. Early reactions to the reemergence of Il'in have ranged from the caricature of his views favored by some of the chauvinist right-wing press to thoughtful attempts by quite a few serious scholars to begin to respond to his thought in a wide variety of fields.

2

Il'in first came to the attention of a fairly broad readership in Russia at the end of 1990, when the journal *Kuban'* republished a short excerpt from *Nashi zadachi* entitled "What Does the Dismemberment of Russia Bode for the World?"[16] In that piece, written in 1950, Il'in addressed in considerable detail the question of what shape the ex-Soviet empire would be in following the collapse of the Soviet government. In early 1991, Il'in's article seemed intriguing to many readers, startling in its historical insights, and copies began to circulate from hand to hand. By the end of 1991, the prophesied collapse had taken place, and Il'in's article was beginning to attract still broader interest; at least one other journal republished the article.[17] During the period 1992–93, events unfolded in such a way as to make Il'in seem possessed of even more striking powers of prophecy, and his article was now circulating extremely widely, provoking intense discussion around the country. Many readers, encountering his article in 1992 or 1993, in the midst of the very events Il'in had foretold, found it astonishing that he, writing in 1950, could have described with such accuracy so many of the developments that were in fact unfolding around them. If Il'in was not literally a household name following this episode, he was known much more widely than before, and a great many readers were motivated to seek out more of his writing. By the end of 1992, not only had numerous other journals and newspapers begun publishing excerpts from a variety of Il'in's works, but the entire text of *Nashi zadachi* had appeared in a two-volume edition that promptly sold out.[18]

In the article "What Does the Dismemberment of Russia Bode for the World?" Il'in supposes that it will seem natural to many, especially in the West, that the empire should be broken up into all of its constituent ethnic and national components in the name (ostensibly) of freedom and self-determination for these peoples. Realistically, he supposes, the rest of the world will suppose it to be to their advantage to underwrite this process of the breakup of the empire with financial aid, developmental assistance, and ideological support to the newly independent elements. Il'in argues that all of this is grounded in a prevailing misconception of the nature of the (true) Russian state, and regardless of the apparent ideological "justification" for such a policy on the part of the rest of the world (which he also disputes), in practical terms it will convert much of the territory of the former Soviet Union into a new "Balkans," a perpetual source of civil war and political instability for the rest of the world, and ultimately turn out to be a disaster not only for the peoples of the former empire but also for the rest of the world.

The flavor of his argument, and an understanding of why his article recently excited so much interest in Russia, can best be conveyed by some extensive quotations.

> Conversing with foreigners about Russia, every true Russian patriot must explain to them that Russia is not an accidental heap of territories and peoples, and not an artificially composed "mechanism" of "administrative regions," but *a living, historically developed, and culturally justified ORGANISM, not subject to arbitrary dismemberment. . . .*[19]
> Dismemberment of an organism into constituent elements never did and never will provide either a recovery of health, or a creative equilibrium, or peace. On the contrary, it always was and will be a diseased disintegration, a process of decomposition, a fermenting, a putrefaction, and a universal infection. . . . The territory of Russia will boil with endless quarrels, clashes, and *civil wars* that will constantly escalate into *worldwide* clashes. This escalation will be completely inevitable due to the fact that the powers of the entire world (European, Asiatic, and American) will invest their money, their trading interests, and their strategic calculations in the newly emerging lesser states; they will compete with one another, securing dominance and "pressure points"; as if that is not enough, imperialist neighbors will come forward and attempt a direct or a disguised "annexation" of the

unstable and undefended new formations (Germany advances on the Ukraine and Baltic countries; England encroaches on the Caucasus and Central Asia; Japan, on the Far Eastern coast, etc.). Russia will turn into a gigantic "Balkans"; into an eternal source of wars; into a breeding ground of troubles.[20]

Rejecting the premise of "a state for every people," he points out that "neither history nor contemporary legal doctrine knows any such rule." Pointing to the contemporary world, he inquires:

> Where are the independent states of the Flemish (4.2 million in Belgium, 1 million in Holland), or the Walloons (4 million)? Why are there no sovereign Welsh cymru and Scottish gaels (0.6 million)? Where are the states of the Croats (3 million), the Slovenes (1.26 million), the Slovaks (2.4 million), the Wends [*vendov*] (65,000)? The French Basques (170,000), the Spanish Basques (450,000), the Gypsies (up to 5 million), the Swiss Ladins [*lodinov*] (45,000), the Spanish Catalans (6 million), the Spanish Gallegos (2.2 million), the Kurds (more than 2 million), and many multitudes of other Asiatic, African, Australian, and American peoples?[21]

Despite the indefensibility of the demand for the dismemberment of Russia, there will undoubtedly be just such a policy urged on the country following the collapse of the Bolshevik regime.

> And thus when after the collapse of the Bolsheviks world propaganda throws into the all-Russian chaos the slogan "Peoples of former Russia, dismember yourselves!" two possibilities will be opened up: either within Russia there will arise a Russian national dictatorship that will take in its powerful hands the reins of government, cancel that ruinous slogan, and lead Russia to unity, cutting off all and any separatist movements in the country; or such a dictatorship will not be formed, and in the country there will commence an unbelievable chaos of movements and returnings of peoples, revenges, pogroms, collapse of transport, unemployment, hunger, cold, and powerlessness.[22]

Conditions in the newly created "states" will be even worse:

> According to the most conservative count, [there will be] up to twenty separate "states," having neither undisputed territories, nor authoritative governments, nor law, nor courts, nor armies, nor undisputed national populations. Up to twenty empty designations. But nature abhors a vacuum. And into those developing political empty spaces, into those maelstroms of separatist anarchy will pour a human depravity: first, adventurers schooled in revolution, under new names; second, hirelings of the neighboring powers (from the Russian emigration); third, foreign seekers of adventures, condottieri, speculators, and "missionaries" (reread Pushkin's "Boris Godunov" and the historical plays of Shakespeare).[23]

The appearance of Il'in's article thrilled the nationalists, of course, not to mention the chauvinists. However, readers of every political stripe

tended to find something striking in his viewpoint, and his historical per-
spicacity seemed startling to most. Such was the first impression of Il'in
gathered by a very large readership in contemporary Russia.

3

Another important source for increasing awareness of Il'in's work has
been the tireless efforts of Professor Iurii Trofimovich Lisitsa, the editor
of the first edition of Il'in's collected works. Professor Lisitsa is a mathe-
matician in Moscow with remarkably wide-ranging interests in philosophy, politics, and religion, and he is also a very enthusiastic student of
Il'in. The *Collected Works* (*Sobranie sochinenii*), several volumes of
which have already appeared, originated entirely in his single-handed determination to recover as much as possible of the complete works of Il'in
and have them published in a carefully edited and fully annotated scholarly edition.[24] In an effort that would normally be mounted only by a team
of collaborating scholars, Lisitsa, working privately and alone, managed
to collect enough material for approximately fifteen volumes of the *Collected Works*, entirely on his own initiative, and compiled them into scholarly editions, volume by volume. This effort required a number of years of
sustained effort, and by the time he had assembled most of the material
needed, Lisitsa had become the leading Il'in scholar in the world (Professor Nikolai Poltoratzky, the Russian émigré scholar who was Il'in's literary executor and for many years the world's most knowledgeable
authority on Il'in, had died in 1990). In the first volume of the *Collected
Works*, Lisitsa published a lengthy historical and biographical essay on
Il'in, based on archival research and other sources. Lisitsa's essay is one
of the two most important publications to date on the life of Il'in, the other
being Poltoratzky's *Ivan Aleksandrovich Il'in*.[25]

Lisitsa's personal enthusiasm for Il'in has become well known in Moscow
intellectual circles, and his frequent publications on Il'in have appeared in a
number of journals and newspapers.[26] The fact that the *Collected Works* are
appearing in an edition of 25,000 copies, at a time of extremely uncertain
economic conditions that have caused great turmoil in the publishing indus-
try, is testimony to the considerable determination of both editor and publishing house (Russkaia kniga) and to their conviction that Il'in's works have
great importance at this particular moment of Russian history.

A special two-volume collection of selected works by Il'in is also being
published in the series of reprintings of works in Russian philosophy issued
as appendices to the journal *Voprosy filosofii* and available only to subscribers of that journal.[27] The first volume, containing Il'in's philosophy of law

and his moral philosophy, has already appeared. Professor Lisitsa also compiled, annotated, and supplied the introduction to these volumes.

Lisitsa's efforts to disseminate Il'in's works and views have not been limited to the *Collected Works* project and his other publications on Il'in, however. Dismayed by the apparently low to nonexistent appreciation for the value of the rule of law displayed by most politicians in the public eye and inspired by Il'in's insistence on the necessity for a high level of legal consciousness (pravosoznanie) on the part of both citizen and ruler in any state worthy of the name, Lisitsa decided to run for election to the post of people's deputy in the Moscow City Council, from the Cheremushkinskii District, in the elections of 1990. His motive in doing so had as much to do with the opportunity presented to engage in civic education in the spirit of Il'in's writing and to bring Il'in's ideas for the reconstruction of Russia before a wider audience as it did with the prospects of actually winning. In his own words:

> My election campaign had two major goals: educational—dissemination of the political ideas of Il'in—as well as moral—enhancing legal consciousness in the city population. I took these goals seriously. I took leave of absence from my job and, using materials that took me many years to accumulate, wrote my platform and paid to publish the major positions of that platform and a separate booklet exceeding fifty pages for those who wanted a better grasp of it.[28]

Lisitsa campaigned tirelessly, going door to door throughout the district, as well as making use of every opportunity for public appearances, to present his platform, which was essentially a digest of Il'in's *Nashi zadachi*. He did not win the election, but presumably a significant number of individuals were acquainted through his campaign with the work of Il'in, which had been one of his main purposes.

Not stopping with these efforts to promote awareness of Il'in's work, Lisitsa also conceived and organized a festive public event in May 1993 in order to commemorate the one hundred tenth anniversary of the birth of Il'in and simultaneously celebrate the appearance of the first volume of the *Collected Works*. This evening of speeches and entertainments took place at the Central House of Workers in the Arts, and the event was reported in several newspapers.[29] All of these efforts of Iurii Lisitsa, still continuing, have contributed more than those of any other individual, save the late Professor Poltoratzky, to the project of recovering the works of Il'in and placing them before the public.

4

Lisitsa's political activity, inspired by Il'in's conception of the values to be promoted in the reconstruction of a future Russian state, illustrates the importance of legal consciousness, or respect for the rule of law, as an element in Il'in's political vision. However, other contemporary Russian figures have invoked Il'in's authority in behalf of very different political programs stressing the element of dictatorship, with no reference to the idea of the rule of law. For example, the metropolitan of St. Petersburg and Ladoga, Ioann, hints at the view that Russia's current condition can be explained by a concerted conspiracy stemming from the West to destroy her power and wealth: "Yes, indeed, we *fear to believe* that everything taking place with us over the past eighty years has not been an accident or the whim of capricious history but *a purposeful attempt to destroy Russia* at any price."[30] Citing a prediction made at the beginning of the twentieth century that Russia would be the dominant power in Europe by the middle of this century, he inquires: "Does this not explain the undying effort of the West to undermine Russian power, to weaken and, if possible, to enslave Russia?"[31] A few paragraphs later in the same article, he quotes approvingly the lines from Il'in's "What Does the Dismemberment of Russia Bode for the World?" (quoted above) that declare that there are only two possibilities in the situation following the collapse of bolshevism —either a "Russian national dictatorship" or chaos. He calls for the dictatorship, citing the authority of Il'in, as justified by the dire crisis and the continuing external threat to the future of Russia. His article is remarkable for its lack of any acknowledgement that Russia's current crises might have in any sense been homegrown, and of course it constitutes a misuse of Il'in, in that no suggestion is made that Il'in's call for a "Russian national dictatorship" was intended as a temporary expedient to prevent the complete dismemberment of Russia by outside forces in the immediate aftermath of a collapse of the Bolshevik regime. Il'in supposed that in the conditions of near total chaos following such an event some extraordinary political force would be necessary to undertake the long-term reconstruction of Russia. However, Il'in is equally clear that such a "dictatorship" would be justified in the long run only by its success in raising the moral, legal, and religious consciousness of the population to such a level that a state based upon the rule of law would become possible. That dimension of Il'in's political thought is often overlooked by polemicists of this sort.[32]

5

Interpreting Il'in's political and legal philosophy is admittedly a complex and subtle task, however, if only because, on the one hand, he placed legal consciousness among the highest of the eternal values defining and justifying his ideal Russian state, and, on the other, he insisted that the most appropriate *form* of such a state was *monarchy*, and not unambiguously constitutional but in some sense of the term *autocratic* monarchy. It may well be that Il'in's usages are sufficiently singular that the standard categories of political theory are inadequate to convey the nuances of his thought. Indeed, according to Poltoratzky, he claimed that contemporary formal jurisprudence failed to grasp the essence of monarchy and could not genuinely distinguish monarchy from republicanism.[33] He insisted that one could have all the formal institutions of monarchy without the actuality, and one might have the actuality in the absence of any of the formal institutions. This should suffice to forewarn us that Il'in's discussion of the monarchical and republican principles does not follow the established paths.

There is a special difficulty involved in assessing Il'in's doctrine of the state: despite working on a manuscript on the topic of the monarchical and the republican principles throughout most of his adult life, he never completed it; his work on monarchy was published posthumously by Poltoratzky in 1979, and that volume was a compilation of several separate manuscripts and lectures.[34] On the other hand, he did complete the manuscript published two years after his death as *O sushchnosti pravosoznaniia* (On the essence of legal consciousness). That manuscript was originally produced in 1919, while Il'in remained in Bolshevik Russia with no hope of publishing it. He continued to rework it throughout his life abroad without ever finding a publisher, and at his death it existed as a completed and polished manuscript. Hence we can speak with slightly more confidence concerning the details of his doctrine of legal consciousness than we can of his doctrine of monarchy.

It is impossible to comprehend Il'in's doctrine of monarchy, or of political forms generally, without understanding something of his conception of legal consciousness, and the following lengthy quotation from *O sushchnosti pravosoznaniia* should at least suggest something of the complex connection between the two:

> The state in its fundamental idea is a spiritual union of people possessing mature legal consciousness and authoritatively asserting natural law in a brotherly, collective cooperation.
> Such is the *idea* of the state. But historically speaking, it only very slowly acquires these characteristics true to the idea and frequently develops a whole series of deep defects, while retaining its appellation. The rectification of these insufficiencies and distortions is possible only through the development, purification, and deepening of *legal consciousness*; thus if the history of the state reveals progress in the sense of a development of the state system, then this progress must be understood as a maturation in the soul

and spirit of humanity. The political structure and legal consciousness form a living, inseparable unity insofar as not a single reform is possible until a definite improvement in legal consciousness takes place; and any reform that is disproportionate to the state of popular legal consciousness will turn out to be absurd and ruinous for the state. The single true path to any reform is a *gradual education in legal consciousness.*

Precisely on this path, and only on it, can the fundamental contradiction between the *idea* of the state and its historical *realization* be resolved. For, on the one hand, the state lives by means of the *legal consciousness* of its people, but the essential characteristic of legal consciousness is the *capacity for self-government*; consequently, in its idea the state can be reduced to *self-government of the people.* However, on the other hand, the sole and the objective *end* of the state is so high and requires from the citizenry such *mature legal consciousness* that historically speaking the people turn out to be *incapable* of self-government, of realizing that end. And thus is revealed a great divergence between the principled form of the state and its historical appearance. Political philosophy must uncover the root of this divergence; the state power must find the path to healing it.[35]

Il'in seems to be employing something like Hegel's distinction between the "rational Idea" of the state, and individual states as given in history, with the possible difference that Hegel's rational Idea arises only after the forms in questions have become actual in some sense in history, whereas Il'in's notion of the Idea may be future referring in some more significant sense.

6

The centrality of legal consciousness in Il'in's doctrine of the state can be grasped from the fact that first of all Il'in describes it as the most important element of social existence, including recognition of the requirements not only of positive law but also of natural law. At the same time, *pravo* (law, right), the ideal content of legal consciousness, itself constitutes one of the ultimate elements of spirit, along with truth, the good, beauty, and revelation.

Referring to these ideas, the contemporary Russian writer Iu.S. Pivovarov has recently pointed out that one is entirely justified in calling Il'in a twentieth-century Slavophile and his work on the monarchical and republican principles "a masterpiece of Slavophilism in our time."[36] More particularly, he argues that Il'in's "serious and *carefully thought out* attempt to create his own, original model of a '*Rechtsstaat*' " is without precedent in the Slavophile tradition, and that in this respect he is a "major reformer" of it.[37] Pivovarov also stresses what too many would-be interpreters of Il'in's theory of the Russian state overlook—that the monarchical state he holds out as a distant prospect is "an extratemporal, extrahistorical, ideal model of Russia, its ideal form" as a permanent structure of values enduring unchanged in the midst of history.[38] In this he shows his essential kinship with his nineteenth-century Slavophile predecessors. Pivovarov expresses himself as sympathetic to all of this and argues that Il'in's view must be taken seriously. However, as one reads farther, Pivovarov's interpretation of Il'in becomes steadily more eccentric. It can be cited as a clear example of the difficulties of interpreting Il'in on the basis of anything less than a full knowledge of the texts: Pivovarov was apparently familiar only with a short excerpt from *O monarkhii i respublike* previously published in *Voprosy filosofii* and makes no reference to *O sushchnosti pravosoznaniia*. Absent a knowledge of the latter, one is highly likely to go astray in trying to interpret the former.

Despite Pivovarov's initial, and seemingly correct, focus on Il'in's remarkable and truly unprecedented combination of a pronounced Slavophilism with a strong commitment to the idea of a *"Rechtsstaat,"* he soon becomes sidetracked in a discussion focusing on the *autocratic* as opposed to the *constitutional* nature of the monarchical principle supported by Il'in. Not being aware of Il'in's claim that the idea of the state cannot ultimately be separated from legal consciousness, he turns to trace the "lineage" of Il'in's theory of monarchy to the so-called "young conservative" theorists of state and law in Germany of the 1920s. Identifying the almost entirely forgotten Carl Schmitt as the leader of that group, and "undoubtedly the greatest theorist of the state in the twentieth century," he tries to make a connection between Il'in's theory and Schmitt's.

Though some of his major works date before the rise of the Nazis, Schmitt was widely regarded as one of the principal apologists for the Nazi theory of the state when it arose (except that Pivovarov somehow seems to think of Schmitt as having rejected the Nazi claims). Schmitt had attempted to ground the legitimacy of the state in the "act of decision," by which he meant the essentially arbitrary act of the sovereign in a situation of extreme emergency (also declared to be such by the same sovereign). There is, of course, no "lineage" to be traced—we know that Il'in's theory had already taken shape before he left Russia, several years prior to the appearance of Schmitt's ideas—and the claim of similarity cannot be seriously sustained in any event. However, with "friends" like Pivovarov declaring that Schmitt is "the greatest theorist of the state in the twentieth century" and linking Il'in to him, one would not need too many enemies.

Having professed to find something like a purely autocratic conception of the state attractive (the genius of Schmitt, etc.) and having attributed such a conception to Il'in, he finally turns out to believe that only a constitutional monarchy could survive into the modern period. Since the Russian monarchy proved incapable of this turn, it has perished, never to rise again.

> Our tragedy, our helplessness at the contemporary crossroads is explained in many respects by the fact that we do not know the society in which we live. . . . We are not able to make a correct diagnosis of its frightful illnesses. To impose on it another utopia, a utopia of an ideal autocracy—even if a "rights-based" one, following Ivan Il'in—does not mean finding a way out. More likely, we would get some sort of new form of totalitarianism or the ideological covering for it.[39]

All of this creates a very curious impression. Why a professed admirer of Carl Schmitt should object to every form of totalitarianism is not entirely clear. In any event, it is unfortunately very clear that the attempt to evaluate Il'in's political philosophy based on a fragment from his posthumously published and incomplete work on monarchy is fraught with peril, both for the interpreter and for Il'in's reputation. Once again, the complexity and subtlety of Il'in's thought proves to be a formidable barrier to any quick or easy summary of his position.

By contrast, a far more informed summary of Il'in's political theory can be found in an article published in the same journal (*Voprosy filosofii*) the previous month.[40] In it, Iurii Lisitsa properly places the doctrine of legal consciousness at center stage. Beginning with Il'in's analysis of all types of social norms (moral, religious, and legal), he emphasizes the natural-law basis of Il'in's conception of rights and hence the role of natural law as an element in legal consciousness. From an explication of that notion, he moves on to the idea of the state and only thence to a discussion of monarchy and republicanism. Apart from Poltoratzky's essay on this problem, upon which he draws in part, Lisitsa's article is the most balanced and authoritative one in print thus far.

7

Turning to another subject, some recent attention has been paid in Russia to Il'in's ethical views, mainly to his famously controversial publication in Berlin in 1925 of *O soprotivlenii zlu siloiu* (On opposing evil by force). The journal *Novyi mir* (New world) published an excerpt from that work in 1991 (no. 10, pp. 210–24). The following year, *Voprosy filosofii* published, in nos. 3 and 4, a *pro* and *contra* on the same problem, using an excerpt from Il'in's book to represent one side of the debate. Finally, the entire text of Il'in's book has just become available in volume one of the two-volume selected works being published in the *Voprosy filosofii* appendix series.

The excerpt from Il'in in the journal *Voprosy filosofii* (1992, no. 4) was preceded by a carefully neutral introduction by N.K. Gavriushin discussing the event of the original publication and the furor following it. He provides a careful and balanced account not only of the origins of Il'in's book in some of his earlier published articles and brochures but of the earlier history of the problem itself in the context of Russian Orthodoxy.[41] Briefly chronicling the negative reaction to Il'in's position, he mentions Berdiaev's famous phrase parodying Il'in's book as "Cheka vo imia Bozhie" (the Cheka in the name of God) but declines to enter the debate explicitly himself. He does point out, however, the "extremely curious" fact that S.L. Frank, who also declined to enter the debate publicly and yet was known to have privately opposed Il'in at the time, came around by the time of World War II entirely to Il'in's position.[42] Gavriushin's article did not purport to add any significant new perspectives on the affair but may have drawn the attention of Russian readers to the existence of Poltoratzky's book on it.

8

One last recent development concerning Il'in should be mentioned. *Moskovskii zhurnal* (Moscow journal, 1993, no. 7) acquainted its readers with the existence of an important new book on Il'in's religious philosophy. The book in question was the work of a German Catholic priest, Wolfgang Offermanns, who reportedly served for many years in the West German embassy in Moscow. Having become acquainted with Il'in's work on religion, he concluded that Il'in was one of the most important thinkers in the Russian tradition, and undertook a multiyear study of his life and works.[43] Several pages from Offermanns's work were translated into Russian for publication in *Moskovskii zhurnal*.

Those pages provide a quick sketch of Offermanns's main conclusions concerning the religious dimension of Il'in's life as well as of his thought. Offermanns points out that despite some significant points of convergence with the original Slavophiles, Il'in remained an exceptionally independent thinker throughout his life. He wrote not as a student of the nineteenth-century tradition of Kireevskii, Khomiakov, or Solov'ev but rather as a student of the spiritual leaders of Orthodoxy, especially Theophane the Recluse (Feofan Zatvornik). Offermanns finds an exceptionally strong harmony between Il'in's life and his work.

> In the highly gifted, spiritual, and strong personality of Il'in, we are without doubt dealing with an exceptional Russian, a prophet, a scholar, and a

thinker, who wanted to show people of his time as well as future generations the true paths to genuine humanity and true belief in God. Il'in was a
Russian religious thinker and simultaneously one who carried out what he
thought and experienced.[44]

Offermanns also emphasizes Il'in's *Russianness*, as well as his
objectivity:

> In all that he thought, did, and wrote, Il'in always remained deeply and
> closely connected with his Russian Fatherland, its culture and religion. . . .
> Russian history and spiritual culture were known to him as to few oth-
> ers. That is evidenced by many of his lectures, papers, and essays, espe-
> cially his obituary for Prince Trubetskoi, who died in 1920, "Spiritual
> Culture and Its Spiritual Leaders," and his lecture read in Zurich, "The
> Essence and Distinctiveness of Russian Culture," in which he logically and
> convincingly depicts the Russian soul, Russian religiosity, and the histori-
> cal origins of the Russian people.
> Despite his strongly expressed national consciousness and struggle for
> national Russian goals in political and spiritual life, he was not a limited
> and one-sided human being. He pointed out many defects in the Russian
> national character, criticized the thought, philosophy, and creativity of
> many of his compatriots, and dissociated himself from all one-sided
> movements. In the midst of all his love for the Fatherland and the Russian
> people, he remained farsighted and open to the world, a person who also
> knew other spiritual cultures and had an excellent command of for-
> eign languages, to the extent that he was sometimes called a
> "Westernizer."[45]

Offermanns was also deeply impressed by the quality of Il'in's Christian belief:

> Il'in's philosophy and creativity provide witness to his deep religiosity.
> The Christian faith in God, in which the Orthodox church lives and which it
> teaches, and the conscious fulfillment of the teachings of Christ, had an
> enormous influence on all the deeds and the philosophy of I. Il'in. First he
> attempted to live himself by the laws of faith and only then, on the basis of
> that religious cognition, created his works, in which he gave account of his
> faith and tried to show the way to the same religious experience. In this
> consists the deep significance of his life and creativity; not only theory but
> also practice proves the meaningfulness of Christianity: to live on the basis
> of it, encompassing life experience thereby in the living word.[46]

Referring to Il'in's single most important work on religion, *The Axioms
of Religious Experience*, Offermanns expressed the only significant criticism of Il'in that he felt moved to make:

> The fundamental work of Il'in, in which are expressed all his most basic
> convictions and views, is the exploration *Aksiomy religioznogo opyta*. Axi-

oms for him are theoretical expressions of spiritually necessary forms of life. They are in his opinion essential and necessary truths of the human spirit, to which correspond in everyday life the fundamental forms of existence supplying the foundations of motivation and action. He wrote the *Aksiomy religioznogo opyta* over many years, deducing and generalizing them from the religious experience of the great teachers of religion. This universal investigation of the religious experience of humanity, however, bears a vividly expressed Orthodox-apologetic character, which Il'in openly acknowledged. That character often compels him to make polemical observations concerning the religious forms and manifestations of the Protestant movement and the Catholic church. On the other hand, he never speaks of negative phenomena in the history of the Orthodox church, which testifies to his definite one-sidedness, something which would have been hard to predict in such a many-sided and educated scholar as Il'in. Precisely in this consists the defect of the investigation of religious experience in question.[47]

His disappointment with the *Axioms of Religious Experience* notwithstanding, Offermanns clearly believes that Il'in was one of the most extraordinary and important figures in the recent history of Russian Orthodoxy as well as Russian thought and views him as a moral and spiritual exemplar for twentieth-century experience.

9

In any survey of reactions to Il'in such as this, not to comment on the power of Il'in's language would be a conspicuous omission. Even the best writers of his generation felt there was something extraordinary in his use of language. He was compared by Archimandrite Konstantin with "Metropolitan Filaret of Moscow—that, along with Pushkin, greatest master of language."[48] Petr Struve was still more elaborate in his praise of Il'in's language:

> I.A. Il'in is an interesting and major phenomenon in the history of educated Russian culture. In the formal sense, he is a specialist in law, but in essence he is a philosopher, that is, a thinker, and in form he is an astounding orator or rhetorician in the best ancient sense of that word.
> When he writes, he is speaking.
> And when he speaks, he captures the mind, charms the ear, enters the soul with some special power present in the living, firm, measured, and forged human word.
> This is not simply "golden oratory." Here not everything is pleasant, not everything is even pretty in the usual sense of the word, but everything is powerful and sharp. This speech is a sharp chisel precisely driven by a strong hand that, whether the listener desires it or not (for Il'in is above all an orator and not a writer!), somehow inscribes something on your soul and carves it in, like an engraver carving on wood.

Il'in is an orator-engraver, that is, a genuine artist with the living word that carves into the soul. Russian culture never before produced one such as he, and he with his face, particular and inimitable, with his original gift, strong and sharp in every sense, will enter its history.[49]

Il'in's use of language is unmistakably powerful, original, precise, and subtle. In trying to estimate the future influence of Il'in in his native land, one should not overlook the fact that he makes his own case before the reader with a rare degree of skill. The longer one is exposed to this language, the more difficult it becomes to dismiss its author.

In the nature of things, this could only be an interim report on the reception of Il'in in contemporary Russia. The acquaintance has been made too recently, the scope of his thought is too vast and unusually formulated to expect that a well-rounded and balanced appreciation of his work and life could have emerged in more than a few readers as yet. However, given the numbers of his works being republished and the intrinsic interest of his thought, especially for a post-Bolshevik Russia, it is safe to predict that he will eventually be established as one of the permanent lights in the Russian intellectual firmament.

Notes

Research for this paper was supported by Grant no. RI–20675–93 from the National Endowment for the Humanities.

1. There are two good published sources of bibliographical information concerning Il'in: N. Poltoratzky, *Ivan Aleksandrovich Il'in: Zhizn', trudy, mirovozzrenie (Sbornik statei)* (Tenafly, NJ: Hermitage Press, 1989); and Iu.T. Lisitsa, "Ivan Aleksandrovich Il'in: Istoriko-biograficheskii ocherk," in I.A. Il'in, *Sobranie sochinenii* (Moscow: Russkaia kniga, 1993), vol. 1, pp. 5–36.

2. The Germans appreciated Il'in's staunch anti-Bolshevik politics, and for a number of years after coming to Germany he was allowed to publish his political views freely. However, shortly after the Nazis came to power, that arrangement came to an end. In a private letter to his very close friend I.S. Shmelev dated 2 October 1934 (located in the Il'in archive at Michigan State University), Il'in explained the following circumstances:

> The natives of this country where I currently live behaved as follows with me. Because I
> (a) am in no way sympathetic either to conversations or plans for the separation of the Ukraine;
> (b) categorically refused to sow anti-Semitism among the Russian emigration;
> (c) displayed absolutely no sympathy, nor will display any, for the dissemination of their party among the Russian emigrants;
> they
> (a) deprived me of the right to work or receive earnings in their country;
> (b) fired me from the Russian Scientific Institute (created *by us*) with no right of appeal;

(c) forbade me to engage in political activity in their country under threat of [incarceration in a] concentration camp.

3. See Poltoratzky, *Ivan Aleksandrovich Il'in*, pp. 139ff.
4. See the "Kommentarii" by Iu.T. Lisitsa in vol. 2, bk. 1, of Il'in, *Sobranie sochinenii*, p. 468.
5. Il'in made no effort to disguise his fierce opposition to the Bolsheviks in the years following their victory. Despite increasing personal risk, he took advantage of every opportunity to articulate his opposition publicly, in lectures and in publications. He was arrested by the Cheka six times between 1918 and 1922—in March, August, and November of 1918, in 1919, in 1920, and again in 1922 (L.A. Kogan, "Vyslat' za granitsu bezzhalostno," *Voprosy filosofii*, 1993, no. 9, p. 74). The records of all six arrests, the interrogations and proceedings, are still held in the archives of the former KGB in Moscow, and, according to Professor Iu.T. Lisitsa, they show that even in the hands of the Cheka, under threat of execution, Il'in remained adamant, precise, and articulate in his opposition to the Bolshevik regime. Similarly, when faced with demands by the Nazis in 1934 that he bend his morals and politics to collaborate with them, he categorically refused, was summarily removed from employment, and was threatened with the possibility of arrest and incarceration in a concentration camp.
6. The words he wrote in his famous defense of the appropriate use of force to oppose evil seem applicable to him: he "did not turn away but immersed his gaze in the very eye of Satan . . . [and] permitted the shape of evil really and truly to be reflected in him, and endured it." The full passage, taken from Chapter 8 of *O soprotivlenii zlu siloiu*, is as follows:

> Is it proper or not to physically put a stop to an evil deed—in that question only he is competent who *saw real evil*, who apprehended and experienced it; who received and carried away in himself its devil's burns; who did not turn away but immersed his gaze in the very eye of Satan; who permitted the image of evil really and truly to be reflected in him, and endured it, without becoming infected; who *apprehended*, but *did not accept the evil*. (Quoted from *Put'k ochevidnosti*, ed. P.V. Alekseev and V.I. Kuraev [Moscow: Respublika, 1993], p. 38)

7. Even before his exile, Il'in's contemptuous view of the wavering of such groups as the "Smenovekhovtsy" was well developed. For example, during the interrogation for his sixth arrest in September 1922, the Cheka agent demanded his opinion of that group and was told, "I consider the Smenovekhovtsy unprincipled, hypocritical political adventurists." Quoted in L.A. Kogan, "Vyslat' za granitsu bezzhalostno," p. 75.
8. This attack appeared in his famous (notorious) 1925 publication in Berlin, *O soprotivlenii zlu siloiu*, and led to several years of sharp, even furious debate among the leading philosophers and theologians of the emigration, causing a more or less permanent rupture with a number of them.
9. See, for example, his "Belaia ideia," published as the preface to the first volume of the collection *Beloe delo: Letopis' beloi bor'by* (Berlin: Mednyi vsadnik, 1926).
10. See N. Poltoratzky, *Ivan Aleksandrovich Il'in*, pp. 123ff.
11. Il'in described the extreme right wing of the White movement, the Black Hundreds, as a "mercenary" group attempting to masquerade their own private interests as "the common good" and, morally speaking, a mirror image of the Bolsheviks themselves. "In order to overcome the revolution and revive Russia," he said, "it is necessary to cleanse the soul—first from revolutionism and, second, from the Black Hundreds." Quoted from his three-part article "Chernosotenstvo—prokliatie i gibel' Rossii" in

Rossiia/Slovo, 1926, no. 88 (1 March); no. 89 (2 March); no. 90 (3 March) (quotation from the first part).

12. For his trouble, Il'in seems to have been repaid mainly in opprobrium. In the letter partly quoted in note 2 above, Il'in continues, explaining what else the Nazis did in response to his refusal to teach anti-Semitism or support the Nazi party:

> (d) spread a set of rumors about me, politically defamatory *from their point of view* (a mason, a Francophile, a Jew-lover, enthralled to the Jews, etc.);
> (e) put out a slanderous brochure in Russian that is also being sent out *to other countries*, in which, among other things, it is asserted
> —that I was "not exiled but *sent by the Bolsheviks*";
> —that I am Griboedov's "Udush'ev, Ippolit Markelych";
> —that *prior* to them I declared myself a Jew-lover, and *in their presence* began to engage in anti-Semitism and give lectures on the Aryan principle;
> —that I am accordingly a weathervane, a careerist, and a mason.
> And *the whole of it* is a lie! (Letter to Shmelev dated 2 October 1934, located in the Il'in archive at Michigan State University)

Disappointingly, one still encounters individuals convinced that "everyone knows" Il'in was an anti-Semitic sympathizer of the Black Hundreds, despite incontestable evidence to the contrary.

13. *Rossiia* (New York), 29 April 1955 (quoted by Wolfgang Offermanns, *Moskovskii zhurnal*, 1993, no. 7, p. 16).

14. Personal communication to the author from Iu.T. Lisitsa, the editor of the *Sobranie sochinenii* now appearing in Moscow.

15. Il'in, *Sobranie sochinenii*.

16. "Chto sulit miru raschlenenie Rossii?" published in *Kuban'* (Krasnodar), 1990, no. 12, pp. 2–7. The five bulletins (nos. 101–5) that together comprise this article were originally circulated by the "Russian Joint Military Union" (Russkii obshche-voinskii soiuz [ROVS]) in 1950; they next appeared together in the two-volume work entitled *Nashi zadachi* published in Paris in 1956 by the same organization. *Kuban'* had previously published two other excerpts of Il'in, in May and June of 1990, neither of which had provoked such extreme interest.

17. Personal communication with Prof. Iu.T. Lisitsa.

18. *Nashi zadachi*, 2 vols. (Moscow: MP "Rarog'", 1992), compiled and introduced by I.N. Smirnova.

19. In the edition of *Nashi zadachi* edited by N.P. Poltoratzky, and published under the title *O griadushchei Rossii* (Jordanville, NY: Holy Trinity Monastery and the Telex Corporation, 1991), p. 171.

20. Ibid., p. 172.

21. Ibid., p. 173.

22. Ibid., pp. 177–78.

23. Ibid., p. 178.

24. Il'in, *Sobranie sochinenii*. As of this writing, volume 1; volume 2, books 1 and 2; and volume 3 have all appeared; volume 4 is imminent.

25. See note 1.

26. His articles on Il'in have appeared in *Voprosy filosofii*, *Literaturnaia Rossiia*, *Moscow*, *Znanie—sila*, *Voskresen'e*, *Moskovskii zhurnal*, *Nash sovremennik*, *Russkii vestnik*, and other publications. He has also written introductory essays and commentaries for each of the volumes of the *Sobranie sochinenii*.

27. I.A. Il'in: Sochineniia v dvukh tomakh, vol. 1, ed. Iu.T. Lisitsa, in the series of appendices to the journal Voprosy filosofii (Moscow: Moskovskii filosofskii fond, Medium, 1993).

28. See his account of the election campaign and its motives in the interview published in Moskovskii zhurnal, 1992, no. 2, pp. 2–5.

29. See, for example, Knizhnoe obozrenie, 1993, no. 19 (14 May), p. 4.

30. "Plach po Rusi velikoi," Sovetskaia Rossiia, 1993, no. 36 (27 March), p. 3.

31. Ibid.

32. This is not the most radical example of the misuse of Il'in's writing in support of extreme authoritarianism. There is an ongoing ideological battle in Russia, conducted mainly in the pages of newspapers attached to the various political camps, in which the authority of a number of the older Russian writers is more or less continually used and abused in ideological set pieces. As S.S. Khoruzhii explained in a paper delivered at the Transnational Institute Conference on "The Renewal of Russian Spiritual Life" at Dartmouth College in July 1992:

> In the background of the Tradition, among its weaker and dubious elements, a hotchpotch of ideas and figures is being thrown together to produce a nationalist-orthodox ideology for the New "Time of Troubles": the fabulous quasi-orthodox, quasi-mystics of Sergey Nilus, the authoritarian ideology of Ivan Il'in, the fantastic monarchism of Ivan Solonevich, the theories of Eurasianism. . . . But now the crisis has gone deeper. The defenders of the Tradition today are not Berdiaev, Bulgakov and Frank, but journalists who swear in the names of Berdiaev, Bulgakov and Frank, barely read and largely misunderstood by them. And the vulgarisers of the Tradition now are not the Eurasians (who produced some fresh ideas as well as vulgarisation), but more journalists who are busy fighting the others fiercely and vulgarising the vulgarisers. (From "Russian Religious Philosophy: Present State and Future Prospects" [unpublished paper], p. 5)

33. Poltoratzky, Ivan Aleksandrovich Il'in, p. 194.

34. I.A. Il'in, O monarkhii i respublike, ed. and with preface and appendix by N.P. Poltoratzky (New York: Sodruzhestvo, 1979). Poltoratzky's appendix to this volume, "Monarkhiia i respublika v vospriiatii I.A. Il'ina" (also published separately by the same press) remains the single most comprehensive and authoritative article on Il'in's doctrine of the state.

35. Il'in, O sushchnosti pravosoznaniia, contained in Il'in, Sochineniia v dvukh tomakh, vol. 1, pp. 182–83.

36. Iu.S. Pivovarov, "Mozhet li spasti Rossiiu samoderzhavnaia monarkhiia?" Voprosy filosofii, 1991, no. 6, p. 78.

37. Ibid., p. 79.

38. Ibid., p. 77.

39. Ibid., p. 84.

40. Iu.T. Lisitsa, "I.A. Il'in kak pravoved i gosudarstvoved," Voprosy filosofii, 1991, no. 5, pp. 146–58.

41. The article in question is "Antitezy 'pravoslavnogo mecha,'" Voprosy filosofii, 1992, no. 4, pp. 79–83.

42. Frank's changed view appeared, according to Gavriushin, in his book S nami Bog (Paris: YMCA Press, 1964).

43. Offermanns's book, Mensch, werde wesentlich! Das Lebenswerk des russischen religiösen Denkers Ivan Iljin für die Erneuerung der geistigen Grundlagen der Menschheit, was published by Erlangen in 1979, in the series Oikonomia: Quellen und

Studien zur orthodoxen Theologie unter Mitarbeit von Erich Bryner und Karl Christian Felmy, edited by Fairy v. Lilienfeld.

    44. Ibid., p. 17.

    45. Ibid.

    46. Ibid. p. 18.

    47. Ibid. p. 19.

    48. Quoted in Il'in, *Sobranie sochinenii*, vol. 1, p. 6.

    49. From Struve's "Dnevnik politika," quoted in Poltoratzky, *Ivan Aleksandrovich Il'in*, p. 135.

V

Finding Philosophy Under
Soviet Rule

The previous sections of this volume have been devoted to the ideas of Russian thinkers who flourished either before the Soviet period or beyond the grasp of Soviet authorities, in emigration. This does not mean, however, that the Soviet period itself produced nothing worth including in Russia's philosophical patrimony. For all the Stalinist strictures and despite the forced emigration or imprisonment and liquidation of many nonconformist thinkers, free philosophy was not totally stamped out in Russia under Soviet rule. A few thinkers survived who preserved the intellectual traditions of the past; still others came to maturity during the Stalin years with an almost miraculous independence of mind—the products of which, however, they were compelled to disguise in various ways. Happily, the contributions they made under the nose of Stalin and his communist successors are now being discovered and recognized for their philosophical merit. This final section of the volume will address those Soviet-era thinkers, with special reference to two who are now much in the public eye—Aleksei Losev and Mikhail Bakhtin.

Admittedly some of the independent Soviet-era thinkers did not survive for long in the oppressive intellectual climate of Stalinist Russia. A case in point is Gustav Gustavovich Shpet (1879–1937), the phenomenologist, aesthetician, and semiotician who was a prominent figure in Russian philosophical life at the time of the Bolshevik revolution. Shpet was neither a religious thinker nor a person with strong political views, but his Husserlian philosophy cost him his professorship at Moscow University in 1921. He escaped the mass deportation of 1922 and was able to continue publishing until 1927; in 1935 he was arrested and exiled to Siberia, where he was executed in 1937 on charges of "anti-Soviet activity." From that time until the publication of a relatively brief article about him in the fifth volume of the Soviet *Philosophical Encyclopedia* in 1970, Shpet's name was virtually unknown in Russia; for many years his family was not even informed of his fate. Only with glasnost did Shpet's thought come to life once more. In 1989, three of his major works were reprinted together as a single volume in the first series of appendices to *Voprosy filosofii*, and that volume was followed by other republications, conferences, and a growing periodical literature devoted to his philosophy.[1] The Shpet revival is an example of an intellectual rehabilitation in contemporary Russia that is motivated by purely philosophical rather than political or ideological concerns.

Of the thinkers who did manage to survive beyond the 1930s or to achieve some degree of intellectual independence during the Stalin years, none did so without difficulty and without in some way coming to terms with Marxism. Fortunately, "coming to terms" did not necessarily require sincere belief. The communist monopoly on intellectual life under Stalin, while oppressive in the extreme, was never absolute. It allowed for varying degrees of devotion to Marxism-Leninism, from flaming, militant advocacy to respectful lip service combined with selective silence. It allowed a scholar like Valentin Ferdinandovich Asmus (1894–1975) to do scholarly work in the history of Western philosophy, logic, and aesthetics and to inspire his Moscow State University students with his seriousness of philosophical purpose in the face of constant threats from the authorities.[2] Somewhat later, it allowed the appearance and maturation of thinkers as independent and individual as Aleksandr Zinov'ev (b. 1922) and Merab Mamardashvili (1930–1990), both of whom enjoy a following in postcommunist Russia.[3]

Even within the doctrinal parameters of Marxism itself, it was possible, particularly after Stalin's death in 1953, to engage in serious philosophical study and discussion in the USSR. Both Zinov'ev and another respected Soviet philosopher, Eval'd Il'enkov (1924–1979), first made their names as interpreters of Marx's dialectical method in *Das Kapital*. On many other subjects as well, in a variety of philosophical fields, genuine philosophical issues were joined and positions defended, all under the rubric of "Marxist philosophy."[4] Granted, Zinov'ev was forced to emigrate in 1978 after the publication abroad of his biting satire on Soviet life, *The Yawning Heights*, but Il'enkov remained in the USSR as a prominent Marxist philosopher until his death.

Not surprisingly, however, the genuinely Marxist philosophy that was alive in Soviet Russia has little appeal to Russian philosophers today. Il'enkov, recently the subject of an admiring monograph by a Western philosopher, is now largely ignored in his homeland.[5] When *Voprosy filosofii* in 1990 published a panel discussion on the subject "Is Marxism Dead?" the prevailing answer among the nine participants was affirmative. Even those who saw continuing vitality in Marxism were careful to qualify their assessment: only one of them defended the Leninism side of Marxism-Leninism, and all believed that Marx was as much wrong as he was right, so that only some of his ideas were worth preserving.[6] Some Russian writers who still publicly call themselves Marxists offer portraits of the German philosopher that are scarcely recognizable: K.M. Kantor, for example, argues that for Marx the motive force of history was not economics but cultural values and ideals, and Kantor puts Marxism on a par with Christianity in dedication to humanistic principles.[7] On the whole, Marxist philosophy appears to be no longer an intellectual force of great significance on the Russian scene, and the specifically Marxist portion of the Russian philosophical heritage is not being explored. Ironically, now that it would be possible in Russia to engage in serious critical study of Marxist philosophy, freed from the blinders of Marxism-Leninism, there is little interest in doing so.

There is great interest, on the other hand, in two thinkers—Aleksei Fedorovich Losev (1893–1988) and Mikhail Mikhailovich Bakhtin (1895–1975)—whose relation to Marxism was uncertain and who were considered philosophically suspect by communist authorities throughout their careers. Besides being almost exact contemporaries, the two had much in common. Both were arrested and punished for their freethinking under Stalin: Losev spent three years (1930–33) in prison and in labor camps, working on the White Sea Canal; Bakhtin was exiled for six years (1930–36) to remote Kazakhstan. Both were stricken in their prime with severe physical impairments—in Losev's case, blindness, and in Bakhtin's, a chronic bone infection that eventually required amputation of a leg. Both supported themselves from the mid-1930s on by teaching in relative obscurity in provincial schools and pedagogical institutes, without ever receiving major academic appointments. Neither was allowed to work as a professional philosopher; both did their philosophizing at the margins of their formally permitted occupations—Losev as a classical philologist and aesthetician, Bakhtin as a historian and theorist of literature. Both, finally, were brilliant and productive scholars who, by the end of their lives, were widely regarded as the leading figures in their fields.

Because Losev is far less known in the West than is Bakhtin, some additional information about his life and work may be useful. As a philosopher Losev had two careers—one before 1930 and the other from 1953 until his death.[8]

Educated in the classics, physics, mathematics, and music in his home city of Novocherkassk and at Moscow University, Losev was an active figure in the cultural life of Moscow throughout the decade of the 1920s.

During that time he became director of the section of aesthetics of the State Academy of the Arts, where he specialized in music theory, and from 1922 to 1930 he also lectured on aesthetics at the Moscow Conservatory of Music. Like Gustav Shpet, he was strongly drawn to the phenomenological philosophy of Edmund Husserl then popular at the Academy of the Arts, and also like Shpet he avoided being deported along with other non-Marxist philosophers in 1922. During the last four years of the decade, Losev published an astonishing cluster of eight books, beginning in 1927 with such titles as *Music as a Subject of Logic*, *The Philosophy of the Name*, and *The Dialectics of Artistic Form* and ending in 1930 with *The Dialectics of Myth*.[9] The books brought him a dual reputation—as a talented philosopher (in intellectual circles) and as an "enemy of the people" (in communist government circles).

In his first philosophical career, Losev developed a dialectical version of Husserl's phenomenological method and applied it to the analysis of language, myth, and art. It is this early work of Losev's that Alexander Haardt has taken as the subject of his essay below. Haardt believes that Losev's chief contribution to the phenomenological movement in Russia consisted in his analysis of the consciousness of time as it relates to the perception of music, and Haardt details this analysis in his essay, showing Losev's debt to ancient philosophy, especially Neoplatonism, as well as to Husserl in the elaboration of his distinctive version of phenomenology. Haardt's essay shows the levels of philosophical erudition and insight available to the Russian reading public as early as the 1920s and only now available again after the long intellectual drought that accompanied communist rule. *Music as a Subject of Logic*, *The Philosophy of the Name*, and *The Dialectics of Myth* were republished together as a single volume in the 1990 series of *Voprosy filosofii* appendix volumes,[10] and, as Haardt indicates, other books and articles by the Losev of the 1920s are being republished as well, suggesting the rebirth of the phenomenological tradition in Russian philosophy that was initiated by Shpet and Losev. These early works of Losev's figured prominently in an international conference on his thought held in Moscow in October 1993.[11]

The initial publication of Losev's eight non-Marxist books in the late 1920s was possible because at that time individuals were still free to publish their works privately. But those very books stimulated communist authorities to eliminate that troublesome freedom in 1930. Losev made no secret of his idealist sympathies and of his special scorn for "dialectical materialism" (which he dismissed as "a crying absurdity" in *The Dialectics of Myth*), and in May of 1930 a campaign against him was mounted in the controlled communist press; he was called (among other things) "an instrument of black reaction and obscurantism" and the last bastion of "the 'inner' front opposing Marxism."[12] When the Sixteenth Congress of the Communist Party convened in June, Stalin's trusted lieutenant Lazar Kaganovich used Losev's works as glaring proof that literature must be completely controlled by the state. "We are not yet exercising sufficient vigilance," Kaganovich proclaimed to a receptive audience; "the private author should be under the yoke of the proletarian dictatorship." Following the congress, private publishing was made illegal.[13]

Losev's ensuing arrest and imprisonment marked the beginning of a long period of silence, coinciding with the darkest years—from 1930 to Stalin's death in 1953—of Russia's philosophical dark ages. During this period of almost a quarter century, Losev was able to publish nothing but a translation of Nicholas of Cusa and some literary source notes appended to another author's book on Polyclitus. Originally sentenced to a ten-year term, Losev was released late in 1933 (along with his wife, who was a prisoner in another camp) through the intercession of E.P. Pashkova, the wife of Maksim Gor'kii. But academic and professional posts befitting his qualifications were closed to him, and he was obliged to take a succession of teaching positions in the provinces, until finally, in 1944, he was appointed professor of classical philology and general linguistics at the Lenin State Pedagogical Institute in Moscow, a position he was to keep until his death.

Losev's second career as a publishing philosopher was made possible by his willingness to present himself not as a philosopher but as a classical philologist and aesthetician, and of course to embellish his writings with the customary obeisances to Marxism-Leninism. Beginning in 1953 with an essay on ancient Greek mythology, which he prefaced by acknowledging the "genius" of Joseph Stalin,[14] Losev produced first a stream and then a torrent of scholarly works, eventually including thirty-four additional books and hundreds of translations and articles on ancient and modern literature, linguistics, and the theory of art and music. In many of these works his announced, relatively narrow topic concealed a discussion with far broader philosophical content and implications. His crowning achievement, an eight-volume work with the title *A History of Ancient Aesthetics*, is actually an exhaustive study of Greek and Roman philosophy and culture that established Losev as Russia's greatest authority on the thought of the classical world.[15] Also valuable for their broader philosophical significance are his book *The Aesthetics of the Renaissance* and his studies of the philosophy of Vladimir Solov'ev.[16]

Losev's plentiful obeisances to Marxism-Leninism were never enough to make the communist state accept him as one of its own, but they have clouded his legacy in postcommunist Russia, for they raise the question of what his philosophical beliefs really were in his second career. Was Losev's coming to terms with Marxism simply a matter of *pro forma* gestures designed to ingratiate himself with the authorities, or did it reflect sincere beliefs? Most of his present-day admirers accept the former explanation; Losev's Marxism, writes Viktor Erofeev, was a "Potemkin village."[17] But in addition to convicting the philosopher of sustained hypocrisy, that explanation must face a large body of conflicting evidence.

Losev's bows to Marxism took the form not only of ritual phrases but of the deliberate use of Marxist principles and methods, as is evident when he persistently explores the social setting of ideas, stresses the importance of dialectics throughout the history of thought, and points to what he calls the "elemental and integral materialism" that pervaded the philosophical thought of antiquity. Moreover, beginning in 1954 Losev spoke directly of having been "converted" to Marxism; as late as 1985 he insisted to an interviewer that the process had begun in 1925, when he read Engels's *Dialectics of Nature*, and was capped in 1934 by reading Lenin's *Philosophical Notebooks.*[18] Commentators who take these statements of Losev's seriously argue that those who reject them are distorting Losev's thought for their own, chiefly religious purposes; Isai Nakhov speaks disparagingly of the "religiously inclined Losevites who prefer faith to reason and objective argumentation." (These "Losevites," incidentally, include national patriots such as Pavel Tulaev, whose views are discussed in chapter two above.) Nakhov claims to find intimations of Losev's later Marxist orientation even in his writings of the 1920s, and he contends that although the philosopher may not have been a "one-hundred-percent Marxist," his Marxism was not an "ornament" but was "substance itself."[19]

The difficulty with a position like Nakhov's is that there is also much evidence to the contrary, particularly evidence that has come to light in recent years. In 1992, the publication of excerpts from conversations with Losev by one of his confidants made it clear that, in the first half of the 1970s at least (when the conversations took place), Losev was a devoutly believing Christian of the Russian Orthodox faith.[20] Furthermore, the last years of Losev's life were spent in intensive study of Vladimir Solov'ev, the Russian philosopher who had most appealed to Losev ever since his youth; and Solov'ev, Losev wrote in the introduction to his first monograph on the philosopher in 1983, was "an idealist from start to finish . . . [and] also a fideist from start to finish," who philosophized entirely "outside Marxism."[21] But the most stunning revelation of Losev's spiritual orientation came only after his death, at a Russian Orthodox memorial service in Moscow on 18 October 1993, commemorating the one-hundredth anniversary of his birth, when it was announced that Losev and his first wife had secretly taken monastic vows in 1929 (that is, midway through his supposed "conversion" to Marxism!).[22]

What, then, are we to make of Losev's own testimony that he was a Marxist? The most charitable interpretation is that he seriously thought he could accommodate the genuine insights of Marxist philosophy within a framework of essentially religious and idealist belief. He would not have been the first thinker to believe that what Nakhov calls "the rational kernels" of Marxism could be combined with Christianity; Nikolai Berdiaev was another religious, antibourgeois Russian philosopher who believed it, but who enjoyed the luxury of discussing it openly because he lived in emigration. Had Losev been at liberty to explain himself fully, he, too, might have advocated a melding of Marxist and Christian principles. Certainly Losev did not deny the importance of the material and social dimensions of being that are emphasized in Marxism. As his widow, Aza Alibekovna Takho-Godi, points out, Losev strove not for a fleshless idealism but for a synthesis of the material and the ideal, such as he found in his paragons Plato and Solov'ev.[23] When Dzhimbinov writes regretfully in his essay above that Losev "was nearly turned into a Marxist" under Soviet rule, he is testifying, perhaps unwittingly, to the genuineness of Marxism's appeal for Losev.

Just as Losev philosophized in the guise of classical philology and aesthetics, Mikhail Mikhailovich Bakhtin (1895–1975) philosophized in the guise of literary and linguistic theory. As Caryl Emerson relates in her richly detailed essay that concludes this volume, in postcommunist Russia Bakhtin is increasingly cast as a philosopher rather than simply a literary scholar.

Like Losev, Bakhtin created a stir in the late twenties, particularly with his pathbreaking book *Problems of Dostoevskii's Creativity* (1929); was punished for it by being removed from the centers of Russian intellectual life for a time (six years in Kazakh exile); and subsequently was tolerated as, teaching at Saransk Pedagogical Institute, he slowly made a reputation through additional publications, which in Bakhtin's case were not only brilliant but uncompromising. Far more influential than the cautious Losev and with his fame spread beyond Russia, Bakhtin is now regarded by some in the West as not only Russia's greatest literary theorist but "one of the leading thinkers of the twentieth century."[24]

Surveying the present-day enthusiasm for Bakhtin as a philosopher in Russia, Emerson finds that (again like Losev) Bakhtin is claimed by both Marxists and religiously oriented thinkers. The Marxists' claim is based not on any testimony on his part (Bakhtin, in Erofeev's words, "did not build Potemkin villages")[25] but largely on the ground that Bakhtin's opposition to formalism and his "dialogic" theory of language as a social activity were open to Marxist readings and were in fact given such readings by his followers Valentin Voloshinov and Pavel Medvedev (whose books are sometimes attributed to Bakhtin himself). Emerson finds such evidence unconvincing, particularly in the face of Bakhtin's explicit repudiations of Marxism. Similarly unconvincing, she believes, are the efforts by religious nationalists to co-opt Bakhtin for their illiberal cause; it is true, of course, that Bakhtin found Russian Orthodoxy intellectually interesting and remained a believing Orthodox Christian all his life, but Emerson does not see the religious dimension of his thought as central or enduring.

To the Marxist and the Christian interpretations, Emerson counterposes a portrait of Bakhtin as what she calls a "moral philosopher of narrative." By this she means that his moral philosophy is bound up with his conception of the novel as an open-ended world of subject–subject relations in which multiple potential realities are confronted at every turn and the reading of which thus constitutes a kind of moral education of an Aristotelian variety: it sharpens the ability to make proper choices in the absence of certainty and finality. Emerson predicts that Bakhtin's novelistic approach to morality will remain interesting to us long after we have forgotten Bakhtin the supposed Marxist and Bakhtin the religious thinker. If she is right, Bakhtin will have made his own distinctive contribution to the philosophical patrimony of both Russia and the world.

Notes

1. G.G. Shpet, *Sochineniia* (Moscow: Pravda, 1989). See also O.G. Mazaeva, ed., *Shpetovskie chteniia v Tomske—1991: Tvorcheskoe nasledie G.G. Shpeta i sovremennye gumanitarnye issledovaniia* (Tomsk: Izdatel'stvo Tomskogo universiteta, 1991); V.G. Kuznetsov, "Germenevticheskaia fenomenologiia v kontekste filosofskikh vozzrenii Gustava Gustavovicha Shpeta," *Logos* (Moscow), 1991, no. 2, pp. 199–214; and the 1992, no. 1, issue of *Nachala*, which is wholly devoted to works by and about Shpet.

2. N.V. Motroshilova, "In Memory of a Professor," *Soviet Studies in Philosophy*, vol. 28, no. 2 (Fall 1989), pp. 59–65. The survival of a limited philosophical culture in Stalinist Russia through the influence of figures such as Asmus has also been described recently by other Russian memoirists; see, for example, the following articles in *Russian Studies in Philosophy*: A. Piatigorskii and V. Sadovskii, "How We Studied Philosophy: Moscow University in the 1950s," vol. 32, no. 4 (Spring 1994), pp. 66–88; and V.N. Sadovskii, "Philosophy in Moscow in the Fifties and Sixties," vol. 33, no. 2 (Fall 1994), pp. 46–72.

3. On Zinov'ev, see a roundtable discussion entitled "The Social Philosophy of Alexander Zinoviev" in *Russian Studies in Philosophy*, vol. 32, no. 2 (Fall 1993), pp. 48–93. On Mamardashvili and his circle, see the memoir by Piatigorskii and Sadovskii cited in the preceding note and M.K. Mamardashvili, "A Beginning Is Always Historical, i.e., Governed by Chance," *Russian Studies in Philosophy*, vol. 32, no. 4 (Spring 1994), pp. 48–65.

4. See James P. Scanlan, *Marxism in the USSR: A Critical Survey of Recent Soviet Thought* (Ithaca, NY, and London: Cornell University Press, 1985).

5. See David Bakhurst, *Consciousness and Revolution in Soviet Philosophy: From the Bolsheviks to Evald Ilyenkov* (Cambridge: Cambridge University Press, 1991). For a critical response, see the review by Taras D. Zakydalsky in *Canadian Philosophical Reviews*, vol. 13, no. 4 (August 1993), pp. 134–37.

6. "Is Marxism Dead? A Discussion Among Soviet Philosophers," *Soviet Studies in Philosophy*, vol. 30, no. 2 (Fall 1991), pp. 3–74.

7. K.M. Kantor, *Istoriia protiv progressa. Opyt kul'turno-istoricheskoi genetiki* (Moscow: Nauka, 1992); see also K.M. Kantor, "Two Designs of Universal History," *Soviet Studies in Philosophy*, vol. 29, no. 4 (Spring 1991), pp. 35–58. For a critical discussion of Kantor's views, see V.M. Mezhuev, "Marx against 'Marxism'," *Russian Studies in Philosophy*, vol. 32, no. 3 (Winter 1993–94), pp. 22–27.

8. The closest thing in print to an adequate biography of Losev is the brief article by his widow, Aza Alibekovna Takho-Godi, entitled "Aleksei Fedorovich Losev," *Soviet Studies in Philosophy*, vol. 28, no. 2 (Fall 1989), pp. 30–44. On Losev's philosophy, see Alexander Haardt, *Husserl in Russland: Phänomenologie der Sprache und Kunst bei Gustav Špet und Aleksej Losev* (Munich: Wilhelm Fink, 1993).

9. *Muzyka kak predmet logiki* (Moscow: Izdatel'stvo avtora, 1927); *Filosofiia imeni* (Moscow: Izdatel'stvo avtora, 1927); *Dialektika khudozhestvennoi formy* (Moscow: Izdatel'stvo avtora, 1927); *Dialektika mifa* (Moscow: Izdatel'stvo avtora, 1930).

10. A.F. Losev, *Iz rannikh proizvedenii* (Moscow: Pravda, 1990).

11. The conference, held at Moscow State University on 18–23 October 1993, was entitled "A.F. Losev: Filosofiia, filologiia, kul'tura. K 100-letiiu so dnia rozhdeniia A.F. Loseva." Selected papers delivered at the conference are being prepared for publication.

12. For a more complete description of this campaign, with references to the original sources, see James P. Scanlan, "A.F. Losev and the Rebirth of Soviet Aesthetics after Stalin," in *Contemporary Marxism*, ed. J.J. O'Rourke, et al. (Dordrecht: D. Reidel, 1984), pp. 224–25.

13. Ibid., p. 225.

14. For references and a discussion of this article, see ibid., pp. 225–27.

15. A.F. Losev, *Istoriia antichnoi estetiki*, 8 vols. (Moscow, 1963–92).

16. A.F. Losev, *Estetika Vozrozhdeniia* (Moscow: Mysl', 1978). Losev's principal writings on Solov'ev are listed in note 9 of the introduction to section II of this volume.

17. Viktor Erofeev, "Poslednii klassicheskii myslitel'," in A.F. Losev, *Strast' k dialektike: Literaturnye razmyshleniia filosofa* (Moscow: Sovetskii pisatel', 1990), p. 7.

18. Ibid.

19. Isai Nakhov, "Losev i marksizm: Uroki odnoi zhizni: 1893–1988," *Svobodnaia mysl'*, 1991, no. 15, pp. 80–89, especially pp. 82, 83, and 86. On Tulaev's relation to Losev, see Pavel Tulaev, ed., *Vokrug Loseva: Tri filosofsko-prakticheskie vstrechi* (Moscow: Sobor, 1990).

20. V.V. Bibikhin, "Iz rasskazov A.F. Loseva," *Voprosy filosofii*, 1992, no. 10, pp. 139–46.

21. A.F. Losev, *Vladimir Solov'ev* (Moscow: Mysl', 1983), p. 3.

22. The author was present at this memorial service for "the monk Andronik [Losev]."

23. Takho-Godi, "Aleksei Fedorovich Losev," p. 40.

24. Katerina Clark and Michael Holquist, *Mikhail Bakhtin* (Cambridge, MA: Harvard University Press, 1984), p. vii.

25. Erofeev, "Poslednii klassicheskii myslitel'," p. 10.

ALEXANDER HAARDT

9 | Aleksei Losev and the Phenomenology of Music

In the context of the Russian reception of Husserl as it developed between 1914 and 1930 in the areas of language theory and aesthetics, the early work of Aleksei Losev occupies a central place.[1] His most important contribution within the "phenomenological movement" consists in the development of a phenomenology of the consciousness of time, which he (independently of Husserl's related analyses) presented in an essay entitled "The Phenomenology of Absolute, or Pure, Music," written in 1920–21.[2]

Contrary to Husserl, for whom the apprehension of music, and especially the hearing of a melody, was interesting only as an illustration of his general insights into the constitution of the consciousness of time, Losev tries by an analysis of music as a temporal art to work out its specific structures.

Like all of his early work in the first two decades of the century,[3] Losev's theory of musical time is also determined by an intensive dialogue with ancient, and, in particular, Neoplatonic, theorems and models. Here the close ties between musical theory and mathematics in Platonic–Pythagorean metaphysics comes to mind, as do Plato's definition of time in the *Timaeus* as a numerically expressed picture of eternity (of the Aion) and Plotinus's related interpretations.[4] In taking up this theme of ancient Neoplatonism under the conditions of contemporary philosophical consciousness, Losev's main point of reference lies in Husserl's method of eidetic description, which played an important role in the Soviet discussion of aesthetics at that time.[5] Yet phenomenological discussions of essential structures have in Losev's philosophy of language, art, and myth a purely heuristic character. Their purpose is to bring the specific subjects of discussion into full view. The actual development of these structures in all their complexity is reserved for the principal relevant dialectical-systematic parts of the corresponding theories.

Losev's interpretation of the experience of music passed through a number of stages between 1916 and 1925. His prephenomenological conception of music is expressed in 1916 in two essays on the aesthetics of music that were strongly influenced by Vladimir Solov'ev's metaphysics of total-unity (*vseedinstvo*) and by Schopenhauer's theory of art.[6] In his subsequent "Phenomenology of Absolute, or Pure, Music" (1920–21), Losev construes this conception on a phenomenological plane and so modifies it at the same time. But inasmuch as phenomenology is not able to cope with the antinomic structure of musical experience—the antithesis between formlessness and form in music—so a transition to a dialectical theory of music becomes necessary for Losev. This is expressed in the essays "Music and Mathematics" (1924) and "The Logic of Musical Form" (1925).[7] But these essays, too, are based on a phenomenological analysis of the structures of meaning, for which reason the Russian aesthetician still characterizes the later versions of his theory of art as (dialectical) phenomenological conceptions.

In the following pages we shall sample the development of Losev's thinking about the theory of music and thereby focus on the methodological question concerning the complementary relationship between phenomenology and dialectics as well as on the problem in the history of philosophy that is raised by the relationship between modern and ancient conceptions of time in Losev's analyses of music.

Losev's earliest works, published in 1916, do not yet show any recognizably phenomenological influence. The works in question are (leaving aside a study in the history of philosophy concerning the notion of Eros in Plato) two essays on the aesthetics of music, dealing with the operas of Rimskii-Korsakov and Verdi.[8] The conception of music contained in these essays is strongly influenced by Schopenhauer's philosophy of art and by Nietzsche's *The Birth of Tragedy from the Spirit of Music* but also by Solov'ev's metaphysics of total-unity. According to Losev's early metaphysical interpretation of music, "pure musical being" (to use his words) retraces the pre-individual "essence of all things," the "interior life of the spirit." In music, primordial, inherently undifferentiated chaos strives toward the "universal freedom of the total-unity"; in the experience of music the eschatological transfiguration (*preobrazhenie*) of the chaos of the world is anticipated.

According to Losev, music contains a particular sense of the world (*mirooshchushchenie*) that is opposed to the interpretation of reality made by abstract thought (*chistaia mysl'*): the latter considers each object in its distinctiveness, whereas music expresses the essential ground of all things, wherein they are all one. The career of cosmic events and that of music are placed side by side: just as primeval chaos shapes itself of its own accord into the structured cosmos, so too the formless musical entity presses on toward a form and generates structures and pictures.

The Phenomenology of Absolute, or Pure, Music

As distinguished from these early statements about particular works of music, Losev attempts in his "Phenomenology of Absolute, or Pure, Music" (1920–21) to provide a general theory of music. He is concerned here with "pure," "absolute" music, that is, with autonomous instrumental music without vocal accompaniment. Just as in the early essays, the leitmotif of his analysis is the tension between form and formlessness in music, but here the antithesis is expressed in carefully thought out terminology.

The full title of Losev's essay—"The Phenomenology of Absolute, or Pure, Music from the Viewpoint of Abstract Logical Knowledge"—points to the perspective and the provisional nature of Losev's treatment. It refers on the one hand to a more complete, more comprehensive elucidation of musical structures, to a dialectical theory that surmounts the abstractness of descriptive phenomenology. On the other hand, by indicating the provisional nature of his depiction, Losev draws a particular conclusion from Husserl's program of returning "to the things themselves." To get away from mere words, preconceived ideas, and traditional theories and so to arrive at the things themselves and describe them precisely as they appear was possible only by deliberately reflecting first on current conceptions in order to criticize their limitations.

With regard to the "true phenomenon" of music, this means that it is not immediately comprehensible. Only in stages does everyday consciousness, tied as it is to the categories of the spatial and real world, attain the "phenomenological view" of the eidos music.[9] The forms of thought and perception, accustomed as they are to everyday life and the positive sciences, must be changed if the musical phenomenon is to be comprehended adequately.

In the first stage music is understood as an experienced succession of notes in time, in contrast to the order of things in space. While spatially present objects can be clearly differentiated from one another, in music the notes appear to melt and pass into each other. The multiplicity of notes that make up a work of music is regarded as being whole and coherent, as an agitated coherence of elements melting into each other.[10]

With the help of the metaphors of melting and flowing together, Losev outlines a specific form of time that of itself cannot be made objective and measurable. "Musical being," he writes, "since it does not live in space, also does not live in spatially measurable time. It demands a kind of time that exists without space and that can be measured with no ruler."[11] This structure, or rather lack of structure, of a temporal succession that is subject to no measurement and in which the perceived notes melt into each other is first introduced as a mere construct. That "musical time" really does have this hypothetical property can be confirmed, however, according to Losev, by reflecting on elementary forms of the experience of music.

> In introspection, where there are no exact partitions, we find that states of consciousness follow on each other without this change ever meaning the loss of the previous state. The elements that succeed each other are as it were intertwined with each other. To hear a melody does not mean hearing the first note, then forgetting it immediately, hearing the second note, and so on. Hearing a piece of music means rather that its succeeding parts are being continually joined together.[12]

From this description of the experience of music comes the conclusion, which Losev himself called astonishing, that in musical time there is no past. "The work of music is a continual present without progression into the past, because its every heard detail is there not in itself but rather exists only in interpenetration with all the other details."[13]

With these analyses of the form of time peculiar to the experience of music, Russian phenomenology links up with the philosophy of life of Henri Bergson, who distinguished between physical and experienced time (durée pure). This distinction is to be found in his "Essai sur les données immédiates de la conscience" (1888), a work of great influence in Russian philosophical and psychological discussions of the first two decades of the century. As is well known, Bergson opposes the order of physical objects to that of the facts of consciousness. If spatially present things can be clearly differentiated from each other and can accordingly be counted and measured, the facts of consciousness are experienced only in an interpenetration (pénétration mutuelle) through which they elude any kind of determination and quantification. The form of time of immediate experience can only be described when consciousness withdraws from all spatial notions into itself. Then it experiences time as sheer duration, whereas the differentiation of past, present, and future is only possible when experienced time is regarded in terms of space.

The Russian music theoretician uses Bergson's distinctions as the basis for his own phenomenology of music—to be more precise, for the first stage in his analysis—but in the end he regards them as deficient. By contrasting musically experienced "sheer duration" with physically measurable time, music is still being described from the limited viewpoint of the abstract intellect and defined simply through negation of the structures of the spatial and real world. But such a purely negative definition of music is still indirectly subject to the intellectual categories so negated. In this way the elements of heard music can be thought of as flowing into each other only when they are compared with the mutually clearly differentiated things of the physical world. In the context of a different comparison, the structure of music would possibly appear quite different.[14] Also, the dependence of the conception of music developed here on the categories of objectifying thought leads to contradictions, since the notion that the notes "flow into each other" presupposes that the elements blending were first thought of as separate. The suspension of past, present, and future in the flow of experienced music also implies a prior contrasting of these time planes with each other. In this way—through the purely negative reference to the concepts of objectifying consciousness—the unobjectifiable essence of music can only be apprehended antinomically. With regard to this antinomy, Losev takes a phrase from Nicholas of Cusa and characterizes the structure of music as a *coincidentia oppositorum*.[15]

Nevertheless, for the Russian art theoretician the criticism of this antinomic characterization of the essence of music does not mean that he intends to exclude this method from his aesthetics of music. Rather, the failure of abstract intellectual thought in the antinomy is for him a necessary intermediate stage on the way to a more comprehensive dialectical theory that is capable of solving these antinomies and of reconstructing the musical object in its entirety.

Besides the phenomenological description of characteristic musical structures there are also in the "Phenomenology of Absolute, or Pure, Music" trains of thought and notions from Losev's earlier aesthetics of 1916, which was substantially affected by Schopenhauer's and Nietzsche's metaphysics of will. Thus music is characterized as a depiction of that essential ground of all things in which good and bad, happiness and suffering are fused with each other.[16] Music is referred to as overcoming the ruptured nature of material existence, and the striving of primeval chaos toward the logos is also mentioned. All these themes from Losev's earlier metaphysically determined aesthetics are now, from the newly gained phenomenological standpoint, relativized as "mythological" modes of thought. Thus, in the context of his phenomenology of music, in a chapter entitled "The Musical Myth," Losev gives a very emotionally colored, "poetic" description of musical experience in which the themes just mentioned are incorporated. Losev attributes this poetic-metaphysical text to a "relatively unknown German author,"[17] but it coincides in language and content so much with Losev's own conception of music as propounded in 1916 that we may regard him as the author of the text. It is presented as a mythological parallel to the previous discursively conducted analysis of music, as an "empirical description of how, from the ocean of the alogical musical element, logos and mythos are born."[18] As an expression of fundamental musical experience, these descriptions depict the basic experience of music, which Losev interprets with the help of phenomenological ways of thinking.

The Logic of Musical Form

If the metaphysical-"mythological" aesthetics of the early Losev is still present as the background in the "Phenomenology of Absolute, or Pure, Music," the Neoplatonic-dialectical theory of music developed in the later works also makes itself felt. Thus already in 1920–21 the concepts of phenomenology, and in particular the central term 'eidos', are interpreted in a few passages on the basis of Neoplatonic traditions. Here eidos stands in contrast to logos, the traditional concept of a concept. If eidos is the plastically present essence of a thing, then its concept contains an abstract blueprint that yields the method according to which an eidos should be reconstructed from its elements.[19] The logos interprets the individual elements of a thing in the form of a definition without being able to yield the basis for their coherence. But this basis is present in the dialectical development of the eidos of the particular thing, and accordingly it becomes clear what motivates the joining of the individual elements into a whole.

The central problem of Neoplatonically inspired aesthetics that interprets art as a representation of an eidos consists, with regard to music, in mentally coordinating the temporal character of music with the super-temporality of the eidos. In the paper "The Logic of Musical Form" (1925) on the theory of music, Losev attempts to resolve this problem by having recourse to Plato's definition of time, according to which time is to be understood as a numerically expressed picture of eternity (of the Aion).[20] If in the analyses of the experience of music up to that point the correspondence to eternity had seemed to consist in the fact that past and future are abolished in enduring present time, now the eternal character of time is seen in numbers that are embodied in the flow of time. Musical time is spoken of over and over again, like a leitmotif, as "the life of numbers." Losev regards numbers as the principle of the structuredness of all meaning. Furthermore, they are the precondition for the possibility of differentiating significances.[21] In counting, the counted units are regarded as being different and at the same time as being in a sense identical. In this way numbers are determined by a combination of the categories 'identity' and 'difference'. Moreover, each number "demands" the transition to the following number. This ability to increase is contained in the definition itself. Moreover, the previous number survives in the transition to the following number, while at the same time being at rest in itself. Therefore a number can be defined as "agitated rest." Finally, insofar as each number as a *particu-*

lar structure of meaning belongs to the category of "something" or being, it becomes clear that, in his definition of the concept of number, Losev is having recourse to the five basic concepts—identity and difference, rest and motion, and being—introduced in Plato's late dialogue the *Sophist*.[22]

After reconstructing the supratemporal dimension of the stream of time —its numerical "framework"—Losev proceeds to the concept of time itself. This is achieved dialectically in the following way: a number—like every other category in a dialectical thought process—attains definiteness only by contrast with an other. The other of a number can, as its counterconcept, be defined as "a compact blending, a melting together of elements."[23] A number thought of as in an identity with this blending element yields time. The sheer "melting" itself, in which the separate factors cannot be distinguished and cannot be defined, is not enough to constitute time. Only when these factors can be distinguished from each other as separate entities, inasmuch as the melting is structured in the manner of the interrelationship of numbers, do we have time as the embodiment of number.

In a further step, Losev inquires in due course about the otherness of time. This shows itself to be precisely that which is determined in terms of time—as motion. If its duration is measured, then "pure time" is objectified as the unadulterated "life of numbers" and made concrete as a spatiotemporal aspect of the object in motion.

Since Losev, in the phenomenological part of his inquiry, distinguished between the time of consciousness and cosmic, measurable time—and thus, following Bergson, separated experienced and physical time from each other—the central importance he gives to numbers in the dialectical derivation of musical time is surprising. Musical time is defined here as the "life of numbers," in which connection Losev is falling back on a Neoplatonic interpretation in which no distinction is yet drawn between experienced and cosmic time. Of course the form of time here is also the structure of cosmic life—that is, of the life of the world-soul, which shows itself in the regulated movements of the heavens and which can indeed be measured through them.

Does this falling back on a Neoplatonic interpretation of time in his late dialectical theory mean that Losev revokes the distinction between experienced and physical time that is central to his phenomenology of music? In order to answer this question, the structure of musically experienced time as developed in the "Phenomenology of Absolute, or Pure, Music" must be compared with the time that has been interpreted dialectically as the "life of numbers." When this is done it becomes apparent that the phenomenological conception of the temporality of musical experience as a pure flowing of elements into each other—as the suspension of past and future in "sheer duration"—is an integral part of the dialectical theory. But in that theory the "flowing into each other" is understood to be merely one dimension of time, a dimension that only in unity with the supratemporal frame of the numerically expressible structures yields time in its true meaning. If the numerically structured form of time is supplemented by the flowing structure of experienced music, then the difference between it and physical time is not yet abolished. On the contrary, only "pure time" (conceived of as the "life of numbers"), by being transferred to spatial events, yields objectified and physically measurable time. Contrary to Bergson, it is therefore not through the numerical structuring that objectified time is distinguished from "pure" and also experienced time but rather only through its objectification to the form of time of physical occurrences.

Notes

This essay was translated from the German by Desmond Durkin.

1. The most important works in the Russian reception of Husserl between 1914 and 1930 are a number of books by Losev and by Gustav Shpet (1879–1937), many of which are now being republished in Russia (as well as abroad) for the first time since 1930.

The relevant books by Losev are: *Filosofiia imeni* (Moscow: Izdatel'stvo avtora, 1927; reprinted in Moscow in 1990 and 1993); *Dialektika khudozhestvennoi formy* (Moscow: Izdatel'stvo avtora, 1927; reprinted in Munich in 1983); *Muzyka kak predmet logiki* (Moscow: Izdatel'stvo avtora, 1927; reprinted in Moscow in 1990); *Dialektika mifa* (Moscow: Izdatel'stvo avtora, 1930; reprinted in Moscow in 1990). A German translation of the last work by E. Kirsten was published in Hamburg in 1993, and an English translation by Vladimir Marchenkov is in preparation.

The relevant books by Shpet are: *Iavlenie i smysl: Fenomenologiia kak osnovnaia nauka i ee problemy* (Moscow: Germes, 1914); *Esteticheskie fragmenty*, 3 vols. (Petrograd: Kolos, 1922–23, reprinted in G. Shpet, *Sochineniia* [Moscow: Pravda, 1989], pp. 343–471); *Vnutrenniaia forma slova: Etiudy i variatsii na temy Gumbol'ta* (Moscow: GAKhN, 1927). The first of these works was translated by Thomas Nemeth as *Appearance and Sense: Phenomenology as the Fundamental Science and Its Problems* (Dordrecht: Kluwer, 1991).

Interpretations of the phenomenologically oriented writings of Shpet and Losev are to be found in Alexander Haardt, *Husserl in Russland: Phänomenologie der Sprache und Kunst bei G. Špet und A. Losev* (Munich: Fink Verlag, 1992).

2. A. Losev, "Fenomenologiia absoliutnoi, ili chistoi muzyki, s tochki zreniia abstraktno-logicheskogo znaniia." This text, composed in 1920–21, was published in Losev, *Muzyka kak predmet logiki*, pp. 5–100, and most recently in A. Losev, *Iz rannikh proizvedenii* (Moscow: Pravda, 1990), pp. 193–390 (the edition cited here). Husserl's "Vorlesungen zur Phänomenologie des inneren Zeitbewusstseins," edited by Edith Stein, was not published until 1928 by Martin Heidegger. In the works of Husserl available to Losev between 1900 and 1913, the problem of time is for the most part left aside. These works are the *Logische Untersuchungen* of 1900–1901 (also in

the second edition of 1913, with the exception of the sixth *Untersuchung*, the second edition of which did not appear until 1921); the essay on Logos, "Die Philosophie als strenge Wissenschaft" (1910–11); and the first book of the *Ideen zu einer reinen Phänomenologie* of 1913.

3. This is the only period that concerns us here. Losev's Marxist-oriented later work is excluded.

4. See in this connection Johannes Lohmann, *Musiké und Logos. Aufsätze zur griechischen Philosophie und Musiktheorie*, ed. Anastasios Giannarás (Stuttgart: Musikwissenschaftliche Verlags-Gesellschaft, 1970). See also Plotinus, *Über Ewigkeit und Zeit (Enneada III, 7)*, ed. W. Beierwaltes (Frankfurt/Main: Klostermann, 1967).

5. The most important conveyor of Husserlian phenomenology to Russia was Shpet, who studied under Husserl in Göttingen before the First World War and who, in his book *Iavlenie i smysl*, gave an original interpretation of Husserl's *Ideen zu einer reinen Phänomenologie und phänomenologischen Philosophie I* (1913). Influential in the discussion about the theory of literature was Shpet's *Esteticheskie fragmenty*.

6. This can be deduced from Losev's two essays of 1916: "Dva mirooshchushcheniia (Iz vpechatlenii posle 'Traviaty'), in *Studenchestvo zhertvam voiny* (Moscow: A.A. Levenson, 1916), pp. 105–22; and "O muzykal'nom oshchushchenii liubvi i prirody (K tridtsatiletiiu 'Snegurochki' Rimskogo-Korsakova)," in *Muzyka*, 1916, nos. 251–52.

7. The two essays appeared in Losev's *Muzyka kak predmet logiki* of 1927.

8. A. Losev, "Eros u Platona," in *Iubileinyi sbornik prof. G.I. Chelpanovu ot uchastnikov ego seminara v Kieve i Moskve* (Moscow, 1916), pp. 52–79, reprinted in *Voprosy filosofii*, 1988, no. 12, pp. 121–39. The operas are Rimskii-Korsakov's "Snegurochka" and Verdi's "La Traviata."

9. Losev, *Iz rannikh proizvedenii*, p. 207.

10. Ibid., p. 210.

11. Ibid., p. 237.

12. Ibid., p. 238.

13. Ibid., pp. 210–11.

14. Ibid., p. 228.

15. Ibid., p. 279.

16. Ibid., pp. 225–27.

17. Ibid., p. 257.

18. Ibid.

19. Ibid., pp. 216–17.

20. Plato, *Timaeus*, 37C–D. On Plato's doctrine of time in the *Timaeus*, see Gernot Böhme, *Zeit und Zahl: Studien zur Zeittheorie bei Platon, Aristoteles, Leibniz und Kant* (Frankfurt/Main: K. Klostermann, 1974), pp. 17–158.

21. Losev, *Iz rannikh proizvedenii*, p. 316.

22. On the problem of the five fundamental concepts in Plato's *Sophist* and Plotinus's interpretation of them, which became decisive for Losev, see Karl-Heinz Volkmann-Schluck, *Plotin als Interpret der Ontologie Platons* (Frankfurt/Main: K. Klostermann, 1966).

23. Losev, *Iz rannikh proizvedenii*, p. 328.

CARYL EMERSON

10 | The Making of M.M. Bakhtin as Philosopher

There exists a widespread notion that Bakhtin was a philosopher only in his very first works of the Vitebsk–Nevel' period, when he was planning to create a philosophy of law, morality, and aesthetic activity. . . . [But] Bakhtin remained a philosopher in his philosophical-culturological work as well . . . even in his literary-historical study of Dostoevskii.[1]

"*[In my 1929 book on Dostoevskii,] I couldn't speak out directly about the most important questions.*"
"*About which questions, Mikhail Mikhailovich?*"
"*Philosophical ones, the ones that tormented Dostoevskii his entire life, the existence of God. I had to equivocate all the time, back and forth. . . .*"
"*But all the same in your first chapter you settled accounts with philosophical criticism and demonstrated its inadequacy for explaining the main thing in Dostoevskii. . . .*"
"*Yes, perhaps,*" *M.M. answered,* "*but that was all literary scholarship*" *(again with a slight grimace).*

—Sergei Bocharov, interviewing Bakhtin on 9 June 1970[2]

"*You were [during the 1920s] more of a philosopher than a philologist?*"
"*More a philosopher. And such have I remained until the present day. I am a philosopher. I am a thinker. But in Petrograd we were all caught up in such concerns as: What is philosophy? Neither one thing nor the other. One had to be a specialist.*"

—V.D. Duvakin, in a taped interview with Bakhtin during the spring of 1974[3]

I

It is rarely a wise thing to assess thinkers during the time of their boom or cult. But the case of Mikhail Bakhtin presents us with a posthumous career (1975 to the present) so intriguingly bent by the needs of postcommunist scholarship and society that the temptation is great to record some of its more curious trajectories. What are its directions and distinguishing marks? How does this domestic image differ from the

Bakhtin—carnival king, toppler of hierarchies, patron saint of open-ended, egalitarian dialogue—that has become canonical in many Western treatments of his thought? Any answers must be partial and provisional. This essay offers one cross section of opinions, *circa* the winter of 1993–94.

To open on the broadest possible picture, contemporary Anglo-American and Russian images of Bakhtin differ in many particulars, but in one important aspect they coincide: there as well as here, Bakhtin is no longer perceived primarily as a *literary* critic. On American campuses this can be explained in part by the fact that literature itself is ceasing to be the central concern of many prestigious literature departments, whose members seek, through ambitious multicultural agenda, a more direct impact on real-life worlds. To those inclined to such politicization, Bakhtin has seemed to offer inspired support. His irreverent ideas on the novel and on the liberationist potential of carnival appear to invite a release from institutional constraints, from closed-down worlds, from the isolation and irrelevance of much academic thinking, and from all those written and unwritten laws that keep the marginal and unofficial forever at bay.

In Russia of the early 1990s, however, Bakhtin is being read in quite a different key. It is hardly surprising that to formerly Soviet philosophers and literary specialists the phenomenon of a radically politicized literature is so repellently familiar from their own Stalinist past that they take special pains to locate, among their rehabilitated and canonized scholars in the humanities, methods or world views that offer an alternative to power-centered readings. In the postcommunist context, what many Russians consider desirable and genuinely revolutionary is precisely a return to self-reliant, transcendent, and private values, both in literary texts and in one's life —what they call, simply, "the chance to live a normal life in a normal country." But this newly deideologized, demaximalized Bakhtin does not advocate anything like ethical relativism; here Russian and Western Bakhtins differ. Although a small, articulate, fantastically trendy-sounding, and almost untranslatable postmodernist minority in the capitals is indeed making up for lost time on Bakhtin (and on many other Russian thinkers), all in all Bakhtin has appealed to compatriots rereading him today as a philosopher of old-fashioned (that is, pre-Bolshevik) neohumanist and religious inclinations.

In addition to the neohumanism now sought in Bakhtin's thought, there is a second related trend: an exacerbated interest in carnival. But this interest is not so much in carnivalized *literary* texts as it is in the real thing, the raw down-dirty street variety, and it is cast in a far from celebratory vein. Understandably, the idea of rogues, fools, the Grinning Lie, and the immortal body of the people that never dies no matter how much you torment it arouses less rapture in Russia today than in the West. Carnival is seen as a Stalinist concept, even by those trendsetting Russian enthusiasts of French cultural theory who have been moved to apply radical Western "demystification" strategies to the carcass of Marxist-Leninist practice.[4] In the successive and deepening winters of Russia's discontent, Bakhtin's more ecstatic carnivalesque categories are applied to literary criticism second and to the real-life anarchy of everyday life first. In that unmediated capacity, they often terrorize where they once had liberated, precisely as real-life carnival has long been documented to do.

As my epigraphs suggest, the case for Bakhtin having been "a philosopher all along" is now well under way. The shift came at the turn of the decade. The first full-length Russian book on Bakhtin, Vladimir Bibler's *Mikhail Mikhailovich Bakhtin, ili poetika kul'tury* (Mikhail Mikhailovich Bakhtin, or a poetics of culture) (1991), was also, significantly, the first book to appear in any language that "specifically talked about him as a philosopher."[5] In 1991, the St. Petersburg historian of ideas Konstantin Isupov founded a periodical, *M.M. Bakhtin i filosofskaia kul'tura XX veka* (M.M. Bakhtin and philosophical culture of the twentieth century); in 1992, the leading journal of the profession, *Voprosy filosofii* (Problems of philosophy), featured a large, previously unpublished excerpt (devoted largely to Shakespeare) from Bakhtin's dissertation on Rabelais that was followed, in 1993, by an entire forum on "M.M. Bakhtin and his Circle"; and in 1992, a handsome volume appeared under the aegis of the Institute of Philosophy of the Russian Academy of Sciences, *M.M. Bakhtin kak filosof* (M.M. Bakhtin as philosopher).[6] What might explain this migration of critic and historian of literature into professional philosophical territory?

Several factors have contributed. First is the fact that Russian philosophy itself was "professionalized" at a very late date, and the Russian philosophical establishment traditionally has been quite generous toward *filosofstvovanie*, "amateur philosophizing," which is practiced—often at a high level of eccentricity and self-confidence—by Russia's greatest cultural, religious, and literary figures. (Think of Dostoevskii, Tolstoi, Solzhenitsyn, writers who never doubted their competence to utter moral or metaphysical truths alongside their fictional worlds, and their Russian readers concurred.) In addition, there has been the belated appearance (in the 1970s and 1980s) of Bakhtin's writings from the early 1920s on selfhood and ethics, which at last provided us with a point of genesis for his more familiar, mature work on literature.[7] These early writings also make it clear that Bakhtin's final essays from the 1960s and 1970s on culturology and the philosophy of education are not new developments but a return to the concerns of his youth.[8]

Reading Bakhtin as a philosopher has other advantages. There has been, for example, a growing impatience among many Russian Bakhtin scholars toward those critics (in both the East and the West) who fault Bakhtin for treating his subject matter in a one-sided way. (It should be noted that harsh criticism of the Dostoevskii and Rabelais books as acts of *literary interpretation*, which began in the West only in the mid-1980s as a sort of postcult backlash, was common in the Soviet 1960s when those two revised Russian editions first appeared; and that this commentary was often of high academic calibre.)[9] Reexamining Bakhtin today, philosophers intimate that the focus of the earlier criticism had been misplaced. Bakhtin, they contend, was no mere library researcher or literary critic. He was a *"myslitel'*," a "thinker," and although spectacular insights on literature do abound in the monographs on Dostoevskii and Rabelais, such local tasks as literary theory or the explication of a satisfyingly whole image (whether of texts or of creative writers) was not his primary concern. Much as the contemporary American philosopher Martha Nussbaum has argued for reading Henry James's novels as "works of moral philosophy," as studies in perception designed to discourage abstract paraphrase and encourage qualities of moral attention through the "intense scrutiny of particulars,"[10] so, they argue, should Bakhtin's passion for the novel be viewed as a pursuit of "philosophy by other means." Bakhtin, in a word, invokes literature primarily to illustrate a philosophy for living and not the other way around.

A final reason why "Bakhtin as philosopher" has proved so attractive might be traced to the very success of the cult. Serious students (as well as casual users) of Bakhtin's thought have long been embarrassed by the mindless seepage of such loosely construed terms as 'dialogue', 'carnivalization', 'unfinalizability', and 'loophole' into every possible discourse and into a huge number of disciplines. One result of this inflation has been the assumption that to analyze the world "in Bakhtin's spirit" means to be radically ambivalent, playful, relativistic, uninterested in resolution, and in hostage to the Other to the point of self-cancellation—in short, to be a nihilist in the realm of meaning and value. Many Russian scholars, sensing here an all-too-familiar anarchism, have attempted to halt the proliferation of this side of the cult. They urge that Bakhtin's thought be understood as an originary philosophy, valuable more as a model for constructing a responsible personality (what Bakhtin called an "architectonics of the self") than for its critical methodology—since "Bakhtinian method," once applied to an object, too often yields only predictably unfinalized carnival doubles or else predictably endless oscillations.[11] As Gary Saul Morson has recently argued, just because Bakhtin believed that the world is nondetermined and that (in William James's words) "possibilities may be in excess of actualities . . . and [still] form part of the truth," we should not assume that Bakhtin intended to say that anything goes, that all positions are negotiable, or that past choices can be undone.[12]

Irritation over this terminological inflation and imprecision is increasingly present in Russian overviews of Bakhtin's legacy. Exemplary here is an essay from 1993 by A.M. Ranchin entitled "The Bakhtin Temptation."[13] Ranchin laments the banalization of Bakhtin's ideas and our frequent confusion of their message with their formal mode of argument (that is, open-endedness might be a virtue in narrative and novels might embody that virtue, but Bakhtin is not tentative or ambivalent in arguing this idea). Ranchin points out that Bakhtin's own critical manner is in no sense jesting, apologetic, or illogical. Bakhtin was not a deliberately paradoxical or "carnivalized" thinker; he was no prophet, no "carrier of a secret," no creative writer with tantalizing devices up his sleeve, and—although he, too, could employ Aesopian language when necessary, like any serious intellectual working under Soviet conditions—he never courted obscurity for its own "poetic" effect. Ranchin and others argue that Bakhtin was simply a respectable philosopher: consistent, methodical, a little tedious, and one who propagated his ideas with stubborn single-mindedness.

What are those ideas? Here, in brief, are the philosophical givens of Bakhtin's world: The human psyche is a dynamic entity designed to know things from the outside, not the inside. To know something about the world, therefore, we must be in a state of "participatory outsideness" to it—that is, external to it, but external in a special, implicated way.[14] From this outside position, we come to know inanimate, inert objects and conscious subjects in two fundamentally different ways. (That is, our relations with another consciousness differ from our relations with a rock or from the relations of two rocks with each other.) It should be emphasized that Bakhtin was not opposed to the study of objects; he respected structuralism and the exact sciences for what such systematic world views could accomplish in the realm of subject–object and object–object relations. But his concern was always with the humanities, which deal with subject–*subject* relations, and it is this special axis that defines his reflexes toward the world.

An outside position *vis-à-vis* another consciousness, therefore, provides neither party with a secure ledge upon which to sit and watch, unchanged by the view. Another way of making this same point is to remember that dialogue is not the same as "intertextuality." Languages and texts do not talk to each other, *people* talk. During this process there is no single semiotic code or set of codes, ready-made and nonnegotiable, to which meaning can be referred. Which is to say: we make use of signs, but we are not reducible to them and not defined by them. Humans talk, flare up, fall asleep, commit follies, and forge unexpected links; and whereas texts and languages might indeed provide the ground for such activity, only

human consciousness can make it happen. In Bakhtin's view, consciousness is an energy that is always more creative and exciting than any of its
extracts or residues, such as system, ultimate resolution, or equivalency.

Strictly speaking, then, I cannot "analyze" the content of another consciousness at all. To know this content at all, I must, from my own position, participate in it, converse with it, and assume that in turn I will be
changed by it. Bakhtin was made nervous by methodologies that claimed
to observe objectively or disinterestedly any human source—whether of
voice, behavior, deed, or information. This does not mean, of course, that
we have no right to impose form on what we see, hear, and experience.
Again, one of the services that outsideness can, and must, provide is the
finalization of another person's *image*; such transitory consummation is a
gift we continually bestow upon others—and others upon us—as we pass
through each other's purviews and crave definition. A bestowal of form
cannot, however, finalize another's content or personality.

How, then, do the closing-down impulses of form and the opening-up
impulses of content interact in optimal subject–subject relations? Overall,
Bakhtin is optimistic about the balancing act required to construct a self
successfully, both in life and in art. The procedure is as follows: others
finalize us from without by bestowing images upon us; we internalize these
images and counter them with new content and syntheses from within;
subsequent outsiders then answer and enrich us with yet more images. That
an outsider might take pleasure in hostile or sadistic finalizations of us—
images we could not internalize without desperate damage to the self—
does not prey on Bakhtin; and certainly his readings of Dostoevskii and
Rabelais emphasize the sunny, open, ultimately reinforcing aspects of this
procedure.[15] But as Bakhtin has been refashioned from literary critic and
literary historian to "philosopher of consciousness" over the past few years,
a darker side has emerged. Recently published jottings from Bakhtin's
working notebooks for the war years (1943–46) are helpful in constructing
this revised image.

In these wartime notebooks, transcribed with heroic ingenuity from
faded, crumbling notebooks and first published in 1992, Bakhtin made the
following note: "The position occupied by consciousness while creating an
image of the other and while creating an image of one's own self. At the
present time this is the central problem of all philosophy."[16] The larger
context of this comment makes clear that, for Bakhtin during this period,
each of those two relatively stable realms referred to above—"open" content and "fixed" form—is simultaneously a locus for positive creative activity and the potential site of irreversible transgression. To be sure,
Bakhtin's temperament is not the sort that dwells for long in existential

darkness. But the mode of thought revealed in these notebooks, along with the lengthy and frank discussions with Bakhtin recorded in the early 1970s and now appearing in the Russian press,[17] lends a new seriousness to the familiar, altogether too benevolent Bakhtinian categories of dialogue, loophole, and doublevoicedness. These recently published materials also help us reconstruct Bakhtin's philosophy of the self for the wiser 1990s— not the self in any society, but the self as it might have appeared to a thinker and survivor in *Stalinist* society.

So, relatively open content, relatively fixed form: What are the hopes and dangers of each? "Content," in Bakhtin's world view, is largely the province of personality: fluid, hopeful, full of potential, capable of surprising combinations and renewals. Bakhtin eventually came to see the *personally uttered word* as the most efficient, flexible vehicle for the content-energy of personality. The temptation and desecration peculiar to it is the lie; in fact, the open form and protean creativity characteristic of personalized utterances are precisely what invests lying with its enormous power. ("The lie," he remarks in his wartime notebook, "is today's most ever-present form of evil. The phenomenology of the lie. Its extraordinary heterogeneity and the subtlety of its forms. Reasons for its extraordinary omnipresence. The philosophy of the lie. The rhetorical lie. The lie in artistic form" [p. 155].)

If the dark side of the word-strung personality is the lie, what then of forms and images? The image, as we have seen, is essential for our practical functioning in the world—and for artistic and cognitive finalization as well. We confront one another as images, delineated by spatial boundaries and identified with our finished deeds; humans are so constituted that we continually bestow images on others (with what Bakhtin calls our "form-shaping" power). Not surprisingly, the temptation and corruption peculiar to images—and here one cannot help visualizing the vast hectoring poster art of the Stalin era—is a deadening "thingness," a "todayness" that is "always ready to pass itself off . . . as a servant of the future" (p. 154). Artistic images can embody a "deadening force," Bakhtin writes, which is why they are so easily imposed on an object from a distance, at second hand (*zaochno*) and without love. According to Bakhtin, the image (and, in fact, artistic form in general) bears traces of this inevitable violence. Image-making activity is profoundly vulnerable to *abusing* the privilege of outsideness. And here we sense a possible source for Bakhtin's somewhat baffling ecstasy over the carnival grotesque, with its aggressive defiance of proportion and its delight at deformation. During those rigidly dictated Stalinist years, so saturated with approved prototypes, Bakhtin seems to have feared the potential tyranny of perfect form, the immutability and uninterruptibility of any icon that was too fixed in place. A force that could give us a *seemly* image would most likely know only one way to welcome an approaching idea, consciousness, or historical world view: here *you* come again, stay as you are, you are what you always were, it's all over.

In brief: As these new primary materials come into print, Bakhtin's own received image has undergone a thickening and, as it were, a darkening. His heretofore benevolent optimism about language loses some of its inspirational naïveté.

> The word does not know whom it serves [Bakhtin wrote in his 1943 notes]. It emerges from the dark and does not know its own roots. Its serious link with terror and violence. The authentically kind, unselfish, and loving person has not yet spoken, he has realized himself in the spheres of everyday life, he has not attached himself to the official word, infected with violence and the lie; he is not becoming a writer. (P. 154)

II

The second half of this essay will touch briefly upon three controversial points where the previously "literary" Bakhtin has been recast as a philosopher of subject–subject relations. The first area concerns Bakhtin's politics. Was Bakhtin a Marxist, as many claim (and if not a Marxist politically, then perhaps in his general sympathies and philosophical orientation)? The second area concerns Bakhtin's Christianity. What does he share with Russia's religious idealists and neohumanists, and does this restored "vertical dimension" of his thought, so eagerly sought in today's postcommunist climate, introduce a desirable corrective into the largely horizontal axis of everyday interhuman dialogue? And finally, if Bakhtin's aesthetics does offer an alternative to "power-centered readings," how might it follow for Bakhtin that the nineteenth-century novel is the abiding genre through which to pursue "moral philosophy by other means"?

This last question—which intersects politics, philosophy, and art—returns us to the parallel between Martha Nussbaum on Henry James and Mikhail Bakhtin on the nineteenth-century novel. The convergences are striking. Both critics are philosophers who consider a certain sort of novel the perfect place for particularity and ethical fine-tuning; both insist that novelistic language, although extensive, is noncompressible, unparaphrasable, and utterly efficient to its task; and the reading of novelistic scenes that both critics produce presupposes that literary theory can do without politics (can perhaps do *better* without politics) but will fare poorly without an ethical philosophy.[18] What philosophical tasks can the novel accomplish better than all nonnovelistic genres? Juxtaposing rhetorical strategies to artistic ones in his 1943 notebook, Bakhtin wrote: "Rhetoric, in all its fraudulence, strives to evoke precisely terror or hope. . . . Art (authentic art) and cognition strive, on the contrary, to free us from these feelings" (p. 153). In its anti-Aristotelian resonances, the statement is curious. Freedom from terror we can understand, for that is the moral kernel—such as there is—to a carnival approach to the world; but in what ways should art and cognition free us from hope? Around this paradoxical statement I would like to organize my subsequent remarks on Bakhtin as Marxist, as Christian thinker, and as moral critic. For it appears that in political matters Bakhtin was neither a holy fool nor a utopian, although he did employ Aesopian language and did insist on using the materials at hand to construct an ethics for his time.

To begin with politics. There are two ways to make Bakhtin a Marxist. One can go the route of conflation, that is, include in the canon the texts from the 1920s published under the names of Bakhtin's intellectual associates Valentin Voloshinov and Pavel Medvedev (avowedly Marxist thinkers) but attributed by many to Bakhtin himself, thereby broadening the definition of "who Bakhtin is."[19] Or one can keep to the texts that Bakhtin unambiguously authored but broaden the concept of Marxism, moving off the force-fed dialectic, ugly calls to class-based terror, and uninhibited political opportunism characteristic of the applied Russian variant—"Marxism-Leninism"—in order to endorse something softer, more flexible, and more theoretically appealing. (This approach has proved popular among left-wing social theorists in the West; as one such scholar, the sociologist Michael Gardiner, demonstrates in his 1992 monograph *The Dialogics of Critique: M.M. Bakhtin and the Theory of Ideology*, some portions of Bakhtin's thought can indeed be made compatible with the "warm stream within Western Marxism, which has been more favorably disposed toward the value of utopian theorizing and ethical humanism.")[20] In a variant on this second view, one can keep to Bakhtin's signed texts but metaphorize, or metastasize, his terms out of all recognition—that is, one can broaden Bakhtinian categories and detach them sufficiently from their contexts so that some values common to Marxism and to Bakhtin are indeed uncovered.

There are problems with both approaches. Although most Russian scholars continue to endorse the conflationist position (that Bakhtin was the responsible author of the entire corpus), the "disputed-texts" dispute, in the absence of new verifiable evidence, has ended in a draw.[21] Attempts in the West to float Bakhtin in the direction of what are arbitrarily labeled

uniquely Marxist concerns (labor, value, struggle, exchange, "otherness"—
as if only Marx spoke of those matters), thereby crediting him with an
ideology by association, have not proved persuasive.[22] And as regards
writing Bakhtin in to "warm-stream Marxism," postcommunist survivors
are understandably appalled at the effort expended by Western intellectuals
(who are, after all, free to choose other starting points) to utilize a thinker
of Bakhtin's force and originality to "modify" or "reclaim" such an obviously fraudulent body of thought. Surely, they reason, a flawed system—
and especially a wholly hypothetical system like Marxism, with so
disastrous a diagnostic, economic, and political record in the real world of
human beings—can simply be *rejected*, not tinkered with or warmed up.
Here we might consider, as a sobering corrective to the warm-stream
school, Bakhtin's own comment at the end of his life on the fate of his
family's neighbor in Orel, Prince Dmitrii Sviatopolk-Mirskii. D.S. Mirskii,
in one of those sadly circular twentieth-century biographies, emigrated in
1920 to England, wrote his acclaimed *History of Russian Literature*, became a British Marxist and Eurasian, repatriated in 1932, was arrested in
1937, and died in the Gulag in 1939.

> Yes [Bakhtin remarked apropos of his neighbor from Orel], a typical mem-
> ber of the intelligentsia, absolutely naive. That's how I imagine the English
> Communists. For the English Communist Party is highly peculiar. There are
> almost no workers in it. There are only lords and members of the intelligen-
> tsia. In a word, it's the exoticism of being different from everyone else. And
> Sviatopolk-Mirskii was just such a Communist from among the lords.[23]

The strongest case against the influence of Marxism on Bakhtin's
thought, however, is testimony from Bakhtin himself. He has long been on
record against the dialectic, which he repeatedly opposes to genuine dialogue. In his many discussions of social stratification and its resultant
"languages," he never gives any priority to economic or class considerations. (In contrast to his Marxist associates, Bakhtin—with the utmost consistency—insists on centrifugal impulses in general and in perpetuity; for
were these forces ever to coalesce into a "social class" or any other organized group with a battle plan, centripetality would have triumphed.) And as
regards those laughing and atemporal "interludes," carnival and Menippean
satire, their jesters are far too committed to having a good time to build
alternative political structures of the sort that a Marxist revolution man-
dates (after all, sustained antagonism, to be effective, requires that people
exercise memory, hold grudges, and not grin back). Bakhtin's entire concept of time as something open, and of experience as interpersonal and
laden with potentials, argues against the teleological, impersonal, and col-

lectivist impulses in Marxist thought. One of those recently published interviews with Bakhtin has served to confirm the matter. In 1974, Sergei Bocharov asked Bakhtin outright about his political sympathies, and Bakhtin replied: "Marxism? Never. Like many others I was interested in Freudianism and even spiritualism, but I was never a Marxist, never in the slightest."[24]

Why should Bakhtin's non-Marxism matter? On one level, it makes him more interesting: that is, it transforms his intellectual position *vis-à-vis* his Marxist colleagues from labored ventriloquism or overcautious window dressing into a genuine dialogue. But it also matters for reasons having to do with that 1943 statement on the rhetorical lie and its close connection to terror and hope. Of course Soviet Marxism brought terror in its wake. But it also brought a type of fraudulent and tantalizing hope. Its utopian slogans isolated the present from both past and future; nourished on the idea that we can start over afresh, that the corruption of the present will not distort the already predetermined radiant future, it worked to anesthetize the personalities who participated daily in that present. They were to receive their identity not from individual deeds or decisions undertaken in a concrete time and place but rather from timeless class and state virtues that "belonged to no one." Bakhtin considered this sort of thinking a particularly dangerous type of *samozvantsvo*, "pretendership."

"Today [*segodniashchnii den'*] cannot help lying," Bakhtin wrote in 1943. "When it perpetrates violence, today always passes itself off as a servant of the future. But this future is a future continuation, a continuity of oppression, not an exit into freedom, not a transfiguration" (p. 154). Bakhtin spoke eloquently against the delusion encouraged by official rhetoric, that an ethical identity could be based on noncontinuity and noncontiguity. According to him, such delusions were the result of "theoretist" thinking and a misreading of the relationship of content to form. In this regard, of course, Bakhtin resembles the Aleksandr Herzen of *From the Other Shore*.

It is worth noting in this context that even during the period of his most extravagant carnival enthusiasms—with their utopian disjunctures, robust laughter, and folklore devices to defy death—Bakhtin's philosophical goal was quite specific. Laughter is a virtue because it can frustrate, and at times even triumph over, terror in lives that have become maximally insecure. Bakhtin never pretended that carnival procedures could be of much help in creating an *ethical* personality. If anything, his passion for the *Bildungsroman* and the old-fashioned nineteenth-century novel is an outgrowth of his conviction that under nonterrorized conditions honest cognition and authentic art (especially the art of the novel) require above all an attention to continuities and a personalist ethic. From this perspective, Bakhtin's active dislike of Marxism, his indifference both to the radical aesthetics of the twentieth century and to most of the modernist masterpieces produced by that aesthetic, are all of one piece.

The evidence is convincing, then, that Bakhtin did not share the dominant political philosophy of his own era and place. In spirit he was a philosophical pluralist—what Isaiah Berlin would have defined, broadly, as a liberal temperament. But except for some early remarks critical of "representational procedures," which he considered insufficiently personalistic and wanting in humility,[25] Bakhtin did not address the specifics of political liberalism, nor did he define himself *vis-à-vis* the regrettable Russian tradition of legal nihilism.[26] There are indications that such questions interested Bakhtin greatly at the beginning of his career; but to our great loss, there is no extant trace of a tract Bakhtin had planned to write in the 1920s on the "ethics of politics."[27] The positive side of Bakhtin's political views therefore remains obscure. We know he was negatively disposed toward Marxism. What about his debt to those belief systems that Marxism specifically condemns and hounds out?

Here we confront a second area where Bakhtin is being remade as philosopher—namely, his relation to Russian Orthodox thought. Was he a Christian philosopher? Did he proselytize through his writings? Or was he drawing on religious culture as an intellectual historian, using Christian motifs in a conventionally academic way? In the 1980s, still a Soviet decade but an increasingly unmonitored one, the heady possibility of drawing such hitherto taboo parallels in print whetted enthusiasm for even the most lax associative exercises. Much was made, for example, of Michael Holquist's assertion in a well-known essay from 1981 that Bakhtin in the 1920s had hoped "to completely rethink West European metaphysics in the light of religious thought; to show, as it were, that philosophy had in a sense always been anticipated by religion."[28] The material on Bakhtin's religious activities before his arrest, so painstakingly gathered by Katerina Clark and Michael Holquist in their pioneering 1984 biography, began to be cited heavily and appreciatively.[29] An essay of mine, "Russian Orthodoxy and the Early Bakhtin," written for a non-Slavist journal, was precipitously snapped up and translated for the second issue of the annual *Bakhtinskii sbornik* (1991).[30] That essay speculates loosely on Bakhtin's "Christian cast of mind": the trinitarian sources for his interpersonalism and relationalism, his concept of a "surplus of visualization" that recalls the plurality of vision within icon space, his fascination with embodiment— that is, incarnation—and his holistic reverence for matter, his points of contact with Vladimir Solov'ev and Nikolai Berdiaev; and then those areas where Bakhtin modified or downplayed aspects of Orthodox teaching, in particular, its preference for mystic cosmology and sacrament over everyday ethics, its emphasis on an immutable past rather than an open, flexible future, and its subjection of the individual to the community in the Slavophile understanding of sobornost.[31]

As once-proscribed points of contact between Bakhtin and Orthodoxy became commonplace, a phase of rebuttals and refinements followed.[32] Among the most articulate of the skeptics has been the Moscow philosopher Natal'ia Bonetskaia, whose essay "Bakhtin and the Traditions of Russian Philosophy" (1993) critically assesses all those integrations that would make of Bakhtin a mainstream religious thinker.[33] Bonetskaia sees in Bakhtin's model of self–other relations a major revision of a Kantian presumption that was widespread at the turn of the century. According to that presumption, knowledge, being limited to personal experience, can never adequately penetrate another person's soul—and thus information can be gathered only "from the inside out," that is, by self-observation. Bakhtin rejects that position utterly. He insists that *it is precisely our own selves that we cannot know*, since the human psyche is specifically set up to work from the outside in, that is, to know others. Bonetskaia proceeds to argue that Bakhtin's peculiar "philosophical anthropology" departs from the thought of major Russian Orthodox figures (Solov'ev, Losskii, Frank, Florenskii) in two crucial ways. First, Bakhtin consistently values *drugost'* and *inakovost'* (otherness, otherwise-ness) over Solov'ev's ideal of *vseedinstvo* (total-unity), and thus he sees more saving grace in the ideal of *vnenakhodimost'* (outsideness) than in *sobornost'* (communality). And second, Bakhtin is consistently reluctant to endorse an originary, transcendental principle (God, genesis), content to ground real existence in immediate experience and ongoing dialogue. Bonetskaia concludes that Bakhtin's philosophy has a dual origin: "he knew Western thought too well not to fall subject to its fascinations"; his philosophy was not marked by Slavophile tendencies, and yet the Orthodox church, which held for him a "purely intellectual interest," inevitably influenced him with its intuitionist teachings (p. 93). Her compromise position on Bakhtin as believer seems sensible, disinterested, and deideologized.

Such disinterestedness is not everywhere the case, however. In fact, the battle over Bakhtin's legacy appears to be waged precisely on this vulnerable religious terrain. In the 1992 anthology *M.M. Bakhtin as Philosopher*, for example, a galaxy of prominent culturologists and philosophers eagerly seek out Christian symbolism, allegory, and the "vertical axis" in Bakhtin's texts—which they now assume was concealed by its author in the ever-present Aesopian reflex of the Russian writer. Several essays argue forcefully against any intimation of ethical relativism in Bakhtin, early or late. A substantial archival section features Lev Pumpianskii's seminar notes from Bakhtin's lectures on Kant and religion, held in Leningrad during the mid-1920s. And the general question of Bakhtin's internal consistency as a philosopher is given serious—and ofttimes nervous—attention. Exemplary in this regard is the opening essay by the eminent Sergei Averintsev, who asks whether Christianity and carnival laughter are compatible. Can there be Eastern Orthodox carnival in the spirit of the West's energetic, witty, irreverent Rabelais? If the Russian Christ never laughed, must Russian carnival be of the Devil? Averintsev concludes that Bakhtin greatly idealized laughter and carnival license in a desperate gesture against the tightening Stalinist noose, and that the entire carnival episode in Bakhtin's work is thus more of psycho-biographical than of literary significance.[34]

As we move into 1994, one final development merits comment. Now that Russian and Western images of Bakhtin jostle one another on the open market, it is perhaps only natural that the question of "Bakhtin and religion" is being drawn into the chauvinistic nationalism that increasingly colors intellectual activity during this most recent winter of the Russians' discontent. A pioneering document in this mode belongs to the old Bakhtin hand Vadim Kozhinov, now a right-wing critic of some infamy.[35] Unceremoniously dismissing Vitalii Makhlin and Natal'ia Bonetskaia—Russian scholars who have acknowledged the influence of Western ideas on Bakhtin and the worth of Western work on Bakhtin—Kozhinov insists that Western consciousness, being "monologic in principle," began to celebrate Bakhtin solely as a new fad to replace the poststructuralist void. He maintains that Bakhtin's dialogism was inspired not by cosmopolitan outsiders (such as the eminent German-Jewish neo-Kantian Hermann Cohen, whom Bakhtin greatly admired) but by the fifteenth-century Russian Orthodox Transvolga hermit St. Nil Sorskii, and that the sources of carnival should be sought not in Rabelais's corrupt Catholic West but in the purifying laughter of the Byzantine-Muscovite holy fool. We can only hope that this phase of Bakhtin's "reclamation as Russian philosopher" passes quickly and leaves little residue.

To turn now to the final question, Bakhtin's moral philosophy as an integral part of his aesthetics of the novel. Bakhtin has proved easy to define by what he is not—not a Marxist, not a religious philosopher—and that list could be greatly extended, for as a thinker Bakhtin coincides with no major coherent twentieth-century movement. Indeed, in his 1992 essay on Bakhtin and Western postmodernism, Vitalii Makhlin enumerates all those categories into which Bakhtin does *not* fit: he is a non-Marxist, nonformalist, nonstructuralist, non-Freudian, nonexistentialist, noncollectivist, nonutopian, nontheologian—"in a word, a nonmodernist."[36] Makhlin asks how we might explain the "grotesquely anachronistic 'influence' of Bakhtin's thought, which ripened at the beginning of the century, in the West of the postmodernist epoch." In answer to this question, he suggests that modernism, with its hierarchical and universalizing impulses, was fundamentally monologic, whereas the postmodern temperament finds something congenial in Bakhtin's passion for noncoincidence, incompatibility, and radical otherness (*drugost'*). But Bakhtin quite clearly is no postmodernist either. In their search for positive attributes, Russian philosophers at work on Bakhtin's thought are right to reconstitute its "vertical axis" in all its ethical and religious dimensions. Their primary goal has been to distance Bakhtin from relativism and from a potential anarchy of values, while retaining in full the philosophical pluralism—the *relativity*, not the relativism—that defines his world view.[37] How might the act of reading novels be part of this task?

For a provisional answer to this question, we might repair to one of the founders of literary criticism, Aristotle. It will be recalled that Bakhtin, in his book on Dostoevskii, paradoxically defines the catharsis at the end of a polyphonic novel as a closure that *opens* things up rather than sums them up—and thus as contrary in spirit to a tragic Aristotelian catharsis of pity and terror, and perhaps in a larger sense also contrary to the whole logic of a poetics based on plot.[38] Aristotle is precisely what is needed, however, in the realm of Bakhtinian moral philosophy: the Aristotle not of the *Poetics* but of the *Ethics*. For in the *Ethics* it is character, not system, that is important, and the primary value sought is not perfect form but phronesis, "practical wisdom," the ability to make proper choices under uncertain conditions in the absence of a whole.[39]

How are novels "Aristotelian" in this ethical sense? In one of his most famous programmatic statements, Bakhtin posits three genre requirements for the novel.[40] A novel must be multistyled and multilanguaged; it must be constructed in a space that is penetrable for both author and reader (that is, we should be able to imagine ourselves "entering the novel" and having something to say to its protagonists); and it must create a type of time that enjoys maximally close contact with the present "in all its open-endedness." Taken together, these genre characteristics continually alert us to a multiplicity of potential realities for every human situation, one of the things that novels are designed to do best.[41] If Martha Nussbaum has suggested that reading Henry James can be a moral education (an education, as she puts it, in the art of becoming "finely aware and richly responsible"), then Bakhtin presumes that such ethical training is implicit for the readers of *all* novels. Bakhtin nowhere spells out this training. I would like to conclude this essay on one way in which a Bakhtinian ethics of reading might be understood in an "Aristotelian" spirit.

My questions begin in the realm of the common reader. Why, once we "already know the plot," do we pick up a novel again? Why, upon multiple readings, do we obtain such exquisite unfaded pleasure from it and learn such unexpectedly varied lessons? Is it because we "forget" the world of the novel, and if so, why do we forget, and what are the dynamics of our subsequent remembering? Bakhtin would say, I believe, that our pleasure and our forgetting cannot be simply the result of an impulse to escape into the fantasy of a created world; such flight might console or entertain us in the short term, but it will not hold our interest in repeated reading sessions, that is, in successive boundary crossings between novels and life. Rather, we reread (and we forget) novels because real time and space are built into them.

For what might it mean, in experiential terms, to design a verbal artwork "in maximally close proximity to the present"? Perhaps it could mean that in addition to internally coherent horizontal ligatures that bind together its own plot—what we remember as the "forward thrust" or logic of the story—there are also ligatures of another sort, infinitely varied, adhesive, and finely tuned, designed to undo the forward plot and to come apart, as it were, at right angles to it, reconnecting with our everyday life and our individual selves at the time of reading. There are more of these reconnections in novels, one could argue, than there are in lyrics or epics or tragedies, which are the special domain of heroes and heroic postures; those loftier genres are often structured to distance, concentrate, transcend, and control an emotion, whereas it is easier to reexperience our unheroic daily selves in the minute-by-minute progress of novels precisely because novels are, in the several senses of the word, prosaic. We forget and must relive long novels, then, not just because they are long and detailed but because they are designed to be dragged out of shape, scene by scene. As we change, so, slowly, does the meaning of the whole novel change. The problems it poses continually feel nonpostponably urgent, freshly unresolved, and full of options for an altogether different resolution. And this, to answer Bakhtin's anxiety, might be artistic form *without* the rhetorical lie.

With the above dynamic in mind, perhaps Henry James, who inspired Martha Nussbaum to see the novel as "philosophy by other means," should have the final word. His famous comment about Russian novels being "big baggy monsters" might not be that far off the mark. James would concur with Bakhtin that the greatest Russian novels tend to begin with character, not with plot; thus their tasty shapelessness. But in a well-designed novel, plot is not just "there." To grasp the plot at all, every reader each time must become freshly implicated in it and "deform" it over a long stretch of time. And by this exquisite aesthetic seepage, moral education cannot be avoided. In a decade or two, I predict, the matter of Bakhtin's Marxism will be in retreat and the religious dimension will have faded. But as a moral philosopher of narrative, Bakhtin will continue to astonish us.

Notes

1. E.V. Volkova, E.A. Bogatyreva, "V bol'shom vremeni kul'tury: M.M. Bakhtin," *Vestnik Moskovskogo universiteta. Seriia 7. Filosofiia,* 1991, no. 1, pp. 48–58, especially p. 51.
2. S.G. Bocharov, "Ob odnom razgovore i vokrug nego," *Novoe literaturnoe obozrenie,* 1993, no. 2 , pp. 70–89, especially pp. 71–72.
3. "Pepel i almaz: Iz rasskazov M.M. Bakhtina, zapissanykh V.D. Duvakinym," *Literaturnaia gazeta,* 4 August 1993. Fuller context in "Razgovory s Bakhtinym," *Chelovek,* 1993, no. 4, p. 152.
4. The most prolific and accessible scholar in this group is probably Mikhail Ryklin, whose "Bodies of Terror" (*Tela terrora*), using Bakhtinian carnival to explain the perversions of Stalinism with visual illustrations from the Moscow Metro, appeared in the first *Bakhtinskii sbornik* (1990) and was translated by Donald Wesling and Molly Wesling in *New Literary History,* vol. 24, no. 1 (Winter 1993), pp. 45–74.
5. N.N. Zubkov, "Dialog o dialoge," in *Arbor Mundi/Mirovoe drevo,* 1992, no. 1, pp. 158–72, especially p. 158.
6. *M.M. Bakhtin i filosofskaia kul'tura XX veka,* no. 1, pts. 1 and 2, ed. K.G. Isupov (St. Petersburg: Obrazovanie/RGPU, 1991); L.G. Gogotishvili, "Varianty i invarianty M.M. Bakhtina," and M.M. Bakhtin, "Dopolneniia i izmeneniia k 'Rable'," both in *Voprosy filosofii,* 1992, no. 1, pp. 115–64; *M.M. Bakhtin kak filosof,* ed. L.A. Gogotishvili and P.S. Gurevich (Moscow: Nauka, 1992).
7. These early writings are now in English, with their antecedents in continental philosophy fully annotated. See *Art and Answerability: Early Philosophical Essays by M.M. Bakhtin,* ed. Michael Holquist and Vadim Liapunov, trans. and notes by Vadim Liapunov (Austin: University of Texas Press, 1990); and M.M. Bakhtin, *Toward a Philosophy of the Act,* ed. Vadim Liapunov and Michael Holquist, trans. and notes by Vadim Liapunov (Austin: University of Texas Press, 1993).
8. See especially "The Problem of the Text in Linguistics, Philology, and the Human Sciences" (1959–61), "Response to a Question from the Novy Mir Editorial Staff" (1970), "From Notes Made in 1970–71," and "Toward a Methodology for the Human Sciences" (1974), all in M.M. Bakhtin, *Speech Genres and Other Late Essays,* trans. Vern W. McGee (Austin: University of Texas Press, 1986).
9. See the debate initiated by Aleksandr Dymshits, "Monologi i dialogi," *Literaturnaia gazeta,* 11 July 1964 and continued on 6 August 1964 and 13 August 1964. A sober, appreciative, but quite skeptical review of the Rabelais book can be found in an essay by the Khar'kov intellectual historian L.M. Batkin, "Smekh Panurga i filosofiia kul'tury," *Voprosy filosofii,* 1967, no. 12, pp. 114–23.
10. Martha C. Nussbaum, " 'Finely Aware and Richly Responsible': Literature and the Moral Imagination" (first published version 1985), in *Love's Knowledge: Essays on Philosophy and Literature* (New York: Oxford University Press, 1990), pp. 148–67, especially p. 148. In her description of the "moral work" required in Jamesian perceiving, Nussbaum stresses the nonreducibility of "the right sort of vision of the concrete," a vision that is the novel's special domain. "It could not be shown well even in a philosopher's example," she argues, "inasmuch as an example would lack the full specificity, and also the indeterminacy, of the literary case, its rich metaphors and pictures" (p. 161).

11. For an articulate critique of the carnivalesque Bakhtin, see K.G. Isupov, "Bakhtinskii krizis gumanizma (materialy k probleme)," in *Bakhtinskii sbornik II: Bakhtin mezhdu Rossiei i zapadom* (Moscow, 1991), pp. 127–55. Joining his voice to that of Aleksei Losev (who reads Rabelais's obscene and dehumanized scenarios as an inversion and parody of Renaissance humanism, not its heroic realization), Isupov argues that Bakhtin, in his procarnival phase of the 1930s–40s, actively undid the humanistic ethics of his earlier periods by sacrificing the "I" utterly to the choral Other, and by replacing memory with a sort of satanic eternal present.

12. The quote is from William James, "The Dilemma of Determinism" (1884), as cited in Gary Saul Morson, "Strange Synchronies and Surplus Possibilities: Bakhtin on Time," in *Slavic Review*, vol. 52, no. 3 (Fall 1993), p. 479. Morson opens his excellent essay on the argument, which he takes to be characteristic of the Russian literary tradition, that "novels are a supreme form of philosophy because, unlike the terribly thin accounts of life found in philosophical tracts, they offer a rich and 'thick' description of human thinking and action" (p. 478). As noted above, Nussbaum pursues a similar thesis based on the novel's spatial "visioning"; here Morson examines its temporal aspect.

13. A.M. Ranchin, "Iskushenie Bakhtinym," in *Novoe literaturnoe obozrenie*, 1993, no. 3, pp. 320–25. Ranchin argues that Bakhtin advocated unfinalizability in narratives and selves but in the analyses that he himself produced he was certainly not ambivalent. He gave no sign of questioning the rightness of his stance in his dispute with the Formalists or Freudians, for example, and the respectful but authoritative tone of the Dostoevskii book, which dispenses firmly with its adversaries in the first chapter, leaves little doubt that Bakhtin considered his reading of the novelist to be the best one around.

14. A clear and nontechnical discussion of the ethical implications of *vnenakhodimost'* ("outsideness") is by E.V. Volkova, a leading Bakhtinist at Moscow State University, in her "Estetika M.M. Bakhtina," a sixty-page pamphlet issued in the popular subscription series Znanie/Estetika, no. 12 (Moscow, 1990). See especially the first three chapters, whose titles (translating them) are: "Via Life, to Introduce Responsibility into Philosophy," "The Aesthetic Event: Outsideness and Dialogue," and "Bakhtin's 'Aesthetic Love' and Kant's 'Disinterestedness' " (pp. 6–36).

15. For one preliminary critique of Bakhtin's benevolence in subject–subject relations, see Caryl Emerson, "Problems of Baxtin's Poetics," *Slavic and East European Journal*, vol. 32, no. 4 (Winter 1988), pp. 503–25.

16. M.M. Bakhtin, "Iz chernovykh tetradei," ed. Vadim Kozhinov, texts transcribed by V.I. Slovetskii, *Literaturnaia ucheba*, 1992, bks. 5/6 (September, October, November, and December), pp. 153–66, especially p. 156 (from 1946). These notebooks date from about 1940 to the early 1960s. Further page references are given in the text.

17. During February–March 1973, the Maiakovskii scholar Viktor Duvakin interviewed Bakhtin on his family, education, and early biography (1895–1920s); a transcript was published in the journal *Chelovek*, 1993, no. 4, as "Razgovory s Bakhtinym" (pp. 140–53), with an introduction by Sergei Bocharov entitled "Sobytie bytiia" (pp. 136–40). In his final session with Duvakin, Bakhtin declared that he did not intend to write his memoirs; Bocharov infers from this that Bakhtin considered his own life and the life of his closest friends to be too "unofficial" for such sanctioned (i.e., officially published) form. These oral recollections are of great interest. Philosophy, we learn, was Bakhtin's first love. At age twelve he began serious reading in the German philosophers, especially Kant (whom he read in German, a native tongue to the Bakhtin brothers through their nanny) and also Kierkegaard (who, Bakhtin remarked, being "half philosopher and half theologian," was considered an "obscurantist" in the Soviet Union); Kierkegaard's philosophy reminds him of Dostoevskii. At Petrograd University

Bakhtin chose to concentrate in classics because there was no single general independent philosophy major.

18. See especially Martha C. Nussbaum, "Perceptive Equilibrium: Literary Theory and Ethical Theory" (1987, 1989), in *Love's Knowledge*, pp. 168–94.

19. The case for and against (but mostly against) conflation is made in Gary Saul Morson and Caryl Emerson, *Mikhail Bakhtin: Creation of a Prosaics* (Stanford, CA: Stanford University Press, 1990), pt. 1, chap. 3, "The Disputed Texts," pp. 101–19.

20. Michael Gardiner, *The Dialogics of Critique: M.M. Bakhtin and the Theory of Ideology* (London: Routledge, 1992), p. 138.

21. The most recent Russian argument for the conflationist position is by Bocharov, "Ob odnom razgovore i vokrug nego," pp. 71–76, based on recollected conversations with the aged Bakhtin; for a cautious and skeptical rebuttal, see N. Vasiliev, "M.M. Bakhtin ili V.N. Voloshinov? K voprosu ob avtorstve knig i statei, pripisyvaemykh M.M. Bakhtinu," in *Literaturnoe obozrenie*, 1991, no. 10, pp. 38–43. Regardless of degree of influence or coauthorship, however, a good case could be made for leaving the signatories where they are, for the differences between Bakhtin's texts and the Marxist texts signed by his friends are significant. Voloshinov, for example, gives priority to "productive relations" and "class struggle" in a society, whereas Bakhtin nowhere singles out economic forces as of determining importance.

22. For one unfortunate example of this approach—appropriating Bakhtin for Marxism by rhetorical methods that, happily, even present-day Russians need no longer employ—in an otherwise very useful essay, see Michael Holquist, "Introduction: The Architectonics of Answerability," in *Art and Answerability: Early Philosophical Essays by M.M. Bakhtin*, pp. xxxix–xlv. For a trenchant critique, see Gary Saul Morson, "Bakhtin and the Present Moment," in *The American Scholar*, Spring 1991, pp. 203–6.

23. From Bakhtin's reminiscences of his childhood and youth, as recorded by Duvakin in "Razgovory s Bakhtinym," p. 141.

24. Bocharov, "Ob odnom razgovore i vokrug nego," pp. 70–71. One could argue, of course, that these postcommunist memoirists are rewriting Bakhtin in their own (wiser) image; and indeed, this is always a danger with reminiscences that are recorded and/or published long after the fact and on the far side of an ideological divide. But Bakhtin's closest associates seem to concur on Bakhtin's non-Marxism. The late Vladimir Turbin, who perhaps knew Bakhtin longest of all as an intimate and a contemporary, had this to say: "Our Russian pride has been the 'eventfulness' [*sobytiinost'*] of our judgments about literature. Afanas'ev was an event, Aleksandr Veselovskii was an event, Potebnia was an event. . . . But Marxism was not able to create any concept-events, even the books of its best adepts like Georgy Lukacs did not succeed." What Turbin calls Marxism's "tedious noneventfulness" (*skuchnaia bessobytiinost'*) would surely have appealed to his friend and mentor Bakhtin. See V. Turbin, "Literaturovedenie? Zachem?" in *Literaturnaia gazeta*, 3 March 1993, p. 6.

25. Bakhtin, *Toward a Philosophy of the Act*, pp. 52–53: "I *can* perform a political act or a religious ritual in the capacity of a representative . . . [but] one has to develop humility to the point of participating in person and being answerable in person."

26. An excellent context for Bakhtin's potential as a political thinker can be found in Andrzej Walicki, *Legal Philosophies of Russian Liberalism* (Oxford: Clarendon Press, 1987), especially pt. 1. As Walicki demonstrates, for all his westernizing disdain of the Russian penchant for sacrifice and utopia, Herzen remained a socialist largely because he remained a legal nihilist, preferring appeals to "moral integrity" rather than legalistic safeguards of individual liberty. The Herzen–Bakhtin parallel is intriguing and merits more work.

27. Bakhtin, *Toward a Philosophy of the Act*, p. 54. Bakhtin projected a four-part

study: part one on the "architectonics of the actual world of the performed act or deed—the world actually experienced"; part two on "aesthetic activity as an actually performed act or deed" and "the ethics of artistic creation"; part three on the ethics of politics; and part four on the ethics of religion.

28. Michael Holquist, "The Politics of Representation," in *Allegory and Representation: Selected Papers from the English Institute, 1979–80*, ed. Stephen J. Greenblatt, new series, no. 5 (Baltimore, MD: Johns Hopkins University Press, 1981), pp. 163–83, especially p. 171.

29. Katerina Clark and Michael Holquist, *Mikhail Bakhtin* (Cambridge, MA: Harvard University Press, 1984), especially chap. 5, "Religious Activities and the Arrest."

30. Caryl Emerson, "Russian Orthodoxy and the Early Bakhtin," *Religion and Literature*, vol. 22, nos. 2–3 (Summer–Autumn 1990), pp. 109–31, translated by Vitalii Makhlin as "Russkoe pravoslavie i rannii Bakhtin," *Bakhtinskii sbornik II: Bakhtin mezhdu Rossiei i zapadom* (Moscow, 1991), pp. 44–69.

31. Although highly sensitive to societal factors, Bakhtin still remains a personalist and an intentionalist. Unlike his Slavophile brethren, he had no interest in dissolving the one in the many, or in claiming—along with such thinkers as Konstantin Aksakov—that an individual voice is "most free in a chorus." In fact, Bakhtin's "sociality" expressed itself in quite the opposite move: in his conviction that each of us constantly internalizes and individualizes the social environment in a series of unrepeatable verbal and behavioral acts, which then, thanks to this slow inward seepage and unique accommodation, become our own distinct personality. This process Bakhtin calls our "nonalibi in existence."

32. See, for example, S.S. Konkin and A.S. Konkina, *Mikhail Bakhtin: Stranitsy zhizni i tvorchestva* (Saransk: Mordovskoe knizhnoe izdatel'stvo, 1993), especially chap. 4, "Arest i prigovor," pp. 171–201. This work by Bakhtin's academic colleagues in Saransk, Semen and Larisa Konkin, is the first full-length Russian biography of Bakhtin, and it provides additional documentation on the religious activities that precipitated Bakhtin's arrest in 1929. The Konkins confirm, for example, that the Resurrection circle was indeed ambivalent about the established church and proselytized among the young; the state indictment accused the circle of contact with the White emigration, anti-Soviet propaganda, and the desire to overthrow the Soviet regime (p. 190). Interestingly, the protocol of Bakhtin's first police interrogation read, under the rubric "Political Convictions": "Marxist-revolutionist, loyal to the Soviet regime. Religious" (p. 181).

Also of interest is the Ekaterinburg scholar Ia.S. Babkina, who undertook to place Bakhtin's ideas on outsideness, dialogue, and author–hero relations "in the context of Orthodox mysticism and dogma"—remarking, however, that she did not intend to enroll Bakhtin "in the ranks of Russian religious thinkers" or Orthodox dogmaticians; she wished merely to show how Bakhtin's spiritual world view permitted him perspectives unavailable to "traditional philosophizing," oriented as it must be toward logic and system. An Orthodox context is important in studying Bakhtin's thought, Babkina concludes, because it helps us to formulate the problem in *his* terms; for "according to Bakhtin, a metaphysics can only be religious" (p. 324). See Ia.S. Babkina, "Idei M.M. Bakhtina v kontekste pravoslavnoi mistiki i dogmatiki," in *M.M. Bakhtin: Esteticheskoe nasledie i sovremennost'*, ed. A.F. Eremeev (Saransk: Izdatel'stvo Mordovskogo universiteta, 1992), vol. 2, pp. 316–24, especially p. 323.

33. N.K. Bonetskaia, "M.M. Bakhtin i traditsii russkoi filosofii," *Voprosy filosofii*, 1993, no. 1, pp. 83–93. Further page references are given in the text.

34. S.S. Averintsev, "Bakhtin, smex, khristianskaia kul'tura," in *M.M. Bakhtin kak filosof*, pp. 7–19. For an alternative view that sees most of Bakhtin's work as a successful extended theological metaphor, see Alexandar Mihailovic, "M.M. Bakhtin and the Theology of Discourse" (Ph.D. diss., Yale University, 1993), especially chap. 5, "Car-

nival and Embodiment in Bakhtin's Study of Rabelais," and chap. 6, "The Word Made and Unmade: Rabelais, Bakhtin and Stalin."

35. Vadim Kozhinov, "Bakhtin i ego chitateli," *Moskva,* 1992, July, pp. 143–51. The essay is remarkable for its self-pitying tone and its gratuitous insults to Michael Holquist, who, Kozhinov claims, was ungrateful, reneged on a dedication, and collapsed in the face of "Western pressure" to modify his original image of Bakhtin as a Russian Orthodox thinker.

36. V.L. Makhlin, "Nasledie M.M. Bakhtina v kontekste zapadnogo post-modernizma," in *M.M. Bakhtin kak filosof,* pp. 206–20, especially pp. 206, 209–10, 219.

37. On ethical relativism and the moral ambivalence of Bakhtin's carnivalesque, one of the best is the Petersburg intellectual historian Konstantin Isupov. In essays on Bakhtin and Aleksandr Meier and on Bakhtin's "crisis of humanism," Isupov reminds us that religiously informed debates on self–other relations were common in the 1920s and well integrated into symbolist obsessions with Eros, the Heart, and Sacrifice. All were seeking "someone to save us"—and Bakhtin was no exception. What saves us, it turns out, is the Other (the other's voice, love, presence, world view), to which anything *of our own* must always be sacrificed. In a cruel symmetry, the integrity of the Other is also constantly swallowed up, in endless regression, by a series of "I's." In Bakhtin's model, Isupov intimates, self and other are in constant hostage to one another. This humility might still work to everyone's benefit as long as a certain benevolence obtains; but the danger comes when "the Bakhtinian humility before a sacrificial victim" is transformed, under pressure of Stalinist maximalism, into an idealization of carnival. For in carnival everything really *is* sacrificed. A new choral "I" absorbs the individual "I"; consciousness reenters a prelapsarian state, a car-nivalized Garden of Eden where it blissfully forgets all it once knew of good, evil, or responsibility; and we are left with the laughter of the Serpent, neither human nor humanistic but simply satanic. See K.G. Isupov, "Mikhail Bakhtin i Aleksandr Meier," in *M.M. Bakhtin i filosofskaia kul'tura XX veka,* no. 1, pt. 2, pp. 60–70; and Isupov, "Bakhtinskii krizis gumanizma," pp. 127–55.

38. "Tragic catharsis (in the Aristotelian sense) is not applicable to Dostoevskii. The catharsis that finalizes Dostoevskii's novels might be—of course inadequately and somewhat rationalistically—expressed in this way: *nothing conclusive has yet taken place in the world, the ultimate word of the world and about the world has not yet been spoken, the world is open and free, everything is still in the future and will always be in the future.* But this is, after all, also the *purifying sense* of ambivalent laughter" (see chap. 4 of Mikhail Bakhtin, *Problems of Dostoevsky's Poetics,* ed. and trans. Caryl Emerson [Minneapolis: University of Minnesota Press, 1984], pp. 165–66).

39. See, for example, Morson and Emerson, *Mikhail Bakhtin: Creation of a Prosa-ics,* pp. 25–27; and Carl A. Rubino, "Opening up the Classical Past: Bakhtin, Aristotle, Literature, Life," in *Arethusa* (Special Issue on Bakhtin and Ancient Studies: Dia-logues and Dialogics), vol. 26, no. 2 (Spring 1993), pp. 141–57.

40. "Epic and Novel" (1941), in *The Dialogic Imagination: Four Essays by M.M. Bakhtin,* ed. Michael Holquist, trans. Caryl Emerson and Michael Holquist (Austin: University of Texas Press, 1981), pp. 11–12.

41. For a probing expansion of these ideas, see Gary Saul Morson, "For the Time Being: Sideshadowing, Criticism, and the Russian Countertradition," in *After Poststructuralism: Interdisciplinarity and Literary Theory,* ed. Nancy Easterlin and Barbara Riebling (Evanston, IL: Northwestern University Press, 1993), pp. 203–31.

Index

Adam, 65
Adiushkin, V.N., 75
Aesopian language, 122, 210, 214, 218
Aesthetics. *See also* Art
  of Bakhtin, 206, 213, 217, 219–22, 225
  as a focus of Losev's philosophy, 189–91, 193, 197, 201–2
  Merezhkovskii on Tolstoi's, 140
  Shpet and, 187
  work of Asmus in, 188
Afanas'ev, A., 224
Ahistoricism, 129
Aion, 197, 202
Akhmadulina, Bella, 19
Akhutin, A.V., 157–58
Aksakov, Ivan, 20–21, 32
Aksakov, Konstantin, 20–21, 32, 225
Aksel'rod, Liubov', 11
Akulinin, Vladimir, 76
Albigensianism, 65
Alexander II, Emperor, 134
Alexander III, Emperor, 134
Alexander III of Macedon (the Great), 129
Alienation, 88–89, 93, 101, 111
Amoralism, 154
Anarchism
  in Bakhtin, on some interpretations, 209
  Chulkov's doctrine of, 145
  as an element in Berdiaev's philosophy, 76, 94, 112, 117
  irrationalistic, in Stirner, 96
  Ivanov's acceptance of, 145
  Merezhkovskii on Tolstoi's doctrine of, 131, 133–34, 144
  mystical, 76, 145
Anarchy, 48, 54, 101, 120, 134, 220
Androgyny, 69
Andronik, monk (Aleksei Losev), 195
Andropov, Iurii, 21
Anna Karenina (Tolstoi), 131
Annenkov, P.A., 101
Anselm, Saint, 154
Anthropology, 44, 107, 110, 112, 218
Anti-Christ, 67, 121, 125, 129–30, 140
Anticommunism, 152

Anti-individualism, 25
Anti-Marxism, 8
Antipositivism, 85
Anti-Semitism, 152, 167, 182, 184
Antirationalism, 24, 39, 154, 159. *See also* Irrationalism
Anti-Westernism, 25, 82, 151
Apocalypse, 4, 121, 124, 138
Apollo, 123
Apollonian principle, 140
Ariman, 113
Aristocracy, 84
Aristotle, 89, 154, 194, 220, 226
Art. *See also* Aesthetics
  Bakhtin on, 211–12, 214, 216
  Christian, 143
  importance of, in the Silver Age, 4, 78
  Losev's phenomenological analysis of, 190–91, 197
  Merezhkovskii on Tolstoi's view of, 127, 132–33
  Russian, Berdiaev's kinship with, 105
  Shestov's rejection of, according to Kuvakin, 156
  as a topic of Il'in's writings, 166
Artsybashev, Mikhail, 138
Asceticism, 124–26
Askol'dov, Sergei, 14
Asmus, Valentin, 18, 154–55, 162, 188
Association for the Complex Study of the Russian Nation, 45
Astrology, 27
Atheism, 11, 52, 88, 90–92, 134, 139–40
Authoritarianism, 117
  as an element in Il'in's philosophy, 9, 151–52, 185
  as inherent in the communist ideal, 96
  as present in some versions of Slavophilism, 58
Autocracy
  as advocated by Uvarov, 48
  Il'in's conception of, 151, 167, 175, 177
  Merezhkovskii's views on, 78, 133–35, 144
Averintsev, Sergei, 17–19, 219

Nationalism. *See* National patriotism, Russian
Nationality, 48. *See also* National patriotism,
  Russian
National patriotism, Russian
  as an element in Slavophile philosophy, 3
  in present-day neo-Slavophilism, 25,
    43–49, 55
  religious, 9, 143, 151, 185, 194, 219
  Russian cosmism and, 27–28
  in the thought of Il'in, 149, 170–71, 185
Natural law, 152. *See also* Law
Natural rights. *See* Rights
Nazis, 165, 167, 177, 182–84
Nekrasov, Nikolai, 11–12
Neo-kantianism, 84
Neo-Leibnizianism, 106
Neo-Slavophiles, 25, 35, 44–49, 56, 151
Neo-Thomism, 110
Neoplatonism, 19, 190, 197, 202–3
Neoromanticism, 115
Neurosis, 52–53, 57
New Age, 27
New Religious Consciousness, 78, 111, 116,
  124
New Testament, 149. *See also* Bible; Gospels
Nicene Creed, 43
Nicholas I, Emperor, 3
Nicholas of Cusa, 191, 201
Nietzschean Marxists, 101
Nietzsche, Friedrich, 86, 156
  Berdiaev's agreement with, 88, 110, 112
  Berdiaev's criticism of, 109
  Bulgakov on, 91
  influence of, on Losev, 198, 201
  and Merezhkovskii, 121, 123–31, 136, 138,
    140, 142–43
  in recent Russian literary criticism, 142
  and Shestov, 150, 154–55, 157, 159–60
Nihilism, 127, 156, 163, 209. *See also* Legal
  nihilism
Nilus, Sergei, 9, 185
Nirvana, 127–28
Nonbeing, 107, 114. *See also* Being; Nothing
Nonresistance to evil (Tolstoi), 135, 167,
  178–79, 183. *See also* Ethics; Evil
Noosphere, 27
Nothing, 113–15. *See also* Nonbeing
Novgorodtsev, Pavel, 13, 73
  as a critic of Marxism, 74, 77, 94–100,
    102–3
  as head of the Moscow school of
    jurisprudence, 77
  as the main theorist of Russian liberalism,
    84–85
  recent republication of, 6
Novel, the, 194, 207, 209, 210, 213–14, 216,
  219–23

Novikov, A.I., 156
Novyi put', 121, 145
Nussbaum, Martha, 209, 213, 220–23

Objectivism (Struve), 84, 100
Objectivization (Berdiaev), 111–13, 117
Obshchina. See Commune, Russian
Occam, William of, 154
October Revolution, 98, 139, 147, 153, 167,
  187. *See also* Russian Revolution
Odyssey (Homer), 121
Offermanns, Wolfgang, 179–81
Old Testament, 113, 149, 156, 169. *See also*
  Bible
Ontologism, 32
Ontology, 113, 116
Orthodox church, Russian, 25, 51, 131–35,
  143–44, 165, 180–81
Orthodoxy, Russian. *See also* Christianity
  as advocated by Uvarov, 48
  Averintsev's encyclopedia article on, 17
  Bakhtin's relation to, 194, 217–19, 225
  as a component of Slavophilism, 25, 28–29,
    33, 42–44, 53
  and current Russian national patriotism, 9,
    25, 60
  doctrine of resurrection in, 29, 69
  and early Russian thought, 8, 50
  historical, as criticized by Berdiaev, 112
  Il'in's commitment to, 149, 151, 167, 179,
    181
  Losev's adherence to, 192
  the place of, in Russian culture, 42, 44–45,
    51
Ostrovskii, A.N., 12

Pacifism, 135
Paganism, 124–25, 130, 136–37
Palamas, Gregory, 44
Paradoxicalism (Berdiaev), 107
Paralleli, 10
Parliamentarianism, 48
Pascal, Blaise, 150, 154
Pashkova, E.P., 191
Passion, 107, 110, 114
Patriotism. *See* National patriotism, Russian
Pavlov, A.T., 53–54, 56
Perestroika, 6, 21–22, 75, 146, 157
Personalism, 106, 115, 225
Personality
  Bakhtin's emphasis on, 209, 212, 216, 225
  importance of, in Berdiaev's philosophy,
    105–6, 112–13, 117–18
  Merezhkovskii's conception of, 136–37, 139
  Novgorodtsev's critique of Marxism for
    excluding, 95
  Shestov on, 155

Peter I (the Great), Emperor, 40, 132
Petrograd University, 223. *See also* Saint
  Petersburg University
Phenomenology, 157, 187, 190, 197–205,
  212
Philistinism, 94, 116, 119, 135
Philology, 189, 193
Philosophical Encyclopedia, 6, 17–20, 32,
  153–54, 187
Philosophical Letters (Chaadaev), 15
Philosophy of history, 4, 28, 32
Philosophy of law, 172, 174, 206. *See also*
  Moscow school of jurisprudence
Philosophy of the Common Task (Fedorov),
  26, 63, 67,
Pisarev, Dmitrii, 5–6, 29
Pisemskii, A.F., 12
Pivovarov, Iu.S., 176–78
Plato, 50, 154, 157, 193, 197, 202–3, 205
Plekhanov, Georgii, 5, 34, 84, 100
Plotinus, 154, 197, 205
Plotnikov, N.S., 73–75
Pluralism, 220
Pobedonostsev, Konstantin, 134, 145
Poltoratzky, Nikolai, 172, 175, 178–79
Polyclitus, 191
Popov, Iu., 19
Popov, V.P., 33
Populism, 4, 81, 83–84, 100
Positivism, 84–85, 89, 91, 100, 122
Postmodernism, 220
Poststructuralism, 219
Potebnia, Aleksandr, 6
Pravda, 22
Pravosoznanie (Il'in). *See* Legal
  consciousness
Private property, 23, 38, 75
Proclus, 19
Progress, 74–76, 81–94, 100, 155
Proletariat, 5, 135, 137
Prometheanism, 88, 117, 137
Prometheus, 130
Protestantism, 53, 110, 116
Proudhon, Pierre-Joseph, 85
Pugachev, Emel'ian, 140
Pumpianskii, Lev, 219
Pushkin, Aleksandr, 11–12, 15, 42, 123–24,
  128, 130, 158, 171, 181
Put' (publishers), 14
Put' (journal), 10, 104
Pythagoras, 197

Rabelais, François, 208–9, 211, 219, 222–23
Racism, 25
Radishchev, Aleksandr, 5, 23, 36
Ranchin, A.M., 210, 223
Rasputin, Grigorii, 26

Rationalism. *See also* Reason
  as a feature of Marxian utopianism, 96
  as linked with individualism, 40
  Merezhkovskii's criticisms of, 128, 133, 139
  in the philosophy of Solov'ev, 28–29
  Shestov's critique of, 159, 161
  Slavophilism as a reaction against, 25, 37,
    40
Razin, Stenka, 140
Reason, 106, 111. *See also* Rationalism
Rechtsstaat. See State, law-governed
Relativism, 207, 209, 219–20, 226
Religion. *See also* Christianity; New
  Religious Consciousness; Orthodoxy,
  Russian; Protestantism; Roman
  Catholicism
  current Russian attitudes toward, 51–52
  as a dimension of Bakhtin's thought,
    217–19, 222, 225
  as a dimension of Shestov's thought, 158
  as an enduring Russian issue, 122
  Marxism as a, 74–76, 83, 85–95, 99
  Merezhkovskii's critique of Tolstoi's view
    of, 127–34
  philosophy of, 4
  as a principal focus of Russian philosophy,
    5, 9, 12–13, 23, 32
  as Tolstoi's highest value, 141
  in the writings of Il'in, 165–66, 180–81
Religious-Philosophical Society (Saint
  Petersburg), 78, 121–22, 132–33, 136,
  144–45
Renaissance, the, 48, 111, 124, 191, 223
Repin, Il'ia, 145
Resurrection, 26, 29, 62–71, 128. *See also*
  Immortality
Resurrection (Tolstoi), 131
Resurrection circle, 225
Revisionism, 84, 87, 90
Revolution of 1905, 4, 131, 133, 135–36, 145
Revolution of 1917. *See* February
  Revolution; October Revolution;
  Russian Revolution
Rights, 54, 84–85, 95–96, 176–78
Rimskii-Korsakov, Nikolai, 198, 205
Rodnianskaia, I., 19
Roman Catholicism, 110, 152, 181, 219
Romanov dynasty, 167
Romanticism, 115
Rosenthal, Bernice, 78
Rousseau, Jean-Jacques, 111, 138, 140–41,
  146
Rozanov, Vasilii, 4, 6, 8, 13–16, 22
Rule of law, 150, 152, 167, 174. *See also*
  Law; State, law-governed
Russian Academy of Sciences, 28
Russian cosmism. *See* Cosmism